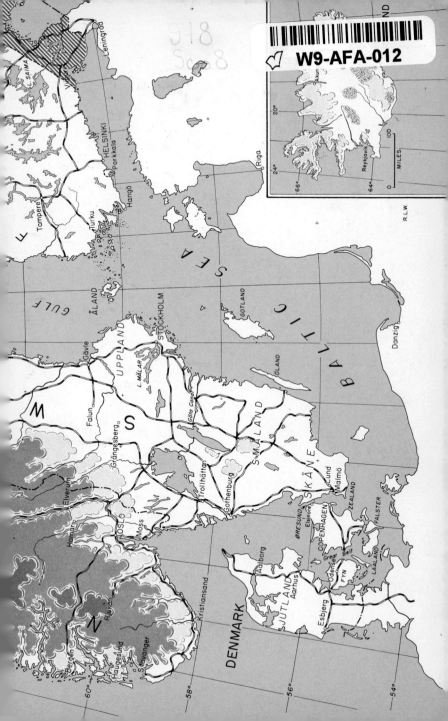

The United States and Scandinavia

THE AMERICAN FOREIGN POLICY LIBRARY

SUMNER WELLES, EDITOR

DONALD C. MCKAY, ASSOCIATE EDITOR

The United States and Britain

BY CRANE BRINTON

The United States and the Near East

BY E. A. SPEISER

The United States and the Caribbean

BY DEXTER PERKINS

The United States and Russia

BY VERA MICHELES DEAN

The United States and South America
The Northern Republics

BY ARTHUR P. WHITAKER

The United States and China

BY JOHN KING FAIRBANK

The United States and Scandinavia

BY FRANKLIN D. SCOTT

IN PRESS

The United States and Japan

BY EDWIN O. REISCHAUER

THE
UNITED STATES
AND
Scandinavia

By

Franklin D. Scott

HARVARD UNIVERSITY PRESS
Cambridge, Massachusetts
1950

Distributed in Great Britain by
GEOFFREY CUMBERLEGE
OXFORD UNIVERSITY PRESS
LONDON

ENDPAPER MAP BY R. L. WILLIAMS

PRINTED IN THE UNITED STATES OF AMERICA

CONTENTS

MAPS

INTRODUCTION

In the tragic world in which we find ourselves this autumn of 1949—a world in which mankind's brief search for peace seems already on the part of many governments and peoples to have ended in a feeble and supine acquiescence in the inevitability of war—a world in which the Western democracies regard the Atlantic Defense Pact rather than the United Nations Charter as the symbol of their security—the five Scandinavian countries have suddenly acquired a new and vital significance for the United States.

Norway, Denmark, Sweden, and Iceland are keys to the control of the North Atlantic. They guard the European approaches to Greenland which lies, of course, within the Western Hemisphere. Unless Greenland remains in friendly hands, the safety of the United States will be endangered. But the five Scandinavian countries are also Western Europe's gateway to the north polar cap. In the age of atomic fission we are forced to realize that the air above those icy reaches of the North Pole may well prove to be the scene of any future struggle for survival between the West and the East.

Norway, like Denmark, is a member of the Atlantic Defense Pact. Norway, like Finland, has a common frontier with the Soviet Union. Were Russia to undertake aggressive action, as Hitler did in 1940, to obtain possession of Norway's deep fjords as bases for the new far-roaming and swift Soviet submarines, the United States would be compelled as a measure of self-defense to go to Norway's aid, even if the Atlantic Defense Pact did not exist.

It is because of such strategic considerations as these, as they help to determine the national policy that we have now been forced to evolve, that what these five Scandinavian peoples do, are, and think, has assumed for us a measure of importance which would have seemed inconceivable even a few years ago.

Intimate coöperation between the Scandinavian countries and ourselves, and the firmest kind of an understanding with them, have become imperative.

Yet, urgent as these strategic motives may be, there are further reasons for such an understanding and for such coöperation that may prove to be of even greater significance to the American people should humanity pass unscathed from under the present shadow of impending catastrophe.

It is not only that there are millions of American citizens of Scandinavian origin. It is not only that the cultural ties between Scandinavia and the United States have long been close and are constantly increasing. It is not only that the Scandinavian countries have long been among the most worthy members of the family of nations and admirable exponents of what enlightened international relationships should be.

It is still more because we have so much to learn from every one of the Scandinavian countries in the science of democratic government. In Mr. Scott's apt phrase they are advanced and highly practical "schools of self-government." At a time when here in the United States, in Great Britain, and in the majority of the other democracies of Europe and of Latin America our so-called statesmen are at last showing signs of realizing that Western democracy cannot prosper, and probably cannot even survive, unless it finds the means of combining individual liberty with economic security, under the orderly processes of law, we would do well to study what our neighbors in Scandinavia have accomplished. For it is precisely that objective that they have achieved. Scandinavian Social Democracy offers a comforting proof that men occasionally can govern themselves wisely and well. The Scandinavians enjoy a form of government which is indeed a "middle way," a separate path between the right-hand path of uncontrolled capitalism and the left-hand path of Soviet Communism.

The close relationship between the United States and Scan-

dinavia that has now come into being under the compulsion
of a grave threat to the security of the Western democracies,
and under the menace of a new war, may well prove to have
a far-reaching and beneficial effect upon the political thinking
and the political practices of the American people.

In *The United States and Scandinavia* Mr. Scott gives us an
admirable opportunity to know and to understand every phase
of the national lives of the peoples of the Scandinavian countries. With admirable clarity, and with an authority derived
from intimate knowledge and from sympathetic comprehen-
sion, he presents a true picture of the political, social, and
economic forces that have shaped the national destinies of the
Scandinavian peoples.

The United States and Scandinavia is a notable contribution
to our enlightenment at a moment when the success or failure
of United States foreign policy may well spell life or death
for American freedom.

Sumner Welles

FOREWORD

In the soul-trying times in which we live, there are much public talk and many written words about what is called the American way of life. Much of it is good talk and many of the words are true. Yet in the phrases of some, there is an underlying implication that the American is the only way of life which is good; that somehow God has bestowed on us, and on us alone, the secret of the art of social and economic living; that we have a celestial patent on political righteousness and that there is really nothing further for us to do but sit on our hands atop the perfection we have created.

Any careful study and analysis of the history of the Scandinavian countries and of their institutions show how narrow and ridiculous is any such self-adulation on our part.

Quite conceivably, the American way of life is the best way of life for us, living as we do in a far-flung continental empire-republic, still not thickly populated and still containing natural resources adequate to provide the basis for the most generous standard of life which the world has known. But to say that is not to say that the American way of life is the *only* good way of life or even the most democratic.

The fact is that any way of life which is based upon respect for the rights of the individual as against the state and upon the free election of rulers responsible to the people—in short, any truly democratic way of life, is good for those who have built it with blood and toil. Democratic peoples should recognize this and endeavor to learn from each other so that democracy, in all the countries where it prevails, will continue dynamic. Clearly, as soon as it becomes static, it ceases to be democracy.

It is of the essence of Scandinavian democracy that it is still in full course of development. It has found what has been called "the Middle Way" but it has no intention of sitting down in self-satisfaction by the side of that path.

In the pages that follow, Professor Scott has sketched—of necessity, briefly—the history, the geography, the economy, the psychology, the social and political institutions of Denmark, Finland, Iceland, Norway, and Sweden, and also their strategic position in a world now divided between two great opposing forces, democracy and fascist-communism.

The title—"The United States and Scandinavia"—comes close to being a misnomer for there is relatively little mention in the book of dealings between our own country and the Scandinavian lands. Rightly so, and the reason is obvious. If a country without any history is a happy one, then the relationship between two countries which is almost a benign blank signifies the happiest of relationships. It is primarily conflict which is the stuff of most accounts of international relations. From whatever cause it may arise, there has been undisturbed peace and true friendship between Scandinavia and the United States over the generations. The break in formal diplomatic intercourse between Finland and ourselves during World War II was such a tragic but rule-proving exception that it is all but forgotten after five years. For the rest, the story of the relations between the United States and Scandinavia is so exceedingly happy and by the same token so dull (save for the saga of the Scandinavian immigrants) that Professor Scott does well to pass it over for the really interesting story of what the Scandinavian peoples are today and how they came to be so.

These countries, like the rest of Europe, participated in dreary generations of feuds and wars, dynastic and economic and religious. Sometimes allied, more frequently fighting one another; sometimes teamed up with one great power against another, and later shifting sides. And like the rest of Europe, they suffered autocratic or oligarchic government only slightly and intermittently modified by bourgeois parliamentary controls. Actually, liberal political institutions emerged rather later in Scandinavia than elsewhere on the continent. The outstanding fact in recent Scandinavian history is this: That once democracy was implanted—and with it long generations of peace —Scandinavian genius was set free. With only very limited natural resources and with mostly barren and rocky soils, these nations of fishermen, farmers, woodmen, and sailors went forward to carve out destinies for themselves which called forth the respect and even the envy of the civilized world. Free institutions plus free men plus peace equaled prosperity and political stability.

It is only during and since the war that their story has taken on a new interest for us in the United States. Faced with the threat of an aggressive imperialistic power bent on world conquest, all truly democratic peoples are of tremendous significance to us, regardless of how small the countries in which they live.

The real importance of the Scandinavian countries for the United States today is that they exist—that they exist and are doing a competent job of making the principles work by which we also profess to live; that they exist as the outermost bastions of democracy in the cold war; that they exist and are unafraid, prepared to work with us for a peaceful world or to go down fighting for their own ideals, which are also ours, if they are attacked.

Lithgow Osborne
President, The American-Scandinavian Foundation

PREFACE

The study of Bernadotte and the inspiration of Professor (now Sir) Charles K. Webster first took me to Scandinavia. The people and their ways of living then gripped my interest and drew me back. The present survey is one which I have long wanted to write, and I appreciate the opportunity offered by the editors of this series, Sumner Welles and Donald C. McKay.

Essentially this volume is a description of the Scandinavian countries and an explanation of their problems, particularly in their relations with the United States. The history of the northern peoples is but epitomized. One fascinating aspect of the story, the history of Sweden, I hope to deal with shortly in more complete fashion.

For twenty years, both in the North and in America, I have been accumulating facts and impressions about Scandinavia. Scholars, librarians, and archivists; journalists, politicians, and businessmen; workers, engineers, and the-man-in-the-street have contributed both knowingly and unwittingly. Most must pass unnamed, but all are thanked sincerely.

Mrs. Adèle Heilborn of the Sweden-America Foundation aided me far "beyond the call of duty," and lent her office as headquarters during my last stay in the North. The directors of the sister organizations in Denmark, Norway, and Finland lent unstinting assistance. The American-Scandinavian Foundation granted me my first traveling fellowships, the Social Science Research Council aided another trip, and the Viking Fund granted a fellowship for an extended trip in 1948. Northwestern University has been generous in providing research assistance and a leave of absence. Special thanks must go also to the staffs of the University Library in Oslo and to the Royal

Library in Stockholm, also to the Northwestern University Library and the Library of International Relations in Chicago.

The endpaper maps were done by Mr. R. L. Williams. The two maps in the text were drawn by Mrs. Marjorie Sommers, who also compiled most of the statistical tables.

The manuscript itself has been read and constructive criticism given by Dr. Howard E. Wilson of the Carnegie Endowment, Docent Folke Lindberg of Stockholm, Professor Raymond Stearns of the University of Illinois, Mrs. Helen Hohman, Mr. Barry Gilbert, and Professor Leland Carlson. Could I have followed all their suggestions it would have been a better book.

My helpful family deserves a kind of thanks which the words of a preface cannot express.

F. D. S.

Evanston, Illinois
February 1, 1950

The United States and Scandinavia

1. An Introduction to Lands and Peoples

In Oslo just after his election as first director-general of the United Nations, Trygve Lie told an assembly of students that his election had a geographic cause and was not a personal tribute to him. Quite aside from the question of personal tribute, the geographic factors to which he alluded are the most significant and revolutionary influences in the contemporary history of Scandinavia. Until a few short years ago, the Scandinavian countries were alongside the current of international activities; they are now in the vortex of the international current.

When Scandinavia was on the frontier of civilization and conflict the people could choose whether they wished to play the game of international war and politics, or stand aloof. When they did choose to play they could usually do so on other people's grounds. Swedes like to claim, for instance, that their country has never been invaded and, even though the claim is not literally accurate, it is almost so. Does this aloofness of the past have significance in the mid-twentieth century? Is the idea of the marginal position of northern Europe merely an illusion to which wishful thinking clings? What are the geographical realities of today, the pressures, the protective barriers which affect this section of the earth?

"Scandinavia" is to be defined here in its widest sense: the central core of Denmark, Norway, and Sweden, the eastern flank in Finland, the western outposts in the Atlantic Ocean: Iceland and the Danish colony of Greenland. This whole area reaches from the Russian border to the shores of North

America. It is flanked on one side by polar seas, and on the other by the Atlantic and the powers of western Europe. The seventeen million people who inhabit it have a common cultural tradition, have been in and out of various political combinations with one another, and think of themselves as a group. They have their differences, each of the five nations is an entity, yet each is far more different from other nations outside the group than it is from any of the brother nations within the group. Geographical position and community of culture are what make "The North" Scandinavia.

This Scandinavian region needs to be reassessed in the mid-twentieth century because of the changes in its world relationships, and because of its own social and economic development. The countries of the North have been praised to the skies as lands of the middle way, and damned to the depths as selfish and blind in a confused and embittered world. Neither view is correct.

But what is correct? How have the peoples of the North created their high standard of living on the meager resources available to them? How have they developed an essentially peaceful and highly creative culture?

The answers cannot be given in easy simple statements, yet they are neither abstruse nor accidental. To understand them one must assume certain fundamentals: common sense, education, honesty, coöperativeness, hard work, a dash of good luck, far-sighted planning, careful spending, a creative talent, independent spirit, and democratic processes. Progress has been hampered sometimes by distance from supplies and markets, sometimes by pride and stubbornness, sometimes by an overdose of the independent spirit. Difficulties from the outside have harassed the Scandinavians. But progress has been real throughout the area.

As examples of how to live in peace and prosperity, and as more or less unwilling members of the complex twentieth-century world order, these lands of the North deserve study and understanding.

1. WHAT SCANDINAVIA IS

A Mercator projection map pulls Scandinavia apart and distorts the northern shapes. Only a globe can picture something of the basic geologic and geographic unity of the area.

Far back in geologic times the "North" lay buried under the great ice sheet. Slowly the frozen mass receded under the warmth of the sun. The dynamic of geology asserted itself and the land rose, released of its crushing burden. The Baltic Sea took shape as an inland lake in the heart of Fenno-Scandia, the entire land mass comprising what is now Finland, Denmark, and the Scandinavian Peninsula. The Baltic then rose higher and at last broke through a channel to reach the North Sea. Thus was formed Öresund (the narrow sound between Denmark and Sweden), the Danish lands were separated from the Scandinavian Peninsula, and the waters of the Baltic made contact with the wide Atlantic. Boats could then traverse the Baltic and sail out to the British Isles, to Iceland and Greenland and Vinland. The Baltic was a northern Mediterranean, providing pathways for travel and commerce and nurturing a common culture.

The barriers were not the sea, but the vast forests and swamps which lay between Finland and the inhabited parts of Russia. High mountains, marshes, and broad reaches of barrens were what man could not cross. Fenno-Scandia was thus insulated from the East and interconnected within itself and with the West. The region was and remains a natural area of community of culture, with a political history closely intertwined. The islands in the Atlantic were separated by greater distances, yet lay within easy reach of Viking seamen, and have borne the stamp of Scandinavian culture for over a thousand years.

As one looks at this area on a globe he is impressed by how far north it lies, and he wonders how an active modern society with large towns can prosper in latitudes more northerly than Labrador, some of the land above the Arctic Circle. The Atlantic Ocean is the answer. Aided by winds from the west, it keeps the Scandinavian peninsula warmed and watered. The Gulf Stream gives an added touch. But it is the whole breadth of salt water which modifies the winds, creates the temperate marine climate, and makes the lands to the east livable. To the west of the Atlantic Labrador suffers under cold winds blowing off the northern plains.

Tromsö in northern Norway (above latitude 69° N.) has a winter temperature averaging about 37° and a summer average just above 50°. Spring flowers bloom there in February. The mountain backbone of the Scandinavian Peninsula blocks off some of this ocean warmth, but never all of it. Even the west coast of Finland feels something of the moderating influences from the west, though by the time the winter breezes reach Finland's eastern border they have lost their delicacy, and a northern "continental" climate prevails. Generally the Fenno-Scandia area has a climate stern, but not capricious. Hurricanes and sizzling heat and earthquakes are unknown, floods and drought are rare. Moderation is there a habit of nature, though weather has always exceptions.

Summer in these northern lands brings days which linger through long twilight far into the night. In the northernmost parts, for weeks before and after June 23 one may see the sun which never sets, but merely glides low to the horizon and rises again. This is the compensation for the long nights of darkness in the winter, and helps to explain the sunworship in ancient ritual and on modern beaches.

The warmth, the sun, the moisture dropped in frequent rains from the western winds, make crops grow quickly where the soil is good. Yet the glacial terrain of Finland and the Scandinavian peninsula often leaves only small patches of arable land, sometimes in inner valleys like Gudbrandsdal in Norway or in strips between water and rock in the western fjords, sometimes along quiet river mouths in northern Sweden, or in clearings in Finland's forests. The ice sheets scraped off the earlier topsoil, and the present thin covering is geologically recent—on top of rocks 300,000,000 years old (the Alps, for comparison, are but 50,000,000 years old).

Iceland has vast stretches of barren land, and Greenland is only a name given by that early genius of real-estate promotion, Eric the Red. Greenland's real claim to fame is her "icy mountains," which may perhaps be the determining force in the climate of the world. The major food-producing area of Scandinavia is in southern Sweden (Skåne) and in the fertile fields of eastern Denmark on the sedimentary rock plains. Contrasts are great between the grandeur of the western Norwegian fjords with their perpendicular walls and the green shores of the Danish islands creeping out of the sea.

In Scandinavia sea and land exist together, complement each other. Man lives on the land, but draws sustenance from the sea and makes it serve his needs. The sea is not only his highway of commerce, his connective link within Scandinavia and with the lands which lie beyond; it is also his most dependable source of nourishment. "Norway has plenty of food—but it's all fish" is exaggeration based on fact. The fishers of the Lofoten Islands and the whole long coast, the whalers who go out to the south, the fishermen of Iceland who provide that country's only important export, attest the importance of the sea.

In Sweden it is the dozen long rivers flowing southeast from the central mountain ridge (the Keel) which carry timber down to the mills at the river mouths, and it is through the Baltic that ships carry pulp, paper, and prefabricated houses to the markets of the world. It is because the Baltic flowed to the west and opened a sea route through the Danish Sound (Öresund) that Finland carries on more trade with the United States, four thousand miles away, than with next-door Russia; and it is the North Sea which makes Britain the best customer for Danish butter and eggs.

The coast lines of the Scandinavian countries are long and they are usable. Harbors are as full of boats as the streets of Copenhagen are full of bicycles. When the Vikings began to build stream-lined seagoing ships in the ninth and tenth centuries they were simply learning how to use the natural advantages of their harbors; the fjords led to the ocean, and the ocean continued to the lands beyond. It is no accident that these northern countries are leaders in seamanship, and that Norway has one of the largest merchant fleets of the world (far the largest *per capita*).

It is because of the sea that the Scandinavian lands have built a basic cultural unity and maintained it through the centuries; it is because of the sea that they are "oriented" to the south and the west. Their Christianity came to them from the south, from Rome. Finland quite naturally received both her first baptism and her protestantism across the Gulf of Bothnia from Sweden, while Russia was Christianized from Constantinople. The line of religious division ran down the eastern border of Finland and the Baltic states, and this was also normally a line of linguistic, economic, and political division; the Gulf of Bothnia, the Baltic, the North Sea, tied these shores to one another, just as the Atlantic tied western Europe and eastern America.

Scandinavia stands, therefore, united geographically as well as historically. The peoples of the North have intermixed, have carried on their interchange of commerce and ideas among themselves, and have fought their family quarrels. In the greater and more diverse world clan of nations Scandinavia is like a family among and yet apart from the rest.

What, then, are the characteristics of these peoples of the North? The Danes, the Swedes, the Norwegians, the Icelanders—these are the Scandinavian peoples proper, these are the folk whom the racial anthropologists call Nordic. The men tall and blond, the women fair. The racists went too far in apotheosizing this northern type, and disregarded too much the varieties within the type. Nevertheless, by whatever standards one wishes to apply—health, strength, endurance, size, intelligence, even subjective beauty, the Scandinavians must rank high, and here the Finns must be included.

Originally these Scandinavians must have been one people.

Perhaps their ancestors came northward from Asia Minor or the Balkans, and founded the great Teutonic family. As the last ice sheet receded, small groups crept northward to hunt and fish and to settle. Tribal differentiations developed, and by the Age of the Migrations (beginning in the second century B.C.) we know of the Cimbri and soon of the Goths; a few centuries later of Angles and Saxons and Jutes, of Svear and Götar and of the Norse Vikings. As late as A.D. 700 the runic inscriptions found in the three central countries indicate that the people used exactly the same language, but in the Viking period (C. A.D. 800–1100) there grew a consciousness of the oneness of Norway and of distinction between Danes and Swedes.

Gradually environment played its subtle part in selection and modification; immigrating groups (Scotch, Walloons, Germans, and others) affected communities differently; variation in personalities and in experience changed habits and traditions. Hence people and speech are not now the same in urban Copenhagen, in the mining town of Kiruna in northern Sweden, and in the rural valley of Setesdal in Norway.

Books of one country can be more easily read in the other countries when they are translated, but it is a matter of convenience rather than necessity. Any Dane, Swede, or Norwegian can travel in the neighbor countries, use his own speech, and be understood without too great difficulty. In fact, these peoples do not try to learn each other's language, but at their various common gatherings each speaks his own, with an occasional bow to some special idiosyncrasy of his neighbor. Skåne has been a Swedish province for about three hundred years and it speaks and writes Swedish; but it was long Danish territory and still has close cultural and economic ties with Denmark— enough so that a scholar at the Swedish university of Lund can claim he has less language difficulty in Copenhagen than he has in Stockholm.

With Iceland the story is different, for the Icelanders, basically of Norwegian stock since the Viking Age, have really retained their ancient speech—at least their language is most closely akin to that of the ancient skalds (poets) and the saga-writers. Danish, Norwegian, and Swedish have succumbed to modernization within themselves, and to acceptance of a number of words from German, French, and English. The Icelanders are proud to say that they, like the Greeks, always have a word for it. Even for such an invention as the radio the Icelanders utilized one of their own root-words and called it *Sima* (thread), while the Swedes took over "radio" and the Norwegians used "kringkasting" which is their equivalent for "broadcasting."

Language may thus serve as an illustration of the ways in which continuity and originality blend, and similarities and differences exist side by side.

The Finns, related culturally and geographically to their western neighbors, are of different origin. Their ancestors moved, in prehistoric times, westward across the Russian plains, then north into Estonia and Finland. Perhaps their homeland was around the Caspian Sea, or in the Ural Mountains. Related tribes are still scattered along the Volga, and the Hungarians probably originated from the same stock. The languages of these groups are at least distantly related, and belong to a separate development, as do the peoples themselves, not Slavic, not Teutonic. They are all part of the separate Finno-Ugrian group. They are tall, blond, and virile, with broad cheek bones. When they moved across the Gulf of Finland they probably found settlements of Germanic peoples already in their destined country. The Finns absorbed some of these peoples but the Swedish communities on the west coast and the south coast have remained distinct in blood and speech. The Finns themselves have retained definite tribal characteristics in several of the provinces (*landskaper*). Others have moved on and have spread into northern Sweden and Norway and mixed to some extent with the Lapps. Still other related peoples, the Karelians, have occupied sparsely the cold forest area east of Finland but their contact with the Finns is slight.

Within Finland itself about 10 per cent of the people are

Swedish in blood and speech, and the Finnish and Swedish languages are equal before the law. These Swedes have been for centuries farmers and fishers and have clung to their two coastal areas in west and south. But Finland was converted to Christianity from Sweden, and for 600 years was an integral part of the Swedish state. The culture is therefore strongly impregnated with Swedish elements, now so thoroughly absorbed that they seem indigenous. The "pure-Finns" developed a strong nationalistic consciousness in the nineteenth century, and although the nationalist antagonism was and is directed primarily against Russia, the Swedish minority has also suffered from it occasionally. In most things there is no conflict between the two different peoples, and together they are one of the most self-conscious and self-assertive nationalities in Europe.

Life is hard in the northern forests. Returns may seem meager to some; to the Finns they are enough. With patient will and a strength which transcends the physical these people have through centuries of hardship and of war with their eastern neighbors hardened their courage, their *sisu*. They dislike to admit impossibility, their backs are broad and unbending. They love their land with the passion of generations who have suffered to conquer the woods and the swampland, and who can suffer for centuries still. Sibelius' *Finlandia* is a mirror of the popular spirit—somber, strong, intense.

In the north of Finland, in northern Sweden and Norway and to some extent in the northwestern corner of Russia, 30,000 wandering Lapps (who are not related to the other peoples of Scandinavia) still follow their reindeer herds in search of sparse and seasonal pasture. These small dark people speak a language of their own, partly borrowed from ancient Finnish, and also often one or more of the Scandinavian tongues. The more "advanced" peoples which claim sovereignty over the land feel a sense of responsibility to these "little brown brothers." They have set up schools for Lapp children, graciously provided special methods of reindeer-taxation, and have permitted the nomads freedom to cross the frontiers which mean nothing to the Lapps. The Lapps in turn remain an independent, upstanding people (6500 in Sweden, 2400 in Finland, and 20,000 in Norway), deteriorating, perhaps, only when they are induced to settle down and become "fishing Lapps."

In many of the fundamental things, despite their superficial differences, the Scandinavians remain alike. In social customs and outlook on life they are closer to each other than New Englanders to Southerners—even in speech perhaps not much farther apart! In religion all the Northerners once worshiped Odin and Thor together; they passed together from paganism to Christianity. Now they are Lutherans: Finns 96 per cent, Danes 98 per cent, Swedes 98 per cent, Icelanders 98 per cent, Norwegians 97 per cent. The legal systems come from common origins and are dominated by a common philosophy; many modern social laws are formulated in common.

The basic common ideal of individualism is modified in practice by a semi-socialized form of government in each of the five states. Literacy is, for all practical purposes, 100 per cent throughout, and nowhere in the world can one find a higher per capita production and consumption of books. Freedom of expression is an ideal and a practice. Poverty, one might say, is one of the few things "verboten," and great wealth is taxed with severity.

Perhaps the most obvious inherent characteristic of the Scandinavians is their pervasive practicality. They can dream, yes, but they are likely to dream of worldly things. They are scientists and technologists; they are architects and shipbuilders and sailors, skillful, resourceful; they are administrators, long successful in the art of governing themselves.

Exceptions there are, of course: Emanuel Swedenborg was one of them, and Hans Christian Andersen, and Edvard Grieg. Henrik Ibsen recognized and portrayed the inner conflict of man's spirit; in *Peer Gynt* fancy dominates reality, and often a Northerner likes to think he has a good bit of Peer Gynt in himself, though 99 per cent of them suppress the little imp most effectively. Abstract thinking is rare, and a materialistic attitude toward life is deep-rooted. A profound love of nature and of the physical is visible, expressing itself in literature and art, and hiking, bicycling, boating, and skiing in the high fjelds.

Essentially united as one family, yes, but with strong intra-family differences too. Unity is prized, but each member-nationality in the family group has an individuality to maintain even while coöperating with the group. Hence each people and country must be considered independently.

2. THE FIVE COUNTRIES

The diversity which exists within the over-all unity can be seen by a brief introduction to each of the individual countries.

Denmark is the geographic link between the European con-tinent and the North. Denmark has been in closest contact with Germany and western Europe. This is evident in a speech which has been affected by Low German elements, in manners cosmopolitanized by trading and cultural contacts with France, and in architecture influenced noticeably by the Netherlands.

The Danish land seems as open-hearted and as smiling as the people who enjoy themselves in Copenhagen's open-air play-house, Tivoli, or who jostle one another as they stroll along commercial *Strøget* or seaside *Lange Linie*. Springtime views reveal the character of the countryside: green fields dotted with white cottages, thatched or red-tiled, with red window frames; families working together in the fields; cows and their calves, horses and their colts; square-towered white rural churches, solid-built, well-proportioned; wide reaches of sandy beaches; close-packed fishers' villages; an occasional stork's nest pitched high on the roof; dunes and stretches of heath being slowly reclaimed for cultivation; sometimes a small forest of beech or low wooded hills; a folk high school here and there; factories, breweries, shipyards; roadways built in three sections instead of two, one for pedestrians, one for automobiles and wagons, and one for the thousands of bicycles on which Danes go to work or to church or to play.

It is a gently rolling landscape, somewhat like northern Illinois, with only enough woods or undulating country to shelter the cottages from the west wind. There are occasional sections as rugged as southern Iowa, but the highest point in the country is only 536 feet above sea level. This modesty of the landscape seems comfortably appropriate. As Grundtvig put it: "No towering peaks thundered over our birth: it suits us best to remain on earth."

In the west of Denmark is low-lying Jutland, turning her back to the North Sea (the only important port there is Esbjerg, a modern "made" town). In southern Jutland Germans and Danes have pushed and shoved at each other for generations. Eastward lie the islands great and small which make up the bulk of the country: Fyn, with busy Odense and, across the Great Belt, Zealand, on the east shore of which is Copenhagen. To the south are Laaland and Falster and a number of smaller islands; far to the east in the Baltic Sea is ancient Bornholm. On Zealand was the castle of Hròthgar and the scene of the Beowulf epic; to the north, at Elsinore, the ramparts paced by Hamlet.

Across the Sound boats ply busily, as they have for centuries, to the near-by Swedish shores, and through Öresund (the Sound) goes the shipping from the lands of the Baltic out to the world's markets. Copenhagen is a natural crossroads, like Constantinople and Singapore. The sea is in and around Denmark, inviting commerce and travel and fishing.

The Faroe Islands are the last remnant left in Scandinavian control of the once extensive Norwegian holdings in the British Isles. Here some 28,000 farmers and fishermen of Norwegian ancestry live under Danish suzerainty, but with a high degree of local autonomy. These green hills, mist-enshrouded, have not attracted foreign invasion, except as in World War II when Great Britain took them under temporary protection. Far to the west is Denmark's great island, Greenland, but of that more later.

The total population of Denmark is about 4,000,000 (exact

figures are given at the end of the book), and 1,000,000 live in metropolitan Copenhagen. One must say that there is no second city in Denmark, but rather a group in third place: busy and cultured Aarhus (107,000); Odense (92,000); cement and akvavit-manufacturing Aalborg (61,000); Esbjerg built for fishing and commerce (43,000); with no other over 40,000; and a number of small towns.

Denmark is no land of luxurious abundance, but of a carefully nourished sufficiency. Her people live within their means. They export their butter and eat margarine, they boil barley to stretch out the coffee, and they do without the fancy new cars and their grilles with the "dollar grin." And they accept these post-war stringencies more pleasantly than one could expect. Perhaps centuries of experience have taught them to accept limitations. The Danes keep happy doing the necessary.

Sweden. Across the narrow Sound from Denmark lies the southern tip of the northward-reaching Scandinavian peninsula. This southern province of Skåne is geologically as well as culturally linked with Denmark. Here is deep rich soil not scoured off by the ice sheets, here is the bread-basket of Sweden, where the wheat is raised, the oats for the morning oatmeal, the sugar beets and the vegetables. It is the region of beech trees and of the chateaux of the old landed aristocracy. The rolling landscape and the trim white cottages make one wonder if he is not still in Denmark.

But immediately to the north of Skåne begins a new landscape: the beech ceases to flourish, the coniferous trees begin to reign, and the surface of the earth is strewn with rock. Underneath is a different geologic substructure; it is the land of granite and other crystalline rocks, still asserting themselves after thousands of years of erosion. Sediments have filled in enough to support rich farming areas, but sometimes only enough to allow the roots of trees to gain foothold in pancake formation, and often naked rock permits no growth. The south central Swedish province of Småland was less abundant in its production of crops than of people, for from this rock and forest area came a large portion of Sweden's immigration to the United States.

Northward, in a broad belt running from the west coast in a northeasterly direction toward Stockholm and the ancient plains of Upland, is again a fertile agricultural area. The mouths of the northern rivers provide strips of rich delta land, slowly increasing as they rise out of the sea.

For the most part the northern half of the country is timbered, and the slow-growing pines provide Sweden's greatest natural wealth. Lying within the rock in both central and northern Sweden are rich deposits of iron, copper—now almost gone—gold, silver, and a variety of other minerals. It is in the north, too, that the great series of parallel rivers flowing to the Gulf of Bothnia provide resources of water power to give light and energy to the south, and to drive the trains of the country.

Variations are numerous, for the total length of Sweden from south to north is almost 1000 miles, comparable to the distance from the southern tip of Italy's toe to the German Baltic coast. East to west the breadth at most is 300 miles, and the total area is 173,300 square miles—almost the size of prewar Germany, 10 per cent larger than California, and ten times the size of Denmark. So in May, while the farmers till their fields in Skåne, city workers can vacation on skis in the mountains of the north, and enjoy the midnight sun.

Sweden's physical and political boundaries are significant. In the south the sea connects her with Denmark and with Germany; in the west it opens a wide window to Britain and across the Atlantic. Toward Norway in the west rises the Keel, a long high range of mountains, unfortified and peaceful since 1814. In the east the border with Finland is defined but not defended by the fjelds (the upland moors) and the waters of the Torne river, and by the wider waters of the Gulf of Bothnia. Sweden's east and south coast on the Baltic is blessed with skerries and harbors. For many centuries it has been the starting point for adventurers and traders to sail across to the neighbor lands; it has held for Sweden the islands of Öland and Gotland; and it has led fishermen out for many a catch. The same coast has attracted invasion, too, but it was the ancient habit of the Swedes to get there first.

One of the most magnificently situated cities of the world is Stockholm, built on islands and cliffs of rock where sprawling Lake Mälar enters the narrow end of the widening Stockholm archipelago. The early medieval trading center was at Birka, an island in Lake Mälar, but Birger Jarl (thirteenth century) sensed the strategic importance of the Stockholm site, and built a new city. In the last generation it has grown with especial rapidity, and now Greater Stockholm numbers almost 1,000,-000. The second city in Sweden, westward-looking Gothenburg, is a kind of Scandinavian San Francisco, cosmopolitan, commerce-minded, with busy shipyards. The population is 350,000. Malmö, with a population of 190,000, is third, building ships, too, and carrying on the active import and export trade of Skåne.

Norway's heritage is much of nature's magnificence and little of her useful resources. The country stretches 1100 miles in direct line from south to north, 2100 miles along the coast; the whole coast line, if one measures the fjords and bays, is about 12,000 miles, protected on the west by a long chain of outlying islands. The land is shaped like a squash with an abnormally long and bumpy neck. The end of that neck, up beyond Kirkenes, curls farther to the east than the easternmost limits of Poland or Romania.

In width the land varies from four miles to 267, and the total area of Norway proper is 124,556 square miles, about three-quarters the size of Sweden, or a little smaller than Montana. The only long land frontier is the mountainous eastern border with Sweden, well marked but unfortified (1028 miles). Farther north Norway marches for 460 miles with Finland across a rugged country of reindeer, Lapps, and occasional settlers. In the far northeast there is a frontier of 110 miles with Russia, since Finland ceded Petsamo in 1944. But it is the long western frontier of the coast, with its wealth of protected harbors and its deep-cut fjords which opens the windows of Norway to the Atlantic Ocean, Britain, the world of the West.

There is no railway to the north and no complete auto road. Ferries are frequent, and the burden of north-south transportation is borne by coastal boats. To get to Narvik by rail one must cross into Sweden and return on the ore-road through Kiruna. The sea so dominates communications and life that an English visitor once insisted that Norway was really an island like Britain. It is the sea which holds the Norwegian land together; it is the sea which has made Norway a nation; and it is sea and rock together which give Norway its grandeur. Norwegians send out their fishing boats to the Arctic and the Antarctic, catch and process everything from sardines to whales. They have created the world's largest merchant fleet outside Britain and the United States. On the sea Norway is an economic world power.

The earliest settlements in Norway, and probably in all Scandinavia, were made in the far north, where wanderers from Asia came in along the ice-free coast. Here there were birds and fish, perhaps wild animals, and it may be that man lived in this coastal fringe even while the great ice sheet covered the mountains behind him and the whole land south into Denmark. When the later Teutonic and Mediterranean peoples moved up from the south they too came along the warm coastal belt, and moved inward through the rock-walled fjords, finding their small patches of fertile loam and living by fishing and hunting and a little agriculture. As the population increased, men had to seek the inner valleys, where narrow strips of soil along lakes and streams were separated from each other by vast areas of barren, wind-swept fjeld. Intercommunication was difficult, and each cloistered valley tended to inbreed its people and its speech.

The larger unity of Norway was accepted the more easily because nature guaranteed each valley a high degree of autonomy. Whether up in his inland valley, or in a cove of a deep fjord, or in a fishing village on an island in Lofoten, the Nor-

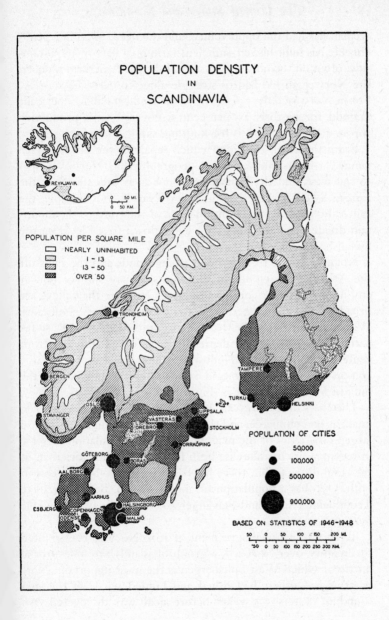

POPULATION DENSITY
IN
SCANDINAVIA

REYKJAVIK

0   50 MI.
0   50 KM.

POPULATION PER SQUARE MILE
NEARLY UNINHABITED
1 - 13
13 - 50
OVER 50

TRONDHEIM

BERGEN

OSLO

STAVANGER

VÄSTERÅS
ÖREBRO
UPPSALA
STOCKHOLM

NORRKÖPING

GÖTEBORG

BORÅS

AALBORG

AARHUS

ESBJERG
COPENHAGEN
ODENSE
HÄLSINGBORG
MALMÖ

TAMPERE

TURKU

HELSINKI

POPULATION OF CITIES

50,000

100,000

500,000

900,000

BASED ON STATISTICS OF 1946-1948

50   0   50   100   150   200 MI.
50   0   50 100 150 200 250 300 KM.

wegian has had the opportunity, and the need, to be independent. He has built his self-sufficient farm on a narrow mountainside, often on the only soil in sight. Like the American pioneer, the Norwegian has had to struggle alone to carve his destiny. For in Norway only 3 per cent of the land is tillable, 1 per cent is good for pasture, 25 per cent is covered with productive forest, and 71 per cent is for hunting, skiing, and photography.

From the Keel, the ridge which separates the Scandinavian peninsula both politically and geographically, Norway slopes to the west, and the Norwegian slope is as precipitous as the eastern Swedish slope is gradual. At Narvik, for example, the railroad climbs steeply along the side of the fjord to the mountain divide, then takes hours to come down to sea level on the Swedish side.

Norway is first to feel the warming winds and the rains off the Atlantic; the clouds in the blue sky may shower rain at any moment. In the southern bulge of Norway the valleys are broader and closer together, but still embraced by mountains. Water cascades from the fjelds in magnificent abundance, so far harnessed in only small degree because of its distance from centers of population and industry. Mineral resources are scarce compared with the deposits in Sweden, but through Narvik the bulk of Swedish iron ore is shipped to foreign markets.

The cities of Norway are built, therefore, not on industry as much as on commerce, and they are neither so numerous nor so large as the cities of the neighboring lands. Population increase in recent years has likewise been less rapid in the cities than in the rural districts, but there has been a considerable increase in both. Oslo has a population of about 420,000, Bergen 110,000, Trondheim 57,000, and Stavanger 50,000. Norway as a whole numbers 3,000,000.

By an international agreement of 1920 Norway was granted sovereignty over Svalbard, a group of islands 250 miles to the north, of which West Spitsbergen is the most important. Norwegians and others had fished and hunted whale in the surrounding waters for years before coal was discovered. An

American company operated mines there in 1906–07, but sold out to Norwegians in 1916. The Dutch and the Swedes tried it, too, but just before World War II the 2000 Russian miners were the largest single group; the Norwegians numbered about 900. The miners were evacuated in 1941, but in 1942 the islands became a theater of war and the end result was almost complete destruction of the installations. After the war both Russians and Norwegians vigorously rebuilt. The Russians were interested in more than coal, and asked for a protectorate, which the Norwegians felt not the least inclined to grant.

In the nineteenth and twentieth centuries the exploring zeal and the whaling skill of the Norwegians have drawn them to still more distant lands of ice. Nansen and Sverdrup and Amundsen have found new seas and ocean currents. Large reaches of Antarctica have been staked out by the venturesome Norsemen, and the surrounding seas are the scene of the great whaling expeditions. East Greenland was wanted, too, but in 1933 the World Court at The Hague decided that Denmark held sovereignty over the entire island, whether settled or not.

Bordering Norway and Sweden on the east is *Finland*. "Oh, why did our forefathers fall in love with these lakes and woods and settle here? Why didn't they keep on moving west? Then someone else could be Russia's neighbor."

Many Finns may agree with this plaint of one of them, but the forefathers did stay, and took possession of the stern land. It is the northernmost country in the world, and one of the most sparsely settled: 4,000,000 people in a land that stretches 720 miles from north to south and 400 miles from east to west. In Europe only Norway spreads out its people more generously; and in comparison with an American state the density is about the same as in Minnesota. The northern sections are more thinly populated than the southern, partly for climatic reasons, partly because settlement moved in from the southwest and south. Here in the middle of the western coast and all along the southern shores still live the 10 per cent of the population who retain their Swedish language and character.

The people have grown from 500,000 in 1750 to 1,000,000 in 1811, 2,000,000 in 1880, 3,000,000 in 1910, and 4,000,000 in 1950. The impressiveness of that growth is emphasized when it is recalled that since 1893 about 350,000 have emigrated to the United States and Canada. The greatest rate of increase came in the stimulating and hopeful first years of independence, 1920–1940.

The land is low lying and nearly 10 per cent is covered with lakes. These factors added to the influence of the Atlantic winds give Finland a climate more moderate than is usual in such northern latitudes. In climate and flora as in several other respects Finland is a transition zone, intermediate between Scandinavia and the east European plains region. Her wealth is in her forests, on which are based her natural industries and her export trade; minerals, fisheries, and agriculture play a comparatively minor role.

Finland has three long land frontiers: 333 miles with Sweden along the Torne and Muonio rivers, 460 miles with Norway along the Tana river and the watershed between the Atlantic and the Gulf of Bothnia, and 775 miles in the east with the Soviet Union. This new-drawn frontier with the U.S.S.R. mainly follows the watershed between the White Sea and Baltic, but at several points it cuts in two economic and old cultural communities. Most troublesome to the Finns is the amputation of the Lake Saimaa-Vuoksi River system, on which the Finns had built much of their lumber industry and lumber transportation.

The seacoast along the Gulf of Finland, the Baltic, and the Gulf of Bothnia measures about 685 miles, broken strategically by the Porkkala peninsula which is under lease to Russia as a naval base; Porkkala is just west of Helsinki and includes a section of the main railway line to Turku.

Finland's industrial centers are many but her cities are few. Helsinki (Helsingfors) is capital and metropolis with a population of 360,000; Tampere (Tammerfors) with a population of 94,000 is a lumber and textile town; while Turku (Åbo), 94,-

ooo population, is the chief western port, and a center of the old Swedish culture.

Iceland, in mid-Atlantic, lies only 180 miles from the coast of Greenland; the northernmost point reaches to the Arctic Circle. The island is a rough oval, deeply cut by fjords and bays, almost 300 miles in length and 194 miles in width. The total area of 40,000 square miles is less than that of Cuba, about the same as Virginia, but the people live in the lowlands, comprising only 7 per cent of the land. The interior is magnificent in scenery, with a hundred mountains up to 6400 feet in height, and geysers, sulphur springs, waterfalls, volcanoes. The weather is even more uncertain than in most parts of the world, and is strongly influenced by the Gulf Stream and by a northern current which brings drift ice and mist. Rainfall in the south averages almost fifty inches a year, but the north is dry though often foggy like the east.

The geographical revolution has affected this northern island directly. Just as it was on the route of the Vikings westward, much more now Iceland lies athwart vital strategic routes. In World War II it was a gathering place or way station for convoys sailing from the west to Murmansk; it was a stopping place and an emergency base for planes between North America and the British Isles or Germany. In the crucial northern hemisphere, in a period of water-borne and air-borne commerce and war-craft, Iceland occupies a key position; isolation is no longer conceivable.

Holding this crossroads position is a population of 138,000 homogeneous, literate, highly intelligent, well-governed folk, alert to the changing world in which they live. More new books are published in Iceland, *per capita*, than in any other country. The "per capita" may not be much, but the significant thing is that publication is a habit, and that since the saga age the children of Iceland, girls and boys, have been taught to read and write. Chief town is Reykjavik (the Smoky Bay), the capital, grown rapidly from a population of 6600 in 1900 to about 46,000 in 1948, with handsome new buildings for the university.

Next in size comes Akureyri, a fishing port of 6000 population, and several towns slightly smaller.

The contacts of the Icelanders have been largely with Danes and Norwegians, but British traders and pirates disregarded prohibitory regulations and visited the island, and Americans edged into a small trade there beginning in 1809, and gained a special license in 1815. But in general the Danes held close control over trade and government.

In the nineteenth century, however, a nationalist movement, inspired especially by Jón Sigurdsson, forced gradual concessions from Denmark. In the 1830's a consultative assembly was established, and in 1874, when Iceland celebrated the 1000th anniversary of settlement, King Christian IX gave this assembly, the Althing, additional legislative powers. In 1903 the Althing won the right to control the ministry, and in 1918 Iceland became a kingdom, united with Denmark through a common sovereign, and using the Danish foreign service to represent its interests abroad. It was then conceded that Iceland might become completely independent by mutual agreement after twenty-five years. World War II hastened the realization of that ambition; Iceland steered her own course after April 9, 1940, and became a sovereign republic on June 17, 1944.

Greenland is the western outpost of the Scandinavian area, only a short jump across the Davis Strait from the North American mainland. Because the island must be neglected in later sections of this volume it will be considered generously at this point.

The world's largest island has an area of 736,500 square miles; it is larger than the combined area of Spain, France, Germany, and Italy. From Cape Farewell in the south to Cape Morris Jesup in the north is 1650 miles, and the greatest width is 690 miles. From the northernmost point it is but 439 miles to the North Pole. Of its vast surface 86 per cent is covered by the inland ice cap, which reaches heights up to 10,000 feet. At the edges it is usually some 100 feet above sea level, and throws off icebergs from many of its glaciers either directly into the sea or into the in-reaching bays and fjords which indent the coast. Some of these more southerly glaciers move at speeds of 65 to 125 feet per day.

Atop the ice sheet the temperatures are always low, but in the coastal regions there is great variation: within the month of February Upernivik has had temperatures as high as 60.8° F. and as low as −44.° F. Precipitation varies from as little as 6 inches per year (Danmarkshavn) to as much as 46 inches (Ivigtut), and it is almost all snow.

Current life on the island has come from the West, both the sparse flora and the animal life of land and sea: reindeer, fox, caribou, polar bear, whales, seal, ptarmigan, even the native Greenlanders, whose Eskimo ancestors came across from northern Canada.

In two areas an ice-free coastal strip is wide enough and conditions are favorable enough so that settlements of people can exist: (1) West Greenland, really the southern stretch of the west coast, where the ice retreats as much as 95 miles from the shore, and where in some places islands dot the coast; (2) East Greenland, about one-third of the total ice-free land, where in one place (Scoresby Sound) it is 186 miles from sea to ice. In East Greenland the land is even more rugged than in the west, with many peaks of over 6000 feet.

Along these two coastal strips a population of some 21,500 scatters itself in small communities; about 21,000 Greenlanders now many of them with a mixture of European blood, and some 600 Europeans, mostly Danes.

Eric the Red made his permanent establishments (985) in the southwest, first in the "Eastern Settlement," now the Julianehaab District, and soon additional immigrants built up the "Western Settlement," now the Godthaab District. In these two settlements around the year 1000 may have lived 2000 people, Icelanders and Norwegians all. It was Eric's son Leif who led the first expedition to explore Vinland; and it was from these Greenland settlements that successive attempts were made by others in the next few years to colonize in North

America. But that was too far, demands for more land were not pressing enough; the Vikings had reached their western limits.

The colony seemed to prosper moderately until the thirteenth century, and we hear in European literature of the importance of Greenland falcons. But Greenland became increasingly dependent on Norway and in the mid-thirteenth century was forced to accept Norwegian overlordship (about the same time as Iceland), though the local Althing was kept. The Norwegians promised to send at least one ship a year, but frequently the ship was lost. When the Black Death laid Norway prostrate in the mid-fourteenth century no ship went out for nine years, "the long forgetfulness." An expedition in 1350 to the Western Settlement found only wild cattle and sheep, no human beings.

Paul Knutson sailed from Norway at last in 1355 to try to check the decline of Christianity; for King Magnus said, "We will not let it perish from the earth." Evidently he did not find much, although the Eastern Settlement still existed. It may have been this expedition, or a part of it, which went on to the American continent and carved the Kensington Rune Stone (dated 1362) in northern Minnesota. If so, it was a first and fruitless phase of the later real Scandinavian conquest of the American Middle West. But Knutson evidently wrote no report on his expedition, and mystery surrounds both its own exploits in North America and the last phases of life in Icelandic-Norwegian colonization in Greenland. Possibly the people, few in numbers and weakened by malnutrition, were overcome by the Eskimos. The colony ceased to exist.

Greenland's "rediscovery" dates from an expedition sent out by Christian I of Denmark in 1472 or 1473, which was attacked by Eskimos in East Greenland, near Angmagssalik (East Greenland being completely different from the old "Eastern Settlement"). The king's purpose was to find a northwest passage to China, which was also the primary aim of later explorers such as Frobisher, Davis, and Baffin. Commercial interest grew as

English, Dutch, and Danes learned from the Basques the art of harpooning whales. The Danish-Norwegian king became annoyed with Dutch claims in Greenland. So in 1666 the Greenland symbol, the polar bear, was added to the Danish royal coat of arms as a reminder to others to keep out. The first new settlement was established in 1721 by the Norwegian Hans Povelsen Egede, named Royal Missionary, and backed by a Bergen trading company.

Trade rivalries and conflicts over fishing led to the declaration of a royal monopoly of trade, 1776. The purpose of the monopoly was to assure the interests of the Greenlanders in culture and trade, and many commissions and self-sacrificing administrators have done their best. Greenlanders have themselves participated in local and district advisory councils. Schools and churches and hospitals have been established. Criticism has nevertheless been recurrent and bitter, and several reorganizations have been attempted.

In 1948–49 the whole monopolistic system was being abandoned, trade put on a basis of free competition, and private Danish capital invited to enter the field. This reorientation was studied by Premier Hans Hedtoft on a trip to Greenland in the summer of 1948, discussed in the local councils and with officials in Copenhagen. It was stimulated to some extent, probably, by the impact of United States soldiers and others in Greenland. But the reasons assigned by Premier Hedtoft had to do with a moderation of the climate in the last thirty years; the diminution of seals, which had made possible a self-contained economy; the increase of cod-fishing, which required sale on a world market; and sheep raising. The changed basis of the economy has been accentuated by a rapid increase in population.

Disputes and complications concerning sovereignty over Greenland have continued. The Norwegian claim was rejected in 1933. The United States, when it purchased the Danish West Indies in 1917, renounced claims to the territory discovered in the north by Admiral Peary. Then came World War II, and the German occupation of Denmark. One year after that occupation, April 9, 1941, the Danish Minister in Washington, Henrik Kauffmann, signed with the United States Secretary of State an agreement which established a wartime protectorate over Greenland by the United States, and permitted the United States to establish military and meteorological bases. But the United States also reasserted that Denmark remained sovereign over all Greenland.

The importance of this vast ice-covered island is both economic and strategic. Most of the native products are of no outside significance, not even the furs are important in world trade, though the natives dress in fox or bearskin trousers, eat the meat, use skins for boats, and in general live from animals. Coal is mined, but only for local consumption. In 1948 the discovery of uranium in East Greenland was reported. But the only important export has been cryolite from the mine at Ivigtût. Cryolite is of great value in the manufacture of aluminum, and this one mine at Ivigtût has almost a world monopoly.

Strategically the island has a double importance. In the first place, the enormous field of ice is a powerful influence on the winds and weather of the North Atlantic, and therefore on all northern and western Europe. A number of different scientific expeditions, primarily Danish and American, have been trying to fathom the mysteries of weather. During World War II the Germans did their best to establish a meteorological post there. In the second place, Greenland like Iceland is on the great circle air route between America and Europe and lies along the pathway of a potential Arctic submarine route. Greenland is in the strategic center of the predicted Arctic warfare.

3. THE UNITY OF THE NORTH

The great expanse of land and sea from Greenland in the west to Finland in the east is unified historically and geographically. The Viking longboats, raiding and crusading, made it one. Language affinities and political institutions attest the interrelationships. Shippers and fishers of all the North mingle in each other's ports. But the pilots and planes of the air have created the real modern counterpart of the sea routes of old. Through changing times and varying techniques the Scandinavians have retained their intimate relations within their area, and have preserved their institutions. The borders have from time to time been threatened, and are threatened in the twentieth century, but so far they have held with tenacity. In a five-way political division the essentials of cultural unity have been deeply engraved. Outside rule has been repelled; immigrants have been absorbed.

These lands and peoples of the North are closely related to each other; they are also closely related to the other countries of western Europe, particularly those bordering on the Baltic and the North Sea. Age-old bonds of culture and commerce connect them with Germany and Britain, and they feel keenly any break in those established and natural ties.

The "island" character of each of the Scandinavian lands influences its entire life. Iceland is the only one which is technically an island. Denmark, however, is made up of many islands and a peninsula connected with the continent by only a narrow neck. The Scandinavian Peninsula and Finland are land-connected only through wide swaths of forest and swamp (except in the isthmus between Lake Ladoga and the Gulf of Finland, where Finland and Russia meet). The island nature of the area, therefore, emphasizes the importance of the sea as a link with other lands and peoples, and has made of the Scandinavians seafaring peoples, using the sea for commerce and fishing and war.

Other pervasive characteristics are sparsity of settlement and vastness of distances; only Denmark is tightly settled, and the distance from Copenhagen to Norway's North Cape, in a straight line, is longer than that from Berlin to Constantinople. Winters lack crippling cold, but in the northern portions they are depressingly long.

The air age and polar flying have come to minimize distance and to add air to sea as a new medium of communication. Airplanes not only knit more closely the territory of the North; they also transform Scandinavia's strategic position. The region was on the edge of land or sea conflicts of the past between the great powers; it now occupies the northern sector between East and West, directly under the air routes between Russia and the United States.

Political shifts outside Scandinavia reinforce the changes wrought by air transportation and a new technology. When four to six powers on the continent vied with one another in the balance of power and bid for the aid or neutrality of the northern states, they had a chance to protect themselves. They were then, as individual nations, relatively strong enough to deserve respect. But now there are not four to six powers juggling the diplomacy of Europe. There are two power centers, and the theater is not Europe but the world. Scandinavia's strategic position has deteriorated politically as well as geographically.

In this new world the Scandinavian countries are individually tiny, and they are no longer on the margin of conflict. Finland is under the shadow of the eastern power; Iceland and Greenland are more or less under the influence of their western neighbor; the central trio is drawn in both directions by competing forces. The revolution in world politics and technology has revolutionized Scandinavian geography.

2. The Heritage

The chief factors in the living heritage of Scandinavia—the broader reaches of its historical perspective—must be appreciated to understand the problems and attitudes of the twentieth century. Only the deeper colors of the broad movements at work in the making of modern Scandinavia can here be scanned. The essential background may be seen in terms of four fundamental shaping forces: *war* which has created states, and fixed boundaries; *religion* which has held people together and encouraged ideals beyond the present and the material; *law* which has defined the relationships of individuals to one another and established order and justice; the *economy* by which men live and through which they have organized for material well-being. These four, expressed in institutions, in literature, in arts, in tradition, afford an insight into a total culture.

1. WAR

In the dawn of civilization in Scandinavia it was war which decided the preëminence of the Nordic invaders over the "little brown folk" who inhabited the inner lands of Sweden or the coasts of Norway. Perhaps tribes like the Herules had fled from the Danube because they had been defeated and decimated in war; new struggle faced them in the North. A reverse movement occurred when the Cimbri moved south out of Jutland and devastated large areas of the Roman Empire before they were subdued and absorbed. The *Svear* and *Götar* and the Danes extended their sway by war and even by the enslavement of conquered peoples. The Beowulf Saga pictured a war-like society, and the Vikings became the terror of their age.

The Viking raids were the second outward thrust of the Scandinavian peoples. The earlier migrations of the Cimbri and the Goths were surges of mass humanity from a backward area into the more highly civilized Roman Empire. The forays of the Vikings were mixtures of trading and raiding carried out not by tribal groups but by small bands of men, sailing in the finest ships of the day, seeking profit and booty and adventure. In the central thrust they raided the coasts of Britain and France, took over the Faroes, Orkneys, Shetlands, Hebrides, and the Isle of Man, and established a kingdom in Ireland; they fought on the shores of Portugal and Normans won control of Sicily. The fleeting raids with which they began in France became large-scale operations and ended at last in the establishment of the duchy of Normandy in 911 under Rollo. From there a century and a half later the mixed descendants of that enterprise went on to conquer England.

In the eastward thrust there was more of trading and less of raiding, when the Swedish Vikings or Varangians traversed Russia via the Dvina and the Dnieper and sailed on to Mikla-gard (Constantinople) through the Black Sea. Here they traded their honey and furs and pitch for the gold and the luxurious products of Byzantine and Oriental civilization. Here in Mik-lagard some of them stayed for a time and served in the Varan-gian Guard, elite soldiery of the Byzantine emperors and em-presses. These "axe-bearing barbarians" fought throughout the Mediterranean, and one of them even carved runic inscriptions on the huge body of a lion statue in the Piraeus. To the north-ward their fellows left runic monuments on the Volga. Others under Rurik and his partners first built an orderly state among the Russian Slavs. Their very name, for the Varangians were called Rus by the Slavic tribes, became at length the name of those tribes themselves, and of the modern Russians.

Far westward across the North Atlantic went another major thrust of the Vikings. Here their beautiful longboats carried warriors and pioneers to Iceland and on to Greenland, and farther yet to Vinland. In their previous thrusts to the south and east, however numerous the Vikings may have been, they lost their northern identity; but in Iceland they created a society which retained their customs and their language longer than did the home lands.

The whole "movement" of these three thrusts was a prodigal dispersion of power, never centrally directed, never quite focused, but with far-reaching results impossible to calculate. In east and west the constructive aspects are clear; in the central push the coasts of western Europe were laid waste, the Carolingian Empire was shattered, and one knows not how much the northern strength and northern ideas of law may have contributed to the process of reconstruction. Nor can we ascertain the effects of this violent outburst on the lands back in the north. Something was learned of Christianity, and the booty brought back in only one or two raids was often greater than the taxes collected through years from peasants and fishermen.

These medieval Scandinavians had their wars and their empire-building nearer home, too. In warfare within the North, Denmark first occupied the central position, and the weight of power swung back and forth like a pendulum. Denmark was the bridge between south and north; also she lay athwart the routes of war and commerce between east and west. Germans pushed north through Jutland, where the still-used central roadway shows evidences of invasion and strife through centuries of both prehistoric and modern times. At the base of the Jutland peninsula lay the ancient land route for trade between France, the North German cities, and the Baltic area, and that region was fought over repeatedly by princes and city states. The Kiel Canal is but a modern device to utilize more fully this age-old route.

Denmark too stood guard over the narrow water passage from North Sea to Baltic; and so through many centuries played a pivot position in the naval wars of commerce which involved England, Spain, France, and Holland on the west,

Sweden, Russia, and the German cities on east and south in all conceivable changing combinations. Denmark's existence hung upon her own agility and the fate of foreign rivalries. The near-by Germans in their weakness or in their strength were the main external influence in Danish affairs. Slesvig (Schleswig in the German spelling) and Holstein, symbol and center of this continual conflict, passed back and forth. War gave and war took away. When through her own strength and that of her allies, Denmark won, she evidenced her prosperity in extensive building and in an increasing population; when she lost, her people suffered privation and waited for another chance.

Denmark did not, however, stand as a passive participant, but was often herself aggressor—not only in the raids of the Vikings, but in the migratory movement of the Angles and Saxons and Jutes, in the later establishment of the Danelaw in north England and in the creation of the North Sea Empire of King Canute in the eleventh century. For a fleeting moment Canute conquered and ruled over Denmark, Norway, and the British Isles. But these lands were too diverse and Denmark was too weak to hold them together. When shorn of this empire ambitious Danish kings strove to extend their power throughout the north and east. Norway and her colonies were united with Denmark in 1389 not by war but by marriage and the diplomacy of Queen Margaret. With control emanating from Copenhagen the Danes held the southern parts of the Scandinavian peninsula, directed Norwegian forces from the west, and won dominion over Gotland and in the lands on the eastern shores of the Baltic.

Thus for a brief period following 1389 the Danes realized the dream of a Scandinavian empire, and exercised hegemony in the famous Union of Kalmar. For four hundred years they played an active game of diplomacy and war. Sweden-Finland was boxed in between the encircling Danes and Norwegians and their frequent allies, the Russians. But Sweden gained the occasional support of Denmark's western neighbors, the Dutch, and she showed a rapidly developing internal strength. By the eighteenth century, Denmark had been pushed back from her eastern position; she was left only Norway and the western possessions in the Atlantic. The Swedes had taken the initiative from their cousins in the south.

The early wars between tribes and traders in central Sweden are beclouded in legend and uncertainty. We know only that out of strife the Swedes and Goths made themselves masters over the other tribes in the east-central area of the Scandinavian peninsula. In the twelfth century the prolific and vigorous Swedes pushed on in a movement of conquest and colonization to control and Christianize the Finns, and to establish in their forest frontier permanent institutions of western culture.

With colonies also on the islands and on the coasts of the Baltic countries to the south of Finland it was natural that the Swedish expansionists should seek power there, and inevitable that they should come into conflict with both the eastward-reaching Danes and the westward-pushing Russians.

In 1523 Gustav Vasa, contemporary of Henry VIII of England, of the Emperor Charles V, and of Martin Luther, by war established Sweden's independence from Denmark, built a national state and a national church, and laid the foundation for further growth. Generations of warfare around the Baltic and the creation of a wide-spreading Baltic Empire led at length to continental conflict. Gustavus Adolphus, "lion of Protestantism," feared that Hapsburg-Catholic success in Germany would threaten the political-religious independence of the North.

In a remarkable speech to the Swedish Riksdag in 1630 as he was about to lead his forces south Gustavus explained that though the Holy Roman Empire had no fleet at that moment and could not cross the Baltic, it would quickly build such a fleet once it reached the northern shores of Germany. Sweden's best protection, said the King, was to fight the enemy on German soil, before she had become too strong and while the north German states could still be of help as allies. It was the 1940–41 argument of "defend America by aiding the Allies" in a seventeenth-century setting. Gustavus Adolphus lost his life, but his policy triumphed, and Sweden won territory in Bremen and Pomerania. The Swedish king also contributed improved techniques and a new mobility to the art of warfare.

Gustavus' successors used the increased power and prestige of the kingdom for further victories: most important was the winning of the southern provinces of Skåne, Halland, and Blekinge from Denmark. It was in this war that King Charles X, after a frustrating campaign in Poland, led his army across Germany, north into Jutland, then on ice across the Little Belt and the Great Belt in a spectacular island-hopping operation, over passages which froze hard enough for such a transit once in a hundred years. That crucial year, 1658, nature obliged the Swedes, and the stunned Danes could not defend Copenhagen. Sweden thus won the agricultural land of the south and the commercial coast of the west, and widened what had been but a narrow wedge of coast between Denmark and Norway.

But the victories of Gustavus concentrated jealousy against a nation with small resources. A half century later Charles XII found himself confronted with a formidable coalition of enemies, and his dashing brilliance in battle was not enough to save Sweden from disaster. Charles conquered for himself only an undying admiration from the romantic heart of the "little man," who still thinks of the impulsive boy wonder as Sweden's greatest king. But Sweden alone was not strong enough to carry through a policy of force. The states of the continent had more men and more guns. Charles lost his soldiers and his empire deep in the plains of the Ukraine. Years later he made a spectacular dash back to the north, but was killed on the Norwegian frontier, and Sweden's age of imperial greatness was over.

Expansion of the power of any state tends to increase the number of its enemies, and to consolidate them in opposition. A small state cannot long survive against pressure from all sides. Both Denmark and Sweden had their brief days of brilliance and power, but they were weakened by internal rivalries and divisions and they lacked the essential bases of manpower and industrial resources for permanent imperial dominion. In the years to come they were even played as pawns in the rivalries of the great powers with one another.

After Charles XII was killed and the Swedish Baltic empire came to its inglorious end in 1721, two small kingdoms were left in the north: Sweden with Finland, and the combined kingdoms of Denmark-Norway. The Norwegian border had been pushed back to the mountain ridge which still marks a natural division between the countries; Jämtland and Härjedalen had become parts of Sweden. In the south, too, the Swedish state had expanded, at the expense of Denmark, and occupied the whole of the lower end of the peninsula; Skåne, Halland, and Blekinge were incorporated into the Swedish state. Denmark-Norway held dominion over Greenland and Iceland and the Faroes—but the Danish king had been forced to mortgage the Norwegian-settled Orkneys and Shetlands for dowry when his daughter married King James III of Scotland (1468). They were never recovered.

In the long struggle for supremacy in the Baltic Sweden had forged ahead, held Pomerania on the North German coast, and won back from Denmark the island of Gotland, "Pearl of the Baltic." She lost to Denmark her brief grip on the southern island of Bornholm, and finally lost to Russia the littoral of Estonia and Latvia where German barons and the merchants and warriors of both Denmark and Sweden had long fought for mastery. To Denmark one imperial right remained: the Danish king continued, as he had since 1429, to collect "Sound Dues" from every ship passing Elsinore between the North Sea and the Baltic.

The external boundaries of Scandinavia in 1950 are surprisingly similar to those of 1721, though intermediate and internal changes have taken place. Slesvig-Holstein was then connected with Denmark and now only the northern section is so connected. Finland's eastern and northern borders were then approximately as today with Viborg belonging to Russia and with the Russian frontier in the north marching for a brief distance with Norway and cutting off Finland from the ocean.

During the centuries of Danish and Swedish imperialistic rivalry Finland and Norway played subordinate roles. The Finns, organized and controlled by the Swedes, made no effective protest against their leadership, and participated as Swedish soldiers in the wars against Russia and in Gustavus Adolphus' campaigns in Germany.

The warfare of the Norwegians was an internal affair, chieftain against chieftain striving for authority over the whole of Norway. Unity came with Christianity out of the wars of the tenth to twelfth centuries: Harold Fairhair united the kingdom about 900, but the divisive elements were still strong; Olav Trygvason and Saint Olav used Christianity as a means of winning a common loyalty; King Sverre at last broke the power of both aristocracy and bishops and established the prestige of kingship. The fighting was bloody and significant, both in the building of Norway itself and in the expansion of Norway overseas. Many independent nobles, defeated or outmaneuvered by the centralizing kingship, then sailed off to build new careers in the islands of the Atlantic, all the way from the Faroes through Iceland to Greenland. In the fourteenth century the male line of Norse kings died out and Norway was united with Denmark. Theoretically Norway remained independent, but the common king resided in Copenhagen and Danish officials directed the fate of the northern partner.

Norway was used repeatedly to threaten Sweden's rear when Denmark allied with Russia to try to drive the Swedes out of the Baltic. The uncertain borderland, for a time taking Norway to within thirty miles of the Gulf of Bothnia, was a place of pillage and burning and terror until in the seventeenth century a shift in power drove the frontier westward to the mountains. The common border between Norway and Sweden has been unchanged since 1660, and a certain *détente* between these two states was reached by 1721.

The eighteenth century was dominated by the imperialistic

wars of the great powers, and the Scandinavian states played cagily for self-preservation. They accepted subsidies from Britain or France, joined one alliance or another, battled with or against each other, cautiously sought a chance to win territory or to expand trade. It was a transition stage in which they reluctantly abandoned the policy of power and turned to the less venturesome, much safer, system of neutrality.

It was during the general turmoil of the Revolutionary and Napoleonic period that war again brought significant changes in Scandinavian boundaries. First, as a result of agreement between Napoleon and Alexander I of Russia the Bear walked into Finland. Battle and treachery combined to yield a swift decision, and Finland was taken from Sweden; the Russians drew the Finnish border to include the Swedish-populated Åland Islands in the Baltic, and in the north swung the frontier far around Sweden toward the Atlantic. This blow to Swedish pride and power, depriving her of the province which she had regarded as part of herself for over 600 years, led to revolution and reorientation. Gustav IV Adolph was removed in a coup d'état by a group of nobles and officials.

A peculiar sequence of events led within a year to the choice of the French marshal, Bernadotte, as Crown Prince and real ruler. But Bernadotte, now Prince Carl Johan, was unhampered either by Swedish tradition or by love of Napoleon. He saw that Sweden had little hope of regaining Finland from mighty Russia. He also entertained the geographic concepts of the French Revolution which meant to him that Norway and Sweden, joined in the same land mass, formed a "natural" geographic entity. Therefore Finland must be forgotten, and Norway must be united with Sweden. The fact that Norway was then united with Denmark could hardly mean much to a soldier who had participated in the wars of the Revolution and of Napoleon and in the recent reorganization of Germany. War must establish what nature intended.

King Frederick of Denmark followed an understandable but foolish policy. When Denmark was attacked in 1807 by Great

Britain he saw Britain as the continuing enemy and clung stubbornly to an alliance with Napoleon, the real threat to all small states. This made it possible for Carl Johan, convinced that Napoleon was soon to collapse, to win agreement from Russia and Prussia and Great Britain that Norway should be separated from Denmark and added to Sweden. This was the price which the Swedish Prince and military genius demanded and received for his alliance in the last coalition against the Emperor of the French.

The Frenchman turned Swede revolutionized the policy of his adopted country. At Åbo, Finland, in August 1812 took place an unprecedented spectacle: the Crown Prince of Sweden and the Czar of Russia embraced each other in real friendship. Alexander turned to watch Napoleon's army destroy itself in the desolating Moscow campaign, and Carl Johan faced about to plan for the final drive on the continent and the conquest of Norway.

After the success of the allies on the continent and the Napoleonic downfall at Leipzig, Bernadotte took his mixed army of Swedes, Russians, and a few others to Denmark and in January 1814 forced King Frederick to renounce Norway. The Norwegians tried to reëstablish their long-lost independence, drew up the constitution of Eidsvold, and elected their Danish statholder as king. It took a short summer campaign and appeals to the pledges of his allies for Carl Johan to assure the union of Norway with Sweden. He left the constitution unchanged, and the day of its original proclamation, May 17, is still the national holiday of Norway. Norway remained united with Sweden under a common king until 1905; the Norwegians then insisted on being independent. The Swedish attitude was summed up: "Let the erring sister depart in peace." Divorce came with bitterness and regret, but without war.

Denmark had, in 1814, by clever diplomacy kept for herself the Atlantic possessions of Norway, but her power and her ambitions had been given an irretrievable blow. In 1848 and in 1864 she was forced to fight against desperate odds to retain the provinces of Slesvig and Holstein. Pan-Scandinavian sentiment was strongly with her, but sentiment did not check the Prussian soldiers. Except for a small occupying force in 1848 the government of Sweden-Norway kept hands off, to the chagrin of the king and of many a citizen; and in 1864 Denmark lost again. Ibsen composed some anguished charges, but Slesvig-Holstein was gone, and even the Prussian promise of a plebiscite went unfulfilled until 1920. Except for these two local, defensive wars in Denmark, the Scandinavians kept out of war from 1814 to 1914, and, except for Finland, on to 1940.

War forged the boundaries of the North; war determined who should control the trade routes and the fisheries; war repeatedly tested the strength of kings and aristocracy. In war were released the pressures of personal ambition and adventure which were later contained temporarily in treaties of peace. Protestantism and the desire for religious independence influenced both the Danish and Swedish phases of the Thirty Years' War. Both personal and national aggrandizement played their parts in the wars of Charles XII and Gustavus Adolphus and Waldemar Atterdag, the fourteenth-century Danish conqueror. As in warfare everywhere, one finds in that of Scandinavia a blend of economic forces and limitations, population pressures, religious and nationalistic ideologies. The peasants asserted their rights in local and national risings, and thus tried to maintain or improve their status. Denmark and Norway were parted by war; Norway and Sweden were for ninety years united by means of war. Finland was torn from Sweden by war and by war gained at last a new independence. Iceland was settled by refugees from internal strife in Norway. Warfare did much to shape the North.

But gradually conflicting forces became balanced within Scandinavia. Boundaries and relative power were established. It became fruitless for the Scandinavian peoples to war among themselves, and dangerous for them to fight such neighbors as Germany and Russia. Out of the fires of experience they learned the destructiveness and the futility of war; they had sufficient intelligence and sufficient inner political stability to reject it "as an instrument of national policy." But still they could not escape it.

2. RELIGION

"We obey the Law and bow before Christ." These words are from an old motto, displayed at Eidsvold in Norway with the picture of a kneeling soldier.

Less tangible than war, but no less an influence in Scandinavian life is religion—both as an impelling force and as a basis of the social structure. The Swedish conquest of Finland was a Crusade, and missionaries marched with soldiers; Christianity formed one of the bonds thereafter tying the two peoples together. In the Thirty Years' War it is impossible to disentangle the intertwined elements of religion, politics, and strategy. In Norway from the time when Olav Trygvason gave the chieftains a choice of sword or cross on to the resistance movement of World War II nearly a thousand years later Christianity and the Christian church have been inextricably linked with the state and the vital interests of the people.

The religion of the ancient gods was bound in closely with the lives of the people of the North. Odin the All-Father was the fountainhead of wisdom; Thor with his miracle-hammer, the god of thunder and of war, was dear to the Viking heart, and so was Loki, the trickster, and Freya, the life-force mother, and the Valkyrie who made pleasant the deaths of warriors in Valhalla. All Northerners believed in these same gods, the *Aesir*, a democratic family community of super-beings, whose lives and loves and hates helped to epitomize and explain the mysteries of the unexplainable on earth.

Beliefs were strongly individualistic, each person having the right to choose his own god-protector. Chieftains, military leaders, chief peasants, acted in the religious rites, and there arose no separate powerful priesthood. Along with this general religious structure persisted beliefs in the *norns* or the spirits that inhabited the forests and the swamps.

The Vikings learned to associate Christianity with the prosperity and the higher culture of the lands they plundered, and foreign traders brought in new religious ideas. Ansgar came north from a Saxon abbey in the ninth century to Christianize Denmark and Sweden, but the converts he won tended to backslide when the missionary had moved on; the ideas he brought were foreign ideas. Then Vikings converted in England or France began to exert their influence at home.

Thus Olav Trygvason came with power and prestige to Norway, and slaughtered those who would not be baptized; it was through him that Leif Ericson became a Christian and was sent to Greenland, where he had more success with the other colonists than with his stubborn father. Many of Olav's conversions were obtained very suddenly, with no real conquest of heart; conversions of the battlefield did not strike deep.

Not surprisingly many of the chieftains combined against the next unifying and Christianizing king, Olav Haraldson, reasserting paganism and their own rights. This new Olav was cut down at the battle of Stiklestad in 1030, but the sequel showed what a ferment had begun to work. Miracles were reported from Olav's body, and at the same time people began to feel the pinch of foreign authority. Half-convinced already, the chieftains and the people began to rethink their deeds and decided that Olav must have been right. They repented their victory, regretted the death of the national leader and the Christian, made him "Saint Olav," and erected Trondheim (Nidaros) Cathedral over his grave. In his memory they joined in a move to reunite Norway.

"The blood of the martyrs is the seed of the church." But as people came haltingly to a recognition of the new faith, so they came with painful gradualness to an acceptance of the teaching of Jesus.

Christ himself was preached at first as a lord of strength, able to humble and to shatter the power of mighty Odin. The apostles were represented as the bodyguard of Jesus, Armageddon as Ragnarök, and Paradise as the old Valhalla. The story of the death of Balder the Good and the Beautiful may well have been an early attempt to reconcile something of the heathen beliefs with the story of Jesus. The annual festivals celebrating the coming of spring and praying to the god of the harvest were so natural to folk dependent on rain and sunshine that they have been merely transformed and kept in a Christian environment; fires still burn on Swedish hillsides on *Valborgsmässoafton* and on Midsummer Eve. The worship of the sun left traces far into the Christian epoch, when the radiant sun symbol was blazoned on altar cloths in medieval churches. Intricately beautiful wood carving on church doors and pagan dragons flaunted atop roofs attest the continuing power of the old traditions as well as the old art forms.

Gradually Christianity, allied with the centralizing policy of the kings, struck firm roots. About 1100, Lund was made the seat of an archbishopric for all the North, and the foreignness of Christianity began to lose significance. Bishops and kings often worked together, even as in those more "civilized" lands to the south. Perhaps most notable is the case of Absalon, bishop of Roskilde in Denmark, foster brother of King Waldemar, who is credited with discovering the site of the merchant city of Copenhagen. The later establishment of separate archbishoprics for Denmark, Sweden, and Norway was both a recognition and a stimulus to the development of national unity. The conquest of Finland in the twelfth century combined the efforts of an English missionary, Henry, and the expansionist energies of Swedish armies.

The adoption and extension of Christianity encouraged an increased cultural borrowing and absorption from the continent and facilitated the growth of peaceful trade. Through Christianity and the Christian Church Scandinavia became culturally integrated with Europe. Yet at the same time Christianity became something different in Scandinavia, for there as in all the other lands of earth into which it expanded, it adapted itself somewhat to native beliefs and to pagan customs.

Individualism was one of the aspects of the old beliefs of the Scandinavians which was retained and emphasized in Christianity as they interpreted it. Luther's "priesthood of all believers" was among them an established concept, therefore some of the theological disputes of the Protestant Revolution were less disturbing in the North than elsewhere. Protestantism came easily. Also it came hand in hand with a reinvigorated nationalism. The Danish attempt to maintain the Union of Kalmar reached an intolerable climax for Sweden in the massacre of 1520 (Stockholm's Blood Bath), when the leaders of the defeated Swedish party were slaughtered after an amnesty, and Gustav Vasa found Protestantism a useful means of augmenting the popular strength of the national rising. The confiscated property of the church was a royal blessing first in Sweden and then in Denmark. For after a decade of defeat and turmoil Denmark too became Lutheran, and then forced Norway to accept the reform.

This element of outside pressure was the most difficult part of the Reformation for Norway; here national sentiment rose in opposition to the change, a futile opposition in the long run. The carrying out of Denmark's policy demoralized faith and national feelings, but it did reinvigorate the Danish language in the northern kingdom. Danish became entrenched as the official and the written language, and Norwegian was forced to be but a "tongue-language," without a written usage.

In theology and intellectual life in general the Reformation was an invitation to new influence for Scandinavians. In Denmark Niels Hemmingsen interpreted the Scriptures to students from all over Europe, and was visited by King James VI of Scotland. Olaus Petri had been a student at Wittenberg and he became Sweden's reforming theologian and a writer of renown in both philosophy and style. A rational and practical attitude gained new strength.

Then gradually coldness and indifference grew within the

churches as a result of their secure position in these northern countries, and the clergy sometimes lost contact with the real soul of the people. Inevitably came reaction from folk who yearned for a more emotional religious experience. In Norway this expressed itself in the popular pietistic movement led by Hans Nielsen Hauge in the early nineteenth century. The "Haugeans" held cottage meetings with prayer and singing, but they did not renounce allegiance to the national church. Nevertheless the established clergy were annoyed, and conservative elements were fearful. Hauge spent ten years in prison for preaching without a license, but his influence expanded.

Discrimination and contempt widened the cleft between religious groups, and dissenting sects like the Quakers found converts. Such groups took a major part in the emigration which began with the sailing of the *Restauration* to America in 1825. In Sweden (and Finland also) similar movements roused the peasantry and the Eric Jansonists were forced to seek a new home, settling at Bishop Hill in Illinois. The ferment in Scandinavia brought first repression, then reform; in Norway, lay preaching was permitted in 1842 and religious toleration was granted in 1845; in Sweden, the Methodists won a number of followers in the 1840's. Events took a different turn in Denmark, perhaps because of the dynamic personality of Bishop Grundtvig, who reinvigorated spiritual life and gave impetus to the broad program of the folk high schools. Religion and education went hand in hand, both geared in closely with the state churches.

In the course of centuries the church established itself in each of the Scandinavian countries as the most broadly inclusive organization outside the state itself. In many ways it is coextensive with the state and functions as a part of the state. The church is still "established" in each of these countries, and a person is born into the church as he is into the political society. A citizen can declare himself a member of another religious organization, but even then, for example in Sweden, the records of his birth and his movements are kept by the parish priest,

and when he wants a liquor ration book he obtains it as a resi-
dent in a parish.

In Norway as well as in Sweden one government department
administers the affairs of both church and education, illustrat-
ing and continuing the long tradition of church interest in
schools. Despite liberalizing laws since 1842 the majority of the
members of the government in Norway must still be members
of the Lutheran state church, and nearly 97 per cent of the
people belong to it. This system facilitates religious instruction
in the schools, and promotes national uniformity and homogeneity. At the same time the very comprehensiveness of
church membership permits a wide range of thought and of
individual liberty. It also puts certain religious matters under
the control of political bodies, introduces some compulsion on
the individual, and produces a certain passivity. People support the church through taxes rather than through voluntary
contributions, and hence may not feel the highest degree of
responsibility for the maintenance of the ecclesiastical establishment or even of charitable enterprises.

The official position of the church and the passivity and
reserve of the membership have made some observers think that
the Northerners are non-Christian, even outright pagan. Many
of the socialist leaders are anti-clerical, occasionally atheist.
One critic has pointed an accusing finger at the sheer physical
display of Vigeland's nude humanity in Frogner Park in Oslo.
Scandinavians are likely to say that they simply treat the body
in a natural, not a pagan way; they express horror instead at the
worship of the machine and the dollar in New York.

The fact is that the free churches, though small, are vital,
and that many religious influences express themselves without
separating their followers from the state organization. The Salvation Army, for example, has astonishing strength, particularly
in Sweden. Various lay groups have active mission stations both
at home and in the far corners of the world.

Most dramatic illustration of the power of the church and
of the basic Christian spirit was the fight of the church in

Norway during the war. It was a fight not just for self-preservation, but, as Bishop Berggrav wrote, "a spiritual struggle against violence and lawlessness." Against a government which defied God the Norwegian Christian was called upon to "obey God rather than man." Both teachers and ministers renounced their state appointments and salaries, but agreed to fulfill their educational and religious functions anyway. The church issued a bold statement of position, "The Church's Foundation," which condemned nazism and was read in churches throughout the land.

Of the 858 clergymen of the state church 797 resigned their places; the people of the parishes took over their support, and the government dared not carry out its threats. Some 28 per cent of the pastors were punished in various ways, and two died as a result of treatment in concentration camps. Seven or eight hundred Jews were taken to Germany; only a handful survived to return to Norway. The church spoke boldly against such brutalities and helped many others to escape capture. Operating "underground" and in persecution the old church rekindled faith and inspired resistance and hope; it could not be intimidated or subdued.

Fanaticism or even deep emotional fervor may be lacking, yet the church occupies a position of prestige, the clergy are respected leaders, moral standards are high, there is a widespread sense of the brotherhood of man, and of social responsibility, and during the recent war the church was a rallying point of faith and action, a bulwark of strength against disunity and despair.

3. LAW

With law shall the land be built,
not by lawlessness laid waste.
—Frostathing Law

Law regulates the relationships of individuals within a community; it is given its character by the moral standards and ideals of society and is thus closely associated with religion.

In Scandinavia the development of law precedes the establishment of the state. Farther back in time than we can know, the chieftains and freemen met in periodic "Law Things" to decide cases and to formulate rules of conduct. The Things were district meetings of the farmer-freemen which brought the force of public opinion to bear upon criminals, and which slowly built up bodies of law which were carefully phrased and just as carefully preserved. In ordinary civil disputes the Thing often acted as a court of conciliation or arbitration, getting the opposing parties to agree on a reasonable settlement.

When a murderer was brought before the Thing both his partisans and his enemies had a chance to present their case; by a clanging of shields the assemblage gave judgment. If the man was judged guilty he was outlawed; there were no police to enforce a verdict, but private individuals might do so if they wished—and if they could. It was a system of controlled personal vengeance, with community sanction through the Law-Thing a matter of vital importance. Gradually there developed rules of conduct that were clear and just, and later real government to enforce the rules.

When the Norwegians settled in Iceland and were faced with new problems of adjustment it was natural that they should go a step farther than they had yet gone and make of the court meeting a full-fledged legislative body, a parliament, the Althing. This oldest legislature in the world, founded in 930, celebrated its thousandth anniversary in 1930. When other Norsemen went to France and won control of the duchy that was to be called Normandy it was not surprising that they should there pool their own experience and methods with those of the natives and that the jury system should develop therefrom—a system of inquest and judgment by one's peers developed in Normandy, taken from Normandy to England, from there overseas to America, and thence back to Norway in the nineteenth century and to Denmark in the twentieth century.

As the chieftains gained power some of them became petty

kings, then slowly gave way before the centralizing tendencies of the strongest. The kings in Sweden and Denmark gradually took over the administration of justice, but in Norway the Things persisted. There the kings came to propose laws which the freemen in the Things discussed and often adopted, with a mutual respect for law so deep that there are no recorded conflicts between king and Thing. Out of the traditions of the old law and the revised formulations there grew in Norway four basic law codes, unified into one code for the entire country in the 1270's.

Some of the clauses of one of these four, the Frostathing Law, reflect not only the law itself, but also the kind of society which then existed, and the philosophy on which it was based:

IV. 5. All free men shall enjoy security in their homes.
VI. 1. The first provision in our law of personal rights is, that every one of our countrymen shall be inviolate in his rights and in his person, both in the kingdom and outside the kingdom.
IV. 58. In three places, in the Church, at the Thing, and at a merrymaking, all men are equally sacred.
II. 4. Every man in the king's dominions must be a Christian.
VII. 1. It is the king's right to command and to forbid, but he must rule according to law.

Landholding was most carefully regulated, each man holding land as the representative of a family; in case of sale the land had to be offered first to relatives, and if sold outside the family it could under certain conditions be redeemed. Slaves were recognized, but had few rights. A freeman had three fundamental duties: to serve in the *leidang* or army, to help in road-mending, and to aid when necessary in church construction; he could not refuse an appointment to meet at a Law-Thing, and he could not bring ale to a Thing.

These laws of the Norse Things were primarily rural in nature, while rules concerning commerce were most highly developed in the later law of Birka, named after the merchant island in Lake Mälar in Sweden. Maritime law owed much to the later development of the Sea Code of Visby, the Hanseatic center on Gotland.

In such a society of equals, making laws for all in great open gatherings, there was no place for absolute monarchy. The idea of divine right was occasionally claimed, but it did not become fixed. In Denmark at last in 1660 the king became really an autocrat, absolute ruler in law and in fact, but this was unique in the North, and was abolished in the revolution of 1848. The basic concept was that the king should be chosen by the people, and strict rules of inheritance were not adhered to: the Swedes chose Gustav Vasa in the sixteenth century, and a French soldier in 1810; the Norwegians elected a Danish prince in 1905. The Scandinavians never wholly forgot the precept that the king must rule according to the law, and they considered themselves to be exercising a natural right when, for example, they dethroned Gustav IV Adolph in 1809 in Sweden.

Most significant of all was the attitude of common responsibility and participation in the making and enforcement of the law. As Nils Herlitz writes:

Sweden was a school of self-government, where the people were educated to look upon the state and the municipalities neither as foreign, hostile powers nor as instruments for promoting their own interests, but as a common concern, for which they had to share the responsibility.*

Throughout Scandinavian legal systems runs a general affinity due to common origins and a somewhat parallel experience and need; on this has been built in the twentieth century a more conscious unity through commissions working to make similar or coördinated laws for each of these countries in social affairs. The total result has been the creation of socially responsible states, but with a citizenry closely critical of the acts of government. There is meaning in the fact that

* Nils Herlitz, *Sweden, A Modern Democracy on Ancient Foundations*, p. 90.

the most common book next to the Bible in a Scandinavian home is a book of law.

Out of these ideas and experiences have grown the governments of present-day Scandinavia, two republics and three monarchies, yet all democratic in nature.

Sweden has the earliest of the existing written constitutions in the north, one drawn up at the time of the overthrow of the Vasas in 1809. Here were embodied the principles of individual liberty, freedom of speech and the press, and the limitations on the king which made possible the further development of constitutional monarchy. The Riksdag, dating probably from 1435, was left with its division into four estates: the nobility, the clergy, the burghers, and the farmers. In 1866 this obsolete structure was changed to the present two-house system, with a First Chamber indirectly elected, and a Second Chamber elected by direct vote, each house being equal in authority. In legislation the constitution provided for agreement between king and Riksdag, each having an absolute veto. Both executive and judicial authority were vested in the king. Within this framework the pressures of democracy in the nineteenth and twentieth centuries transferred the real power from the hands of the king to the Riksdag, the Cabinet (or Ministry), and the Supreme Court. Universal male suffrage was won in 1909 and also proportional representation. Woman suffrage together with woman's right to sit in the Riksdag came in 1921.

In Denmark the absolutism established in 1660, though complete in theory, was for the most part patriarchal and benevolent in practice, and administration was in the hands of a bourgeois bureaucracy. Denmark's misfortunes in foreign politics both discredited the system and for a time fixed it the more firmly on a despondent people. Reform and reaction alternated, influenced heavily by German thought and German officials.

After 1814 a sweeping school reform in Denmark democratized education and gradually the opposition to absolutism gained overwhelming power. A great jurist, Anders Orsted, demanded that the courts consider the meaning of the law, not only its letter or spirit. Grundtvig called for freedom of conscience and political liberty—"Let freedom be the watchword in the North, freedom for Loki as well as for Thor." The July Revolutions of 1830 encouraged demands for a free constitution in Slesvig-Holstein, and in 1831 consultative provincial chambers were established in the duchies. The rigidity of the absolutist system was thus broken, and in 1841 parish and county councils were granted. The European revolutions of 1848 gave the necessary impetus to the next step.

A constituent assembly met, and on June 5, 1849 a new constitution was enacted, abolishing absolutism and setting up a constitutional monarchy. A two-house legislature (Rigsdag) was established with an upper house, the Landsting, elected indirectly and a lower house, the Folketing, elected directly; the basis of voting was equal suffrage of all males over thirty years of age. The individual won the rights of freedom of speech and of worship, and of habeas corpus; the privileges of nobility were abolished; and the executive, legislative, and judicial powers were separated and defined. Such a constitution went far toward real democracy: it was too much for the middle class of the towns, not enough for the small farmers. In 1866 a reactionary constitutional act introduced property qualifications in voting for the upper house, and made the Landsting a bastion of Conservative power.

Against this reversion toward aristocratic authority the industrial workers and the small farmers gradually consolidated their strength, and built powerful political parties. By 1884 the Liberal Left (Venstre) had 69 seats in the Folketing, the Right only 19, and the Social Democrats won two seats. The Left, in its struggle for recognition, sabotaged everything except social reform and at long last, in 1901, the Conservative Ministry resigned. The Conservative party had only 8 seats by that time, the Social Democrats 14, and the Left 76. A new ministry was appointed in line with the legislative majority.

Like the sudden changes of 1660, 1849, and 1866, this one too came without bloodshed, but it was nevertheless a revolution: parliamentary government, with full ministerial responsibility, became an established fact. In 1915 an Act brought the constitution up to date, and established universal suffrage for men and women over 25.

For Norway governmental power before 1814 had rested in Copenhagen. Norway had kept her legal system, and was theoretically a kingdom, but in reality she was governed as a Danish province. Liberal ideas did not perish, and nationalism gained force before 1814, wringing from the king, for example, a Norwegian university in 1811. The constitution of Eidsvold, May 17, 1814, was a thoroughly Norwegian document, combining centuries-old traditions and ideals with the latest thought and practice in Europe and America.

The leaders from different branches of Norwegian life gathered at a country estate north of Oslo that reminds one of Mount Vernon or Monticello. These bureaucrats and farmer-statesmen had read Montesquieu and Rousseau and Locke, as had the framers of the American constitution. The men of Eidsvold knew also the great work of Philadelphia, the Federalist papers, and the various constitutions of the French Revolution. Their document breathed the northern ideal of law-bound liberty, and provided for a government of careful checks and balances. Carl Johan accepted this constitution with only slight changes necessary to the acceptance of the King of Sweden as King of Norway. The electorate was at first only 7 per cent of the population but by 1898 male suffrage was universal, and by 1913 women as well as men over the age of 23 could vote without restrictions.

Norway, like Denmark and Sweden, experienced steady advance in democratic processes through the nineteenth century. The greatest single step was the winning of parliamentary government in 1884, under the decisive leadership of Johan Sverdrup, a veritable Gladstone of the North. Like her sister states, and even earlier than Sweden, Norway built strong political parties, and like the others she built a multi-party system with the Social Democrats gaining steadily increasing power. The safeguarding of freedom is so important that in Norway as in the United States the Supreme Court has won for itself, without explicit constitutional sanction, the right to question the constitutionality of laws.

Finland, for hundreds of years an integral part of the Swedish kingdom, shared in the constitutional history of Sweden. Finns had the same rights as Swedes, and were represented in the Diet of the Four Estates. When Russia conquered Finland in 1809 the liberal Czar Alexander I guaranteed the preservation of Finnish liberties and the country became an autonomous archduchy, continuing independently the laws and political institutions formerly shared with Sweden. Until the Russification policy of the very end of the nineteenth century these pledges were fulfilled; there has been no break, therefore, in the continuity of the Scandinavian legal tradition in Finland. Even local government has borne much the same character of independence and responsibility as in the countries to the west. It was not until 1906, however, that Finland was able to discard the antiquated system of the Four Estates. At the same time she established, as the first country in Europe, complete suffrage for men and women. She then set up the one-chamber Riksdag or parliament which she retained when she won independence.

Iceland's pioneering experience as an independent law-built society was interrupted in the thirteenth century, when Norway made Iceland a dependency, yet internal institutions were not changed. Then control passed to Denmark and the most significant effect was a relaxation of local political activity, finally overcome in the nineteenth century under the leadership of Jón Sigurdsson. Population and prosperity increased and the democratic forces were given new inspiration and new vitality. Subservience to Denmark was abandoned in 1918, when the kingship was left as the only legal bond.

The Scandinavian peoples have lived for centuries with sim-

ilar traditions of freedom and justice, and their political institutions have differed more in detail than in principle. The pace
of political development has often speeded reforms in one
country and retarded them in another, but each has so closely
watched its neighbors that progress in one has had an invigorating effect on each of the others. They have experimented
with forms but they have clung tenaciously to the fundamental
principles of human rights. On this foundation they have created the modern socially responsible state.

4. ECONOMY

Hunting, fishing, grazing and agriculture were the early bases
of economic life in the North as everywhere. Ancient Denmark's garbage heaps, euphemistically called kitchen middens,
give evidences of the life men lived: the bones of fish, oyster
shells in vast quantity, well-shaped tools and weapons of bone
and stone, and later of iron, and musical instruments such as the
lurs. Along the shores of Norway and Sweden are found remains from later periods, among them rock carvings of animals
of the forest and of men in boats.

The primitive methods of earning a livelihood survived
longer in the Scandinavian peninsula than in many parts of the
world, for it was exceptionally difficult there to bend nature
to man's will. Man had to use what he found. Slowly he did
win patches of soil from the forest, and supplemented fishing
with a few small crops. As the numbers of men increased and
pushed farther inland and northward the bear and the deer
retreated or were wiped out, and their economic importance
almost disappeared—except for the reindeer which are still
wealth to the Lapps, and a welcome unrationed meat to all.

Fish remained throughout the centuries the dependable stand-
by in the waters all about the Scandinavian countries. In the
Middle Ages the great market fish was the herring, taken during their run through the Sound along the southern coast of
Sweden (then Denmark). These fish when salted were shipped

throughout Catholic Europe and helped to build the fortune of many a Hanseatic merchant. Control of the fishing grounds became a matter of political importance and a cause of wars. Then suddenly in 1477 the herring for some unknown reason abandoned their Baltic spawning fields and dispersed into the vastness of the North Sea and the Atlantic. Their move upset the economic balance in northern Europe. But fish remained vital in home consumption and domestic economy, and gradually a new world trade was built.

In the early spring of the year the fishing banks of Lofoten off the coast of northern Norway have produced their wealth for centuries, and more and more have gained a place on the world market. In the south of Norway the tiny *brisling* (sardines) have been netted by the million, and canned and sent round the world (labeled now with the picture of King Haakon). In the belts and sounds of Denmark and on the rough sea men have continued to fish, and the fishwives have sold the eels and the green-boned hornfish and herring and dozens of other varieties in the odorous fishmarkets of Copenhagen and lesser towns. To the north men fished for trout and salmon in the inland rivers and lakes and for *strömming* (a small herring) in the waters of the Baltic. The Icelanders have built their export trade from the great fishing banks near by.

Farther afield the Norwegians hunted for whale, and made themselves the world's great whalers. It was a Norwegian Vestfold fisherman who constructed the first harpoon gun for whales in 1868. In 1904 whaling west of Norway was forbidden by law, for the fishermen feared that if the whales were all killed off there would be nothing to drive the small fish in toward land. Then the whalers sought new fields, the richest of them in distant Antarctica.

Forestry must be as old as fishing, providing at first only the humble necessities of logs for cabins and fuel for the fires in the dirt-floored dwellings. It was wood which made the Viking longboats and the oars. Logs were sectioned and fashioned into chairs; dishes were made of wood, and plows; benches were built for eating and sleeping, playthings were carved in the shapes of horses and chickens. Farmsteads had only a few acres under tillage, many acres in slow growing, precious forest. The great tracts of woods distant from settlement were claimed by the kings or the states.

Not all the North had forests. Denmark soon exhausted her beech forests, and Iceland's woods disappeared. Norway had to supply both Iceland and Greenland with wood for boats and building, and she traded wood to Denmark for grain.

From the forests of Norway and Sweden and Finland came the pitch, turpentine, resin, tar, which were large items in the trade of the Varangians with the East and in the later trade of Scandinavia with England. Timber was sent to the continent and to England for buildings and for boats. The British navy and merchant marine found the straight Swedish and Norwegian spruce trees strong and good for masts, and Englishmen bought shipload upon shipload of timber for pitprops in their mines. By the seventeenth century the rivers were being used to float logs down to crude sawmills at their mouths, and here the export trade developed.

Mining is likewise an art inherited from ancient times. At first men merely picked up flints off the surface of the earth in Jutland and fashioned them into hammers and axes. When they found iron over on Fyn the center of population and power shifted to the island where the raw material was available for new tools and weapons. In Sweden bog-iron was found in the marshes and lakes of the south; smelting with charcoal from the forests and adding fine craftsmanship the Vikings of the iron age made armor and swords of wide renown.

Sweden's great copper mine at Falun provided the basis of royal wealth and power in early modern times, and was the chief support for the armies of Gustavus Adolphus in the Thirty Years' War. The mine was chartered in 1347 to the *Stora Kopparbergs Bergslag*, which claims to be the oldest corporation in existence today. For although the copper is almost exhausted, there is still mining for by-products such as the red-clay from which paint is made, which is the reason the Swedish countryside is dotted with deep-red cottages and barns. The copper supplied the shining pots and pans which have hung on kitchen walls for generations.

Other metals and minerals such as gold and silver and nickel are of recent development in Scandinavia, but on the basis of copper, and more especially of iron, manufacturing industries came early to occupy an important place. The Norwegians had a large iron stove industry in the eighteenth and nineteenth centuries. The Swedish Riksdag started a cutlery industry in 1751 (under the old mercantilistic principles). In 1771 the privileges of Eskilstuna, favored center of this industry, were widened, and it became the Sheffield of Sweden, manufacturing fine cutlery for a world market. During the eighteenth century the state granted subsidies to shipbuilding and to many industries and towns, fostering both industrialization and urbanization. Textile industries and others which lacked a natural resource base had difficulties, but industries based on wood and iron saw greater and greater opportunities opening before them in the nineteenth and twentieth centuries.

Agriculture grew from its original position as a supplement to hunting and fishing to become the backbone of economic life. Even fishermen found that it was useful to have some ground to till. The man who built his life upon the land could also hunt and fish, could raise a few pigs and cattle in grassy clearings, and cut timber for his own use or for sale. There was a mutual interdependence in these simple activities, and with them all in proper balance a village of a few families could be almost self-sufficient. Such was a necessity in the isolated fjords and upland valleys of Norway and only a little less so elsewhere.

Oats and barley were the staple crops of early tribesmen, and they have been cultivated in the fields of Jutland, Skåne, and

Upland in central Sweden since soon after man entered those fertile regions. After the discovery of America the potato was brought north and in due course of time was raised to equal dignity with fish; today not even the Irish eat such quantities of potatoes as are raised and consumed in Norway and Denmark and Sweden. Wheat came, too, and rye, but wheat has thrived less well than the old staples. Berries have grown in abundance, especially in the Scandinavian peninsula and in Finland. In Greenland and Iceland agriculture has remained secondary to fishing, but vital nevertheless. Even a meager crop may stave off famine when export products fail.

Land was of such importance that much of the early law is the law of landownership and inheritance. In Norway individual landownership was the rule, for who but an owner and lover of the mountainside patch could make it yield at all? The "odal" law assured to a family continuance of ownership, and safeguarded against partitioning of patches already too small. In Denmark, favored with wide flat fields in the islands and east of the morainic ridge in Jutland, there was more temptation for squires to acquire large areas and to have them worked by peasants. They grew rich on the toil of tenants and beautified the fertile countryside with their castles. Not until the nineteenth and twentieth centuries were those great estates broken up into small holdings, worked by the little men on their own land. Sweden occupied a middle position, with conditions in Skåne comparable to those in Denmark and with conditions in the northern districts similar to those in Norway. In Finland the forest is still being invaded by the plow and settlement is extended by farmer-foresters.

But nowhere is there land enough. This scarcity of land and food is the foundation for the epic of emigration, and perhaps also the basic reason for the careful methods of exploitation of all resources.

Despite their marginal position and their small resources the Scandinavians for centuries have been active traders. They traded for art objects to far away Cathay and their merchants were on the lower Volga in the Middle Ages. They took honey and furs and pitch to Miklagard, and got coins and luxury articles from the East and from Rome. They were the middlemen who brought to the courts of medieval Europe the fish and falcons of Iceland and Greenland, and the Hanseatic League did big business in its "contor" in Bergen and through its merchants in Gotland and Stockholm. Visby, the capital of Gotland, was one of the chief cities of the Hansa, and middleman for the entire Baltic. German merchants were so numerous in Stockholm that they had their own German Church in the heart of the old "city between the bridges."

This trade, however, was based upon the raw products of the North—fish from the sea and the simple products of the forest. Very slowly did the Scandinavians learn to make for export the products of their hands, and much of their imports were but loot from the raids of Viking warriors.

After the Viking period the German merchant cities long held Scandinavia in economic subjection, and it took war as well as economic development to break their hold. Norway suffered most from a persistent rurality, sinking from medieval prosperity to poverty and stagnation, milked both by the German merchants and by Danish officials. Economic and intellectual sterility followed the greatness of the saga age. Many explanations have been offered, such as change of climate and the theory of outworn institutions and inability to establish the democracy which the times demanded. The Black Death (1346–1350) also played its tragic part, destroying a third of the population. Most plausible of all theories is that of Wilhelm Keilhau that Norway simply was too completely rural, suffering from structural weakness. The people were farmers and fishermen, lived in isolated small communities, and seemed unconcerned about the conflicts or the culture of the world outside. Because of this rurality the kings had been forced to grant foreign traders special privileges which became in the end burdensome to the Norwegian people.

The Hanseatic merchants were interested in immediate profits, they did not feel the community of interest in the development of the country as a whole which was essential to prosperity. The attitude of the Germans, and the feeling of the Norwegian ruler, concerned about the utility of trade for his realm, is illustrated by the speech of King Sverre at Bergen in 1186 after some riots in the town:

We thank Englishmen who have brought wheat, flour, honey and cloth, and those who brought flax linen wax or kettles, and any who have brought useful goods, as well as our friends from Orkneys, Shetlands and Iceland. But the Germans take out cod and butter and thus create want, and bring wine, which produces evil and no good. Some of our people have lost lives or been dishonored or beaten. If these Germans wish to keep their lives or their goods they will have to depart immediately, as their visit has been of little benefit to us and to our realm.*

The Hansa bled not only Norway but the entire area became involved in repeated wars with the Scandinavian states, and succumbed at last only because of its political weakness. Then Scandinavia took a new lease on life. Iron works were built in the sixteenth century, new inventions were made—such as the long line with 2000 hooks for fishing—and the Norwegians gained from Denmark control of their own export of fish and sawn timber. Sweden regained her independence in the sixteenth century, and launched into expansion both political and economic. The states of the North vigorously increased their exports and took their place as competitors in world trade. Monarchs and businessmen made common cause under the money-banners of mercantilism. Progress was not spectacular but it was steady through the eighteenth and nineteenth centuries.

The most noteworthy accomplishments of the northerners were on the sea, in this later period as in their earlier lustful impact on the world outside. Settlement had come by way of

* Quoted in Wilhelm Keilhau, *Norway in World History*, p. 88.

the sea, the routes of the Vikings were partly or entirely by sea, the life-giving fish came from the sea, and even the amber of the medieval traders. For many the sea was home.

Shipbuilding was a fine art among the Scandinavians when the peoples of the South were making slow and top-heavy vessels. The Viking longboats were superb in strength and streamlined beauty, swift and seaworthy. One of them, the resurrected Gokstad ship now in the Viking ship museum at Bygdø, near Oslo, served as model for a new-built vessel which sailed the North Atlantic in 1893 to the Chicago Exposition. The Vikings of the tenth century sailed such ships at will through the Baltic, the North Sea, the Atlantic, and into the Mediterranean and the Black Sea.

The Scandinavians continued to build ships, changing their patterns to meet the changing techniques of sail and steam, and the changing demands of commerce. They made sturdy fishing boats and special whalers, and freighters. Their ports were crowded with boats from their own lands and far-off countries.

Norway lost some 1100 ships in the Napoleonic wars; she had enough shipbuilding capacity so that in 1815 she still had 1673 vessels. Through building and buying she had by 1880 some 8100 ships and ranked third in the world; in 1914 she had 3050, two-thirds in steamships, and she ranked fourth in world tonnage. Sweden and Denmark were close behind Norway, all active world traders who participated in the East India business as well as in European and American commerce.

Certain persistent characteristics of this whole economic development can be brought into focus.

The pre-twentieth-century economy of the northern communities was founded directly upon natural resources, and involved little if any processing, except for the small domestic market. Foodstuffs were raised at home, and imported "colonial goods" such as coffee and sugar and tobacco were for a long time rare luxuries indeed. Agricultural life flourished abundantly in Denmark, but on the wind-blown, rocky farms of the more northerly lands farming was a perpetual pioneering. The activities of mines and factories were small-scale. The richest profits were often reaped by the foreign buyers and processers of iron and lumber and even fish. A precarious self-sufficiency was possible on the basis of a meager life.

In resources, psychology, and organization the Scandinavians had the fundamentals for the flowering that was to come. They had soil and sea, timber and ore, and abundant water power. They had learned as people with little that they must stick together and work together. The more isolated they were the more they realized the value of coöperation—as small groups building a house or a boat; as crews on a fishing boat, sharing the catch. Individualism was blended with coöperation.

The part played by the state was an interesting prelude to later developments. The state owned much of the forests, and took an active interest in support of commerce. The Greenland trade was a state monopoly both in the Middle Ages and again in the nineteenth and twentieth centuries, until 1948. The state had guided the foundation of many industrial establishments, and the primary natural resources were regarded as state or community property. The state guided landholding policy and finally provided legislation to keep the land from passing out of the hands of the peasants who worked it, or, as in Denmark, to enable the peasants to gain land. The modern socialistic state is in many ways the natural heir of the paternalistic state of the Middle Ages and of the mercantilistic epoch.

Yet there was freedom for initiative. "Who is chief among you?" a Viking was asked. He replied, "None, we are all chiefs here." Individual freedom was preserved within a voluntary, deeply treasured, social and economic organization. It is the experience with this kind of system and the belief in its possibilities, or even in its necessity, that prepared the Scandinavian people for the "middle way."

Still other facets of Scandinavian culture confirm and widen the impressions of such an analysis. Art gives expression to the individual's love of beauty; and art is not a monopoly of "artists," but a possession of the people. The Swedish program of *vackrare varor för varje dag* (more beautiful things for everyday) encourages appreciation of useful beauty; the flowers which brighten Danish and Norwegian cottages and apartments evidence a love of beauty for its own sake, and a pride in appearance. Literature is a heritage of deep interest and power; it helps to maintain ideals and traditions of ancient and self-conscious peoples, and is a vehicle for constant self-criticism and improvement. Migration has spread people and ideas from the North to all corners of the earth, and has enriched Scandinavia with the ideas of the wide world.

So we turn to an investigation in more detail of these forces of cultural interchange and of the problems and achievements of modern Scandinavia.

3. Scandinavian-American Crosscurrents

1. FIRST EXPLORERS AND SETTLERS

The first connections between Scandinavia and the United States were contacts without influence. Leif Ericson's discovery of Vinland was premature. After the settlements in Russia and Normandy and Sicily and the British Isles and the land-taking in Iceland, too few Vikings remained to people the great New World in the West. Greenland was far from the home base, and its settlements degenerated after a few centuries; Vinland was both too vast and too far, although it was but one step more.

Vinland colonization, however, was not impossible, it was only impractical. There stood no important barrier of either cold or distance to repel sailors who for 400 years crossed the North Atlantic from Norway to Greenland, and who never ceased trading between Iceland and Europe. Several colonies were established in North America, but they were short-lived, wrecked by personal dissensions, trouble with Indians and weather, and most of all by lack of motivation. We have brief saga-accounts of some of the seaboard establishments, especially Leif's own wintering in the year 1000, and the horror of the Amazon Freydis' murder spree some fourteen years after. Evidences of later (fourteenth century?) Scandinavian enterprises in America are sparse and dubious: a skeleton in Canada, some battle-axes and mooring stones and the Kensington Rune Stone in Minnesota (1362?). These things may possibly define the westward limits of Viking wandering, but they carry no other cultural significance.

Not until the seventeenth century did the northerners put down permanent roots in America. The farseeing imperial eye of Gustavus Adolphus visioned a Swedish colony across the Atlantic, and in 1638, six years after his death, a group of Swedes and Finns settled on the Delaware. They brought the log cabin to America, building their cottages and their barns in the style of the homeland 4000 miles away. This was the log cabin which became both the home-building pattern and the social symbol of the American frontier. The colony was soon overwhelmed by the Dutch and then by the English, but the people remained. They gradually blended into the larger community, and left upon it a moral as well as an architectural influence. They were a sober and industrious group, whose pastors came direct from Sweden until the end of the eighteenth century.

2. EARLY INTEREST OF THE OLD WORLD IN THE NEW

The early Scandinavian interest in America and its fresh young society was evidenced in varied ways. Peter Kalm, student of the famed Karl von Linné, visited and studied in North America in the mid-eighteenth century and reported back to Europe on the wonders of the flora and fauna and the society where "each man is a king in his own house." Axel von Fersen was one of the adventurous and liberty-loving Swedish noblemen who played his dashing role in the American Revolution before he became involved with Marie Antoinette. Benjamin Franklin, the scientist and the "worthy bourgeois," was regarded so highly in the North that the Swedish Crown Prince advocated (1768) the reconstruction of the Swedish school system in accord with the principles laid down by Franklin for Pennsylvania.

The Norwegian constitution-makers of 1814 studied carefully the constitution of the United States and the separate state constitutions. Their constitution of Eidsvold carried out the Montesquieu theory and American practice of the separation of powers. One draft incorporated a direct translation of Article XXX of the constitution of Massachusetts, stating the principle of separation of powers and ending with the same dictum that government "should be a government of laws and not of men." Here was a principle inherent in the ancient Norwegian tradition as well as in the state and federal constitutions of the United States.

George Washington fired the imagination of Scandinavian youth of the late eighteenth century. He was the symbol of the noble hero along with Cincinnatus and William Tell. Swedish Archbishop J. O. Wallin, who was in those days young, later wrote a romantic tribute to the bourgeois general, the king-like president—and to Freedom—

> For you the ocean has no breadth
> And the earth has no antipodes.

One of the Norwegian constitution-makers christened a son George Benjamin after the two great Americans. America was both a dream and a reality, and as dream was perhaps more important.

3. THE MIGRATION WHICH HELPED TO MAKE AMERICA

In America the Scandinavian elements, though small in numbers, began soon to make themselves felt. John Hanson, descendant of the early Swedish settlers, was first president of the Congress. Nils Collin, last of the pastors sent out from Sweden in the eighteenth century to the Swedish colony on the Delaware, founded the historical society of Pennsylvania; he was one of those lively and intelligent persons who recognized the crudities and difficulties of early America, and still enjoyed it. Norwegians and Danes were fewer in the early United States than the Swedes and Finns, but gradually they too began to move and soon the stream was a torrent.

The first group migration from Norway sailed in the 54-foot, 39-ton sloop *Restauration* in 1825. In the families which crowded onto the little ship were 52 people, 53 by the time they landed in New York. Except for the birth of the baby the monotony of the long trip was relieved only by the capture of a floating wine keg near the Madeira Islands. This find caused the thirsty emigrants to rock into port at Madeira without their flag hoisted and nearly brought about their arrest and detention. But they were allowed to sail on, and after a voyage of 46 days they landed in New York. Here more troubles awaited them, for the number of passengers exceeded the limits of the immigration regulations. But again there was leniency. They sold their ship (at a loss) and most of them moved to Orleans County, New York, where they bought small farms along the Erie Canal and tried to settle down. Then the beckoning prairies of Illinois led them on westward in the mid-1830's, to the Fox River Valley.

From here their glowing letters home lured more families and young men and young women. The America fever was beginning to burn, and the Middle West became the promised land. For four generations it beckoned, and called with a voice heard throughout Scandinavia.

The "America letters" sent home by ardent pioneers bragged and romanticized; they also contained much sound sense, and occasionally money or steamship tickets. Some of the letters made a direct materialistic appeal, like one of 1856: "and I can tell you that here we do not live frugally, but one has eggs and egg pancakes and canned fish and fresh fish, and fruit of all kinds, so it is different from you who have to sit and suck herring bones." Gustaf Unonius who founded the Swedish settlement at Pine Lake, Wisconsin, wrote many a persuasive letter home. One letter gives some clues to his own thinking and that of many another. He wrote of America:

Work, and honest occupation, is no disgrace. Conventional prejudices, class interest, meanness of public opinion, tyranny of fashion
are not present to hamper every step. Why should I not go to
America, to that country which looms like a shining Eldorado
before the eyes of every adventurous youth, to that country whose
fabulous history compelled our attention from our earliest years at
school. That country which has become the grave of old prejudices,
a cradle for true civic liberty and equality and principles of social
beneficence for new generations.

Warnings were sounded that life was not all ease, that the
changeable rigors of the climate took terrible toll in illness and
death. Ole Rynning, a noble-spirited and educated young man,
a leader of the ill-fated Beaver Creek colony in Illinois, wrote
(in 1838) a judicious *True Account of America*, which became
a popular book in Norway, and one of the best guides for emigrants. But Rynning died the next September.

Those of his colleagues who survived the fever soon fled from
their little cabins in the malarial swamplands. Many must have
yearned for Norway, but they could not return; they had spent
everything on the journey and the land. They died silently, or
they lived to rebuild their fortunes from nothing, some at last
to own good farms. It was the living and the successful who
wrote home, or who went back to visit with high beaver hat
and gold watch chain. The dead and the broken were lost; the
saga of America was a saga of success.

So new and greater waves of migrants broke from the past
and sought the better life in the land across the sea.

Rölvaag in his *Giants in the Earth* has told the tense drama
of those who struggled with nature on the storm-swept prairies
of the Dakotas. The Danes who settled in Iowa or eastern
Nebraska faced conditions somewhat less rugged, as did the
later Icelanders and the Finns in Massachusetts and northern
Wisconsin. But, as with immigrants in general, the first generation had to endure the uncertainties and risks of change and
carry the burden of back-breaking work. They turned the
virgin sod of the western prairies, they felled the timber in the
northern forests, they did housework for those who had mi-

grated a generation or two earlier, they built railroads and carried bricks and stoked furnaces in the steel mills, they laid foundations for a new civilization.

Occasionally some Scandinavian writer or scientist came to view this brave new world and to report to his own people and to Europe. As Peter Kalm had come in the mid-eighteenth century, so came Fredrika Bremer in the mid-nineteenth. The opportunity and the "restless on-ward striving" made a deep impression on this sensitive Swedish writer. She felt the sharp difference between earnest New England and the West, where freedom was "still sowing its wild oats." She reflected the European wonder at the eager search for speed and the mobility of people, "the incessant change from place to place." She analyzed the ideal of the American man as "purity of intention, decision in will, energy in action, simplicity in manner, and demeanor." The woman's ideal she found to be "independence of character, gentleness." She discovered in the New England spirit the "two mainsprings . . . the one is a tendency toward the ideal of moral life, the other impels it to conquer the earth." She recognized America to be the "land of experiment." In her book she frankly said that in America "children have a better prospect . . . for their future than at home. They are admitted into schools for nothing; receive good education, and easily have an opportunity for maintaining themselves." Though slavery and politics worried her the report on *America in the Fifties* was favorable indeed, and gave another impetus to the growing migratory movement.

The upsurging migration of the 1850's was halted by the War between the States, gained new momentum in the later sixties (stimulated considerably by the Homestead Act of 1862), only to be checked by the economic crisis of 1871–72. A new wave then led to the greatest peak, reached in the 1880's with a total of 656,451 Scandinavians coming to the United States. In the twentieth century the Viking inundation began to recede, and by the 1930's the movement was not into, but out from the United States. But already some 2,500,000 Scandinavians had migrated to the New World; hardly a family was left in the Northland without a brother or a cousin in America—in Minneapolis, Rockford, Decorah, Chicago, Seattle . . .

A few adventurous spirits went to South America or Africa, and many to Canada, but 98 per cent of Swedish emigrants found their new homes in the United States, 96 per cent of Norwegians and 88 per cent of Danes. Most of these settled in the upper Mississippi Valley.

They were attracted by the cheap good land and by jobs. They were drawn by the demands of a new society for brain and sinew, by a higher reward for their abilities than they could ever expect to gain at home. And they were drawn too by the principles of social equality in democratic America; many an "America letter" rejoiced that the settler no longer had to tip his hat to the clergyman, and that he had a voice in the affairs of the community. Such letters circulated in Scandinavia from household to household, sometimes were copied dozens of times and passed on, or were published in the local papers. The vision of America was painted in rosy hues; imagination and hope only deepened the colors.

Steamship agents fanned the ardor and the returned "local boy made good" enhanced the legend—the legend which was more than half truth. Migration fed on itself and grew.

On they came, thousands and hundreds of thousands, from the neat thatched cottages of Denmark, from the overpopulated woodlands of Småland, from far north in the land of the midnight sun. They came to the land where life was young. In the first generation they drew together in their own national groups, held by their common background, and by their distance from it. They brought with them many of their old-world prejudices. For example, many retained a strong anti-clericalism, and it took them a few years to realize that in a society with no state church the issues of clericalism were simply not important. Gradually, however, they adjusted to the new environment, and they "Americanized" more rapidly than most newcomer groups. They became aware of American

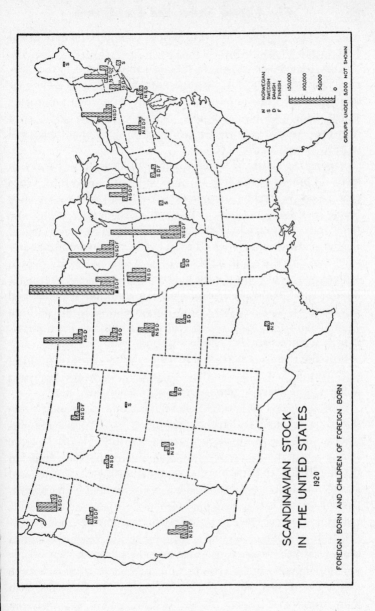

SCANDINAVIAN STOCK
IN THE UNITED STATES
1920

FOREIGN BORN AND CHILDREN OF FOREIGN BORN

NORWEGIAN N
SWEDISH S
DANISH D
FINNISH F

150,000
100,000
50,000
0

GROUPS UNDER 5,000 NOT SHOWN

issues such as slavery and public education and temperance, and they began to speak their minds.

They joined hands with the Greeks and the English, the Germans and the Irish and the Poles, and built a new and great society. They furnished thousands of the "common man," sturdy backbone of America; they hewed timber and mined iron ore. And they furnished in increasing numbers men and women of distinction.

Among the names of well-known Americans of Scandinavian birth or ancestry are those of Senator Henrik Shipstead, Governor Earl Warren, Congressman Andrew Volstead, Senator Irving Lenroot. The voice of Lauritz Melchior has become familiar to millions, and the art of Greta Garbo and Ingrid Bergman and Sonja Henie. Charles Lindbergh came of Swedish stock, as did Victor F. Lawson of the *Chicago Daily News*. Vilhjalmur Stefansson was an honor to Iceland, Eliel Saarinen's architectural genius has benefited both the United States and his native Finland, and Carl Milles has created sculpture on both sides of the Atlantic. The battle of the *Monitor* and the *Merrimac* proved the genius of John Ericsson. Andrew Furuseth was one of the truly great leaders of labor. In the field of scholarship Anton J. ("Vot iss de effidence?") Carlson, Thorstein Veblen, and many others made contributions of note.

Craftsmen and engineers from the North have brought overseas their training and techniques in carpentry, glass making, interior decorating, metallurgy, and the building of bridges. In the seventeenth century they cut down trees and built log cabins; in the twentieth century they measured stresses and strains and built skyscrapers. They were a part of the "migration of skills."

In all walks of life, in positions of leadership and management, in individual roles as artists and writers, in essential but less publicized supporting parts, one found these dependable and intelligent children of the north. By the mid-twentieth century most of them were so wholly a part of America itself, so completely integrated in the new environment, that their origin was forgotten. They assimilated with ease, partly because they willed it so, partly because their inherited ideals and patterns of life were basically the same as the ideals and patterns earlier established in American life and appropriate to the American environment.

Their churches gradually changed from the use of the mother tongue to the English of the new society and of the second generation. Their schools and colleges retained something of the stamp of church and nationality but more and more began to serve a larger community. The day may come when Rock Island's Augustana College is no more Swedish than Notre Dame is Irish (the Notre Dame where Norwegian Knut Rockne was the great coach). Living in mixed communities, working together, intermarrying, the special characteristics of national origin have been submerged, diluted, though not wholly lost. Scandinavians have built themselves into America.

4. THE AMERICAN IMPACT ON SCANDINAVIA

The mass movement of peoples created the new America; it also helped to transform the old Europe.

Even before 1900, authorities in Scandinavia became concerned over the flow of young blood to the west. The predominance of young men in migration upset the ratio of the sexes (leaving only some 100 men for every 105 women), and became a factor in a declining birth rate. Ministers preached that the Lord intended people to live where they were born, and societies against emigration appealed to the young to help build their own countries. Governments asked what was wrong, and the social legislation of the late nineteenth and early twentieth century was partly "appeasement," to try to hold at home the youth who were tempted to emigrate. The legal status of the lower classes was improved, women's rights were extended, and labor gained greatly in power. Or, as with the cotters * in Norway, the class itself was eliminated by emigration; it declined from one-quarter of the total population in 1845 to 3 per cent in 1920.

Sometimes the appeal for social reform came directly from across the Atlantic. P. A. Berg and his wife left Norway for economic reasons, and also, as was often the case, because their dissenting religious opinions made them social outcasts. From Wisconsin Mr. Berg wrote back to the liberal Norwegian Prime Minister Johan Sverdrup that they had found freedom in America and that they enjoyed their Methodist fellowship, but he added: "You, Mr. Sverdrup, are fighting the good fight for democracy and freedom in Norway; keep it up, we are for you, for we have three sons and two daughters still in Norway, and we want them to enjoy at home the freedom which we could get only by leaving." †

Another Norwegian, who had never been to America, held up the United States as the model of all things wise and good. Sören Jaabaek was a radical politician, a Stortingsman (Congressman), close to Sverdrup and other political leaders who were friendly to the United States. Jaabaek published from 1865 to 1879 a small paper with a big rural circulation (for then) of 17,000. He compared the "unjust inequality" of Norway with the assumed new equality of Negroes and whites in the United States; he condemned the suffrage restrictions in Norway and called attention to the coming universal suffrage in America. He praised the early income tax law of the United States, the lack of pensions, the fruitfulness of the land, and the stimulus given to work. He serialized a history of the United States and gave information about migration. Those who migrated found it a good land, if not so perfect as Jaabaek thought. Only a few returned home disillusioned.

Migration was escape for the downtrodden and the embit-

* The cotters or *husmaend* owned small plots of land, but earned most of their meager living by work for the owners of the large farms.

† Original in Sverdrup Papir, Rigsarkiv, Oslo.

tered; the threat of it was a bludgeon with which to force reform from the vested powers. As Dr. Hovde points out with regard to the adoption of religious freedom in Scandinavia: it "was due in no small part to the knowledge that people were emigrating for the lack of it." Jaabaek and others deliberately used the fear of emigration to pry reform from reluctant government and to speed the process of social and economic change.

Migration was itself a potent force on both America and Scandinavia, and it was a means and a stimulus to further cultural interchange. There has been also much vital interplay of commerce and of ideas that is only distantly related to migration.

The lively commerce between Scandinavia and the United States will have to be analyzed later. Here one can but recognize that a large and increasing portion of Scandinavian trade has been with the United States. Millions of dollars' worth of automobiles, sewing machines, typewriters, oil, nylons, plastics, etc., have gone to the North; the United States has obtained in turn large quantities of wood pulp, paper, fine steel, and art objects, especially of porcelain, silver, and glass. Despite the distance across the Atlantic the United States even before World War II ranked next to Britain and Germany in the foreign trade of the Scandinavian states. The Norwegian merchant fleet has carried goods between the United States and all corners of the earth.

5. DIPLOMATIC RELATIONS

Governmental relationships between Scandinavia and America have been long-standing and friendly; they have not involved either momentous conflict or spectacular coöperation, except in connection with the repeated struggle for neutral rights and the freedom of the seas, which is discussed in the story of neutrality.

In commercial relations, however, Sweden and the United

States early joined in a far-reaching and revolutionary attack upon the existing system of the Navigation Acts; they opposed the nationalistic channeling of trade prescribed by the great maritime powers. The United States' first treaty with a non-belligerent was that with Sweden in 1783. Thus early began the coöperation of the new state overseas with one of the small but commerce-minded monarchies of Europe. This first step led on to others, and during the 1820's to separate treaties between the United States and Denmark, Norway, and Sweden which abolished many of the old mercantilistic restraints on trade. Thereafter the ships of the Scandinavian countries could trade freely with the United States, and vice versa, carrying either their own goods or the goods of other countries. The Scandinavian governments were pleased too with the Monroe Doctrine and with the way in which Britain and the United States together blocked the reconquest of the Spanish American republics.

The countries were still both small and far apart, however, and connections were not always close. In 1780 John Quincy Adams wrote: "The North of Europe (excepting Denmark) think very little about us, and in my opinion the longer this inattention continues the better it will be for us. I would rather contribute to increase than remove it."

The United States often had very meager consular and diplomatic representation in Scandinavia. As late as 1810 the government used a British citizen as consul at the important port of Gothenburg.

This underestimation of real interests, the failure to appreciate the world-wide ramifications of commerce and of war, almost led to complications in the Napoleonic period. Then a vigorous young Philadelphian had himself set up as vice-consul in Gothenburg. He, Richard Smith, was in Gothenburg from 1810 to 1812 because he had shipped as supercargo on one of his uncle's vessels bound to Russia. War conditions made the trip on to Russia seem too risky and he and the consignments for which he was responsible were stranded in Sweden. By

1812 Gothenburg played host to some 1200 foreign merchant vessels, anchored far up and down the river—perhaps the largest number of merchantmen ever immobilized in a single port, all afraid of capture by the French or the English. The Americans had been protected often in British convoy, but times were changing. Smith, though far from home, could put two and two together, and expected a United States declaration of war on Britain. He knew that if it came about forty American ships lying with British vessels in the outer roads would be taken captive if the British got the news first.

Hence the vice-consul was alert. When, on July 23, 1812, an American ship arrived, sailing in ballast from New York to Eastport, Maine, he surmised she had not been blown by storm that far off course. The captain was reluctant to say anything for he had orders to report only to his clients in the city. But Smith got from him the news that the United States had declared war on Britain on June 17, and warned the captains. To the astonishment of the British all the American ships moved up river. When the British discovered next day that they had been at war with the United States for five weeks they found also that the American ships had left their protection and were resting under the shelter of the Swedish batteries.

Smith then dashed overland to warn other Americans returning from Russia in British convoy. The captains refused to believe it was a serious war and sailed on. In Copenhagen the British learned of the war and as soon as they were all at sea again every American vessel was taken. If the Britisher had been serving as consul none of the American ships would have been saved.

The major depredations on American commerce were, however, due in this period to France and to her ally Denmark-Norway, and the claims arising out of these seizures cluttered the diplomatic docket for many years to come. Part of the claims dated back to John Paul Jones, some of whose prizes the Danes had given back to the British. In 1809 twenty-three

American prizes were held in Norwegian ports at one time. After long negotiation Denmark in 1830 agreed to pay $650,000 and there was a mutual renunciation of claims.

Disputes of this nature were annoying rather than serious. It is such claims against Denmark and against Sweden and disputes over the interpretation of clauses in the commercial treaties which comprise the diplomatic controversies between the United States and the Scandinavian countries.

Another aspect of diplomatic relations had to do with colonial possessions. As early as 1783, and again in 1845 the Swedish government wanted to sell the island of St. Bartholomew to the United States. In the latter instance it was James Buchanan who rejected the offer on the ground "that the acquisition of distant insular possessions for colonial dependencies, has never been deemed desirable or expedient by the United States."

But conditions changed. By 1917, after fifty years of intermittent negotiations, the United States was glad indeed to get new footholds in the West Indies and bought the Danish possessions in the Virgin Islands. Despite the high price of $25,000,000 the Danish conservatives and some of the Left strongly opposed the sale, but the people as a whole were not so proud in their nationalism, and a plebiscite approved the agreement. The Danes also obtained from the United States a recognition of Denmark's sovereignty over all Greenland.

More significant and more fruitful than these bilateral agreements and disagreements has been the coöperation of the United States and the Scandinavian states in international affairs. Norway especially and the United States, have been concerned with the codification of maritime law. Citizens of the small northern states have often been able to accomplish the kind of things which the United States wanted done, but which it was difficult for Americans to do because of the suspicions aroused by great power activity. Fridtjof Nansen and Count Folke Bernadotte are two outstanding examples. The story of Scandinavian contributions to international enterprise is a long and glorious one, studded with the names of able statesmen: Stauning, Undén,

Hambro, Trygve Lie. In this realm the United States and Scandinavia have usually seen eye to eye and have often acted arm in arm. The 1949 negotiation of the Atlantic Pact has brought most of these states into still more intimate relationship.

6. CULTURAL CROSSCURRENTS

Between the Scandinavians and the Americans there has long existed a basic similarity of thought. Even the Lincolnian interpretation of democracy in his "government of the people, by the people, for the people" had been used nearly twenty years earlier in an unpublished paper written by Johan Sverdrup in Norway. Neither statesman borrowed the phrase from the other; each was independently giving expression to the political philosophy of his society. Henrik Wergeland and Walt Whitman, though they did not know each other, gave voice to common ideals and aspirations; and Wergeland, Norway's romantic nationalist poet of the nineteenth century, proposed a triune federation of Scandinavian states patterned after the federal union of the United States.

The traditions of Scandinavia are the traditions too of America, and center about the struggle for personal freedom and democratic equality. The men of the Icelandic sagas sound much like American frontiersmen, though placed in different surroundings. Hard work and the incessant struggle with nature have characterized both Scandinavian and American. The resultant likeness in thought has made easier all phases of cultural exchange, from religion to industry.

For religion was a field of active interchange. In America the Scandinavian immigrants established their own religious organizations, and they were deeply affected by the evangelistic movements of the midwest in the nineteenth century. The Methodists and the Baptists and the Mormons and other sects also reached across the ocean to preach and convert in Scandinavia. To this day the peoples of the North are amazed at the religious diversity and fervor in America—"The land of revivals, churches, chapels, congregations."

A Presbyterian Sunday School worker from New Jersey, Robert Baird, was one of the most effective apostles to Scandinavia. Mr. Baird went to Europe in the 1830's to preach religious toleration and temperance. He won the highest sponsorships for his temperance program in Scandinavia as well as in Germany. King Carl Johan was deeply impressed by Baird's book (in French) on the American temperance movement, and had it translated and published in Sweden and distributed to every pastor in the kingdom. It was spread in Finland as well.

It was the psychological moment, for the Swedes had begun to worry about themselves. The English pastor, George Scott, helped to promote the movement, as did Swedish leaders like Per Wieselgren. In 1826 the Swedes had shown interest in the work of the American Temperance Society. In the 1830's temperance societies grew up rapidly, Baird traveled about like a conquering hero, and in less than a decade the consumption of *brännvin* and other strong liquors declined from forty-eight quarts per capita to less than six. In Norway legislation aided the cause; many little distilleries went out of business; and coffee replaced *brännvin* as the national drink.

When in the 1890's this wave had exhausted itself, a new working-class movement sprang up to fight demon rum, and this too had strong American support. Yet temperance was but one of the many social reform movements stimulated by American experience and precept.

Religious intolerance was not usually brutal in Scandinavia, but social and political ostracism often plagued dissenters. The Erik Janssonists were something of an exception, yet they as a group of dissenters were thrust out of Sweden in the midnineteenth century, and migrated to set up the Bishop Hill colony in Illinois. Law and practice grew more liberal, but men and women opposed to the state church made up an unusual proportion of emigrants. Visiting preachers from America left their imprint, as did the "America letters" and the stories told by returned emigrants. The Scandinavian countries remained Lutheran but became tolerant. By the twentieth century considerable congregations of Methodists, Baptists, Mission Friends, and Mormons flourished. They and their Sunday Schools, which reached with moving religious force the worker elements of the population, played a significant part in the education and inspiration of the labor and government leadership of the northern lands.

Prison reform in the United States concerned Fredrika Bremer, as it had even earlier interested Crown Prince Oscar. The Prince studied the Philadelphia system of single cells, and the Auburn system of common-work. In 1840 he published a book dealing with the American experiments, and this was influential in the creation of new prisons and new penal methods, more humane and more effective in crime prevention.

In the early twentieth century the Scandinavians looked carefully at American theory and experience with the indeterminate sentence, honor system, and parole, and legal authorities like Harald Salomon and Arne Omsted made extensive study tours in the United States and published their views at home. Norwegian authorities used American experience in railroad law, and they quoted John Marshall on the power of the courts.

The coöperative movement is the most noted example of recent Scandinavian influence on the United States. Marquis Childs' *Sweden, The Middle Way* won an amazing vogue in the United States, and worried sober Swedes, who knew that their angels' wings had been pictured as too lily-white. Through the Hoover Commission and its report and the visits of scores and hundreds of coöperative-minded Americans the Scandinavian countries have become an ideological and practical pattern for that movement in the United States. In Denmark in 1949 the Danes themselves were amazed at the popularity of the course on coöperatives which they offered to American graduate students in Copenhagen.

Educational interchange rose to new heights after World War II, but it had a solid background. The immigrants needed educated clergy and they prized education. Hence they built seminaries and colleges, schools which emphasized the ancestral background but which patterned themselves upon the American system: Upsala College in New Jersey, St. Olaf and Gustavus Adolphus in Minnesota, Dana in Nebraska, Lindsborg in Kansas, Luther in Iowa, Augustana and North Park in Illinois.

Scandinavian pedagogues had come to the United States to investigate new methods as early as the 1840's. School architecture, classroom devices, John Dewey and "progressive education," have all exerted a potent influence. In 1911 Niels Poulsen, a wealthy Danish-American businessman, established the American-Scandinavian Foundation which has been continuously active in promoting understanding of Scandinavian culture in the United States, and in sending American students to study in the North.

Complementing the work of the American-Scandinavian Foundation have been a group of independent but coöperating societies established in the northern countries: Sverige-Amerika Stiftelsen (Sweden America Foundation), Danmark-Amerika Fondet (The Denmark America Fund), Norge-Amerika Foreningen (The Norway America Society), and Islenzk-Ameriska Félagid (Icelandic American Society). During World War II a Finnish-America Society was organized and it has become active in the postwar period.

The American-Scandinavian Foundation in New York estimates that between 1945 and 1949 these sister societies (not counting the Finnish) have sent approximately 2000 students to the United States. The Chicago chapter of the Foundation has brought over some students independently, and others such as the Rockefeller Foundation account for still more. One of the most rapidly expanding parts of the Foundation's work is its trainee program, introducing hundreds of young Scandinavian bank clerks, skilled workers, business managers, to American methods on a work-study basis.

Some of the notable former fellows in this interchange are: Henrik Dam (who won the Nobel prize for his discovery of the vitamin K); Harold C. Urey, atomic physicist, another Nobel winner; Robert Hillyer, Pulitzer prize poet; Bryn Hovde, president of the New School for Social Research, a Guggenheim fellow; the Swedish brain surgeon Herbert Olivecrona. And who can tell of the future potentialities of recent and present scholars—such, for example, as Jens Arup Seip, brought to the United States by the Rockefeller Foundation to study American history and institutions in order that he might return to Oslo to carry on the teaching of American civilization introduced by Halvdan Koht?

Six to twenty scholars per year have gone from the United States to Scandinavia to study forestry, chemistry, art, geography, music, industry, history, literature. They have brought back to the United States minds sharpened in their particular studies and broadened by contact with different customs and points of view. From Scandinavia to the United States have come scores and hundreds of writers, technicians, artists, labor leaders, and business experts, learners of all varieties. They return home after a few weeks or a year or two to spread greater understanding (usually) of American life.

The American Scandinavian Foundation has also published *The American Scandinavian Review*, perhaps the most distinguished journal of any national group in the United States. Hanna Astrup Larsen, daughter of an early president of Luther College in Iowa, through her long editorship established the reputation of the *Review*. It has served as an interpreter of Scandinavia to all Americans and as a bond with the ancestral lands for Americans of northern descent. The Foundation has also published, and continues to publish, classics from the wealth of Scandinavian literature and modern books of interpretation.

In addition to the work of private organizations, governments have taken a hand, especially since 1945. A group of about 100 GI's went to Stockholm in 1946, and similar though smaller groups followed in later years. About one-half of the 250 American students enrolled in a summer course at Oslo University (since 1947) have had GI grants, and in 1948 a group went to Copenhagen. Under the Fulbright Act still more Americans will go to Denmark and Norway. In 1949 Congress passed an act authorizing the use of the remainder of the Finnish debt payments to the United States for scholarships to Finnish students to come to America to study. This eight-million-dollar gesture may become an influence comparable to the Chinese scholarships set up under the Boxer indemnity funds.

Immediately after 1945 scores and hundreds of Scandinavians flocked to the United States to study dentistry, banking, education, journalism, science—though few in the social sciences and humanities. Their own universities had been seriously hurt by war, Germany was closed and England could not be as hospitable as of old. The center for foreign study, for Scandinavians as for most other peoples, had shifted across the Atlantic.

Even prior to this postwar surge the cultural ties between Scandinavia and the United States had been peculiarly strong in certain fields. To American library schools, for instance, had come more student-librarians from Norway than from any other country. The organizer of the city library in Oslo had spent seven years at the Newberry Library in Chicago, and the director (Arne Kildal) of the widespread library extension service of Norway got his own training and inspiration in the United States. The builders of the city library in Stockholm made a tour of United States libraries and many ideas thus gained were incorporated in the new structure as the Swedes adapted and remolded them to fit their needs.

American books were even more important than American library techniques and construction. In 1938 the Oslo public library loaned an average of ninety volumes a day of English and American fiction; the Stockholm library averaged 150 a day—two to four times as much as German fiction and many times that of any other nation. The American authors far outnumbered the English. Among the most popular were Jack London, Upton Sinclair, Dos Passos, Hemingway, Sinclair Lewis—as well as old stand-bys like James Fenimore Cooper (more popular there than at home) and Mark Twain. In the other direction the United States absorbed Ibsen and Hans Christian Andersen, and of recent years especially Sigrid Undset and her *Kristin Lavransdatter*.

Music, often an easy international language, has been interchanged freely. Americans have loved the grave and powerful symphonies of the Finnish Sibelius, and the mysterious blend of the gay and the somber that is found in Norwegian Edvard Grieg. From America the Scandinavians have taken the Sankey-Moody hymns, translated them over and over, and sung them into their own souls. America has modified and popularized the music of Africa and sent it on to the North. There it contrasts oddly with the old folk music but it dominates the dance. In 1948 the master of bebop, Dizzy Gillespie, began his triumphal European tour in Gothenburg—an extraordinary exchange for Jenny Lind, the Swedish nightingale, and for Ole Bull, the Norwegian violinist, both of whom won vast popularity in American tours a century ago.

One's thoughts race on through the innumerable avenues and bypaths of Scandinavian-American cultural interchange. The first private banks of the North in the 1850's were patterned on American models. Many American buildings, some of the most notable skyscrapers, have been built by architects and engineers from Scandinavia. When after World War II a medical mission from the United States went to assess the needs of aid in Poland and northeast Europe, it arrived at last in Helsinki. There the members were so impressed with the practical architectural improvements they saw that they warned their colleagues in New York to postpone further hospital construction until the travelers could give them information on these new devices built into Finnish hospitals. In the other direction a Swedish committee planning a children's hospital to be given to Norway made a flying tour in the winter of 1948–49 to inspect the most recent developments in the United States. They inspected hospitals and blueprints and talked with both architects and pediatricians. Hundreds of engineers from the Scandinavian countries have toured the United States and gained new insights into factory management, technical appliances, new products.

Groups of industrial laborers have been brought across the Atlantic recently to observe and work in American factories for brief periods. Perhaps American labor and management can learn from them some of the reasons why industrial labor relations operate more smoothly in the Scandinavian environment than in the American. These visitors are impressed by the mass production of the great factories, by the mechanical aids that lessen the human burden, and by the fine cars driven to work by the American workers. They consider their housing superior to that of the American workers.

American-made comic strips have captured space in many of the Scandinavian newspapers; Dagwood and Blondie speak Norwegian, Finnish, and Danish too. Newspaper advertisements are increasingly set up in an American pattern, though *Svenska Dagbladet* still looks like the defunct *Boston Transcript*. And every night of the year American movies show in Scandinavia much that isn't true of America.

Oslo University has its own American Institute and has taught regular courses in United States history for many years. Upsala (Sweden) has a lectureship which began to operate in 1948 and an Institute which emphasizes American literature. Copenhagen and the other universities of the North have nothing comparable. The American visitor is amazed at the academic neglect of American studies, and at the same time is aware that a considerable knowledge of America has seeped in from he knows not where. Occasionally one finds a public teaching of the "American language," rare because the intellectuals have long insisted on "Oxford English" and have assumed that "American" was a cross between a Swedish-American brogue and the slang of Hollywood.

Denmark has a unique American institution in the form of a park at Rebild in Jutland. Here a gift from a Danish-born Chicagoan has preserved a large section of natural Danish heath and has established a museum complete with covered wagon, Indian headdresses, and American flags. Nearby in Aalborg was created a Danish-American archive, with valuable material on migration (in 1949 moved to Copenhagen). At Rebild on each Fourth of July American tourists and native Danes in numbers up to 40– and 50,000 assemble for a huge picnic and lengthy oratory. It is a Denmark-American love feast, and lacks only a baseball game to make an American feel fully at home.

The tourists to Rebild and the thousands of others who have sailed to the North Cape or traveled by air and land in the picturesque North have left in their wake American dollars, millions of them. Sons and daughters have sent home parts of their earnings. Mr. O. B. Grimley of Nordmanns Forbund estimated in 1938 that in 100 years Norway had received 3,000,-000,000 kronor from her emigrants, three-quarters of a billion dollars to one country alone! Even if some of this money went to buy steamship tickets to America it is sure that much of it went to buy new clothes, farm equipment, books, food, medical service. Long before the epoch of the Marshall Plan some of the "surplus profits" of a rich America were going back to make life easier in lands which had for centuries "lived on the margin of the possible."

An interesting recent example, given much publicity in the Swedish press, was of a Swedish emigrant boy who became a successful doctor in Oregon. He bethought himself of his little village in southern Sweden, and of his own difficulties in getting an education. He gave $3000, as a beginning, for the use of deserving boys of that village who wanted further education. "It happens every day"—almost.

The great exchange goes on. New experiences stimulate new ideas, new ideas give birth to new inventions. Men come to know and understand one another. The foundation at least is laid for productive coöperation and for continuing friendships.

The manifold influences and ideas from America have been significant and still are. The ideas were felt at first largely through missionaries and returned emigrants and therefore affected the lower classes more powerfully than the intelligentsia. Among the working groups the influence was so direct that, for example, when a controversy within the Independent Order of Good Templars split the organization in the United States the division was mirrored within every Good Templar lodge in Sweden.

The men and women of the North have been deeply moved by American-expressed ideals like the Gettysburg Address and the Four Freedoms, but often they see that American realities do not match the high ideals. They become confused and even embittered at reports of racial intolerance in the United States, of bigotry and materialism and waste and the ruthlessness of man to man. This is partly that they have been taught to think of the United States as the kind of Utopia which could not exist; it is partly that in the homogeneity of their own society it is difficult to appreciate the complex problems of the vigorous, heterogeneous community across the Atlantic, a community great with potentialities but still lacking the unity and stability of the ancient nations of northern Europe.

Yet these two societies, the small and the large, the old and the new, have reacted powerfully on one another. By direct imitation of techniques and by subtle pervasive ideals the United States has helped to make the modern Scandinavia and Scandinavia has helped to make the United States. The New World has been a testing ground for theories born in the Old World; it has helped prove possible "things before held impossible"; it has stimulated by example and by competition the social reform of the North. As people and ideas and ideals have been interchanged the North and the West have grown closer; a great American and a great Scandinavian both spoke of "government of the people, by the people and for the people."

4. Functioning Social Democracy

The social pattern of the five northern countries is marked by superficial diversity and fundamental likeness. The dominant note is similarity, founded on a common cultural tradition, based on geographical proximity, and aided by deliberate coöperation.

Herein only a few facets of the total culture can be surveyed, but the institutions and techniques described will illustrate the habits of thought and the methods of organization characteristic of the peoples. These peoples are realistic. Their institutions emphasize practical accomplishment. Their goal is the freedom and welfare of the individual. That goal, they feel, can be attained only in a well-ordered society, and therefore they engage in planned social engineering. They try nevertheless to keep *society* subordinate to the *person*, and they indulge in no mystical worship of the state. Government, the economic order, education, all are means to an end, not ends in themselves. In the utilization of these means the Scandinavian peoples are guided by past experience, yet not fettered by old forms. The makers of policy constantly experiment and seek for ways to better the lot of man on earth. They are ready to hold to the past, or to borrow, or to create. Hence, as the following pages will show, they have built a functioning social democracy out of a blending of indigenous and foreign ideas and institutions.

1. GOVERNMENT: STRUCTURE AND PARTIES

Government is close to the peoples of the North, it is something fashioned by them for their use. Its nearness is nurtured by homogeneity of peoples and smallness of area; its prestige is preserved by the tradition and the soundness of governmental institutions and the intelligent restraint of officials.

Kingship was of old the major centralizing factor in Denmark, Norway, Sweden, and Finland, and was often the organ through which the common people won relief from the nobility. The bond between people and king is well illustrated in the recent wartime tribute to Christian X by the poet-priest Kaj Munk:

> Today once more you take your morning ride.
> Regal, friendly, Danish, through the city.
> A benison to us—as if to say
> that Denmark keeps her saddle as before.

The history of Sweden may not be the history of her kings; but in both Sweden and Denmark the changing character of the monarchs has profoundly affected foreign policy, domestic prosperity, architecture, and innumerable aspects of everyday life. In recent times a succession of strong personalities, long-lived and popular, has saved the ancient institution and has made kingship a vital factor in national unity and stability.

Family relationships among the monarchs, too, stimulate political interchange and consolidate popular sentiment. Haakon VII became King of Norway in 1905 and through many years his reign paralleled that of his tall brother, Christian X in Denmark. Their father was King of Denmark, their mother was a daughter of Charles XV of Sweden. New ties were created when Haakon's son, Olav, married Swedish princess Martha, and Christian's son, since 1947 King Frederick IX, married Princess Ingrid. That made King Gustav V of Sweden grandfather of the Danish queen and uncle of the Norwegian crown princess.

The progeny of the Bernadottes is so numerous that it has intermarried widely into other royal houses in Europe and outside the blue-blooded lines in both Europe and America. Some have proved their ability beyond the royal palace. Prince

Eugen attained fame as an artist, and Count Folke Bernadotte, who married Estelle Manville of New York, operated usefully and heroically on the international stage in the Red Cross and the United Nations work in Palestine.

The kings in the North reign but do not govern. They are symbols of national unity, and permanent hubs in the revolving wheels of government. They stand above party and represent the nation. They sign laws, but ministerial approval is also necessary, and parliamentary sanction. Their influence is based on personality, not on legal powers. No king has exercised the veto for many years, and the power itself has atrophied as in England. The kings must be members of the Lutheran state church, but ecclesiastical headship resides in the archbishops. Monarchy is a vestigial organ, but recent Scandinavian experience has been comparatively happy with it, the monarchs have been democratic in spirit, and republican agitation, once vigorous, is now defunct. King Frederick of Denmark tells his people that family life is the same for him as for a father whose three daughters are commoners instead of princesses, and he acts as if he meant it.

Iceland and Finland grew within the Scandinavian monarchic tradition, but in their new independent status they are republics with presidents as chiefs of state. In Iceland Sveinn Björnsson served as regent during the war years and was made president when the country became legally independent in 1944. The constitutional term is four years.

In Finland the president enjoys more power than any other northern head of state. He is named by an electoral college popularly elected for the purpose, for a six-year term. On emergency occasions, however, the Parliament has chosen a new president—as in 1944, when Risto Ryti resigned and Gustaf Mannerheim was brought in to end the war. When ill health forced Mannerheim's retirement he was succeeded by the elder statesman, Juho Paasikivi. The government is ministerial in form, and responsible to Parliament, but the president has in law and practice broad powers in foreign policy, in questions of citizenship, a temporary veto in legislation, powers of appointment in church, army, and government, and a limited power of issuing administrative (non-law-making) decrees.

The courts throughout Scandinavia are respected and important, but are not as powerful as in the United States, and their structure varies from country to country. In Norway the constitution of 1814 established a system of separation of powers and the judges have attempted to tread the path of judicial review with John Marshall. Since 1818 the courts have practiced "the right and duty to determine the question whether an administrative act was lawful"; and throughout the North the citizen is protected carefully against possible injustice by officials. Nowhere else, however, have the judges attained as much power as in Norway. The claims they made to power irritated some of their fellow-citizens as early as 1827 when a Norwegian professor wrote to a Danish friend, complaining that the judges "are considered, God knows why, as the patron saints of the idolized constitution." The courts asserted themselves still more after the victory of parliamentarism in the 1880's. Then, while the king was still also the king of Sweden, many Norwegians felt they needed some safeguard against "an accidental Storting majority," and the Supreme Court began to base decisions on the principle that it could determine the constitutionality of legislation. In general, however, the legislative bodies of Scandinavia are supreme in authority, as in England. The job of the courts is to interpret and apply the law, not to question its constitutionality.

Special courts are often set up to deal with special problems such as water power and administrative law. Labor courts are established which utilize a combination of the power of adjudication and the persuasion of conciliation, and which bring together on the same bench trained judges and lay representatives of the parties to dispute.

In each country the basic law is simple and clear, and is available to the public in condensed and codified form. The ordinary home is likely to have a book of law, and the individual can often be his own lawyer. An American is constantly amazed at how few lawyers he sees in courts or parliaments or business. The ancient right of a freeman to plead his own case persists and is practiced. Lay experts are used regularly as assistant judges, as for example in the local courts of Finland and Sweden and in special courts like the Danish maritime and commercial court.

In each country one finds a pragmatic attitude toward law and courts—as toward life in general. Capital punishment was abolished long ago in Norway because it did not deter crime, but wartime treason was something that called for stern measures, so the government simply legislated capital punishment. Means are adapted to the need. Another illustration of this is the way in which labor courts, where the letter of the law seldom has much significance, have become in fact and in name courts of arbitration. This is the practical approach. Of course the basic supremacy of the parliament over the courts is likewise practical, a recognition of the authority of the electorate. It is, for better or for worse, a more flexible system than that in the United States, less flexible than that in Britain.

The parliament is the real power in each country, and in the parliament the will of the people can express itself quickly and effectively. There has been a tendency to unicameralism, also, as in other countries with the ministerial system—for it is difficult for a cabinet to be responsible to two different houses. Finland's *Eduskunta* or Parliament is composed of only one 200-member chamber. This body, elected on July 1 for a three-year term (there was an election in 1948), chooses a Grand Committee of forty-five which serves as a steering committee and names the standing committees. Iceland elects fifty members to the Althing, and then these fifty choose seventeen of their number to sit in an "upper house." This is somewhat like the system in Norway.

Norway's system of parliamentary organization is unusual, a compromise between the bicameral and the unicameral. The Storting is elected as one body, 50 members from the cities,

100 from the rural districts. When these 150 meet, they divide themselves into the 38-member Lagting and the 112-member Odelsting. Both the Storting as a whole and also each house elects a president and a vice-president, and these six officers form an influential steering committee. Fifteen of the seventeen standing committees are chosen from the Storting as a whole, and each reflects the proportional strength of the parties. Bills originating in one house or *ting* commonly pass there first, then go to the other for approval. If agreement is not reached the whole Storting meets and a two-thirds vote is then required for passage. Budget legislation and certain other classes of laws are handled in the first instance by the entire Storting, and in these cases a majority vote is sufficient. The Storting can almost be described as a one-chamber body with two semi-independent committees.

The Danes have worked out a different and even more complicated system for their Rigsdag. The Folketing is a lower house of 149 members elected partly at large and partly through multi-member districts; the term is four years. The Landsting is an upper house of seventy-six members, elected for eight-year terms; half of them are chosen (one-quarter at a time) by the outgoing Folketing, and the other half (one-quarter at a time) by electoral colleges in seven special Landsting districts. Citizens must be thirty-five years of age to vote for the Landsting electors, so the whole system obviously aims at a conservative and slow-changing upper house. This is a bicameral system, but the two chambers meet as one for an opening session and in case of a default in the royal succession; there are conference committees and one joint standing committee; and since 1923 there has been a commission on foreign affairs made up of members from either house.

Sweden likewise has had a two-house Riksdag since 1866, but the two chambers are closely intermeshed. Compensation and dignity are approximately the same in the 150-member First Chamber and in the 230-member Second Chamber. The property qualification for membership in the First Chamber was abolished some years ago. Tenure is for eight years; one-eighth of the members are chosen each year by electoral colleges or county councils in nineteen districts. A member of the Second Chamber serves a four-year term and must reside in the one of the twenty-eight districts from which he is chosen. With about eight members to be chosen from each district the proportional representation system can be applied fairly well.

Proportional representation is the custom throughout the North. The ideal is to have both parties and geographical districts properly balanced in the parliaments; that is often very difficult to manage. In Sweden the population and the representation are large enough that it comes out fairly. In Iceland, with scattered districts, small population, and only fifty representatives, it is difficult indeed. The Icelanders work it out by setting up for the Althing three classes: first, twenty-one of the representatives are chosen from single districts; second, twenty are chosen from party lists; third, up to eleven compensatory seats are parceled out to balance the whole as well as possible. The whole method of proportional representation acts as an encouragement to political parties of principle and special interest.

Disregarding the infinite complexities of party programs and organization we can see a broad common pattern throughout Scandinavia. Five major party groupings account for most of the votes and practically all the parliamentary representation. On the extreme right are the conservatives, a former governing group now relegated to dignified and convinced opposition, scarcely hoping for power, but eager to voice their opinions and to check the excesses of the left. They are the bankers and the big businessmen and the "gentlemen of the old school," men and women with great economic interests, wide experience, and considerable influence.

Second from the right come the agrarians, a class group with definite economic interests which once constituted a separate house in the Swedish Riksdag. The agrarians have become increasingly the representatives of farm interests generally, and of the equalization of conditions between rural communities and urban, opponents of monopolies and high taxes.

In the middle are the liberals, fighting steadily the extinction which overwhelmed their English brethren, squeezed always both from the right and from the left. In Sweden particularly this group has made a notable come-back in recent years, and in the elections of 1948 it won votes from the conservatives and from the social democrats. It represents a variety of moderate, intellectual, and moral convictions, and is mainly urban, professional, and middle-class. It is influential beyond its numerical proportion. It is now attracting youth which wants a vigorous leadership, which questions whether social reform may not go too far, and which feels itself more a part of the wide new world than does the older generation of socialists.

The social democrats (or labor party) are the largest single party group in each of the northern countries, and in each they direct the government. They must operate, however, with a bare majority at best, and usually with less. In Finland in 1948 they elected only one-fourth of the Parliament, and obtained their precarious leadership because they were to the left and because the communists demanded too much for their coöperation in a coalition. Their lack of overwhelming majorities forces them everywhere to be moderate, a fact which very probably strengthens them in the long-run. Every bit of social legislation must be sufficiently needed, sufficiently reasonable in cost, sufficiently well-planned, to win votes from at least some other parties.

The social democrats are moderate Marxists, and represent the industrial workers of the cities and of the small factories, and a small ideological contingent from academic and other groups. They are tied intimately with the trade union organizations, and are in close sympathy with the coöperative movement. In the 1920's and early 1930's they often leaned toward Moscow (most notably in Norway); they were vigorous in denunciation of nazism. Toward the end of World War II they lost many voters direct to communism. Since the war a two-way movement has affected them: disillusionment with Russia has brought back many from the communist fold; disgruntlement with their own policies, particularly isolationism in Sweden, has sent some of the socialists into the liberal parties.

At the left end are the communists, representing dissatisfied workers, strongest always in the poorer economic sections such as northern Sweden and northern Norway. They grew partly because a worker discontented with the social democrats could go nowhere else, partly because of the prestige of Russia in her war against nazism, partly because of sincere conviction. But events in Russia, the unreasonable refusal of capitalist America to disintegrate, the ruthlessness of the 1948 coup in Czechoslovakia, and in general the nationalization and militarization of Soviet communism, brought disillusion and defection. Elections from 1947 on have brought everywhere greater and greater losses. In 1948 the Finnish communist representation in the Parliament fell from forty-nine to thirty-eight (17 per cent), and in Sweden from fifteen to eight. (In Finland the figures are for the coalition of communists and "popular democrats," and it is impossible to estimate accurately how much the communist vote alone would be.) In Norway's 1949 elections the popular vote of the communists was halved, and their Storting representation was cut from eleven down to zero.

Special groups are occasionally of significance, too, such as the Swedish people's party in Finland, a culture-minded minority which won fourteen seats of the 200 in 1948. In Denmark there is a Slesvig party. Nazi parties existed before and during the war, but they were too insignificant to win position in the parliaments. In Norway there is a separate Christian People's Party, emphasizing religious issues but prevailingly "liberal" in outlook.

It is obvious that these parties are parties of classes and special interests. This is particularly true of the agrarians, the social democrats, and the communists. The conservatives and the liberals do not talk about class interests, but they represent the interests and the ideology of special groups, and they become class parties by the inevitable process of elimination: with the farmers and the industrial workers organized in their special parties the conservatives and the liberals have only certain groups left to whom they can appeal.

This ideological-class-interest division of the parties affects the whole legislative process. In the United States interest groups compete within the parties and reach their basic compromises in party caucus and convention. In Scandinavia the parties have more consistent programs, and the necessary compromises of democratic government are thrashed out in the committees and on the floors of the legislative chambers.

Ofttimes ministries must be built through alliances of two or more parties. During crises such as World War II the common practice is for the parties to join in coalition government, to form ministries with members from most or all of the parties, and to postpone programs of party politics. Even in periods of semi-crisis nonpartisan experts are given high position. Finland especially uses non-party figures for presidential and ministerial posts. Another factor that distinguishes party government in these countries from that in the United States is that patronage plays only a small role; an efficient and attractive civil service reaches almost to the top of government.

Government is nevertheless government by party, and elections are fought with debates and party slogans. The programs and activities of these governments can best be seen through the story of what they have done, on the basis of their economic structure, to meet their own social problems.

2. THE COÖPERATIVE MOVEMENT

Soon after the Rochdale coöperative was founded in England in 1844 the idea took root in Scandinavia, but the growth was feeble for the first half century. Around 1900 several societies began to flourish, and phenomenal development followed. The scheme seemed to fit these close-knit communities of the North, where the people were homogeneous and intelligent, and accustomed to working together. Resources were too meager to waste, and any opportunity to save was welcomed.

The coöperative movement became intertwined with the social program and with economics. In each northern country by the mid-twentieth century it was supported by 25 to 50 per cent of the population. The consumers' coöperatives handled from 10 to 40 per cent of the retail trade. Connected wholesale organizations did a large volume of business in import and export, and influenced the entire productive system. Producers' coöperatives sometimes had monopoly control within their limited fields. The whole movement was voluntary, but was usually supported by enabling legislation. It existed side by side with private enterprise and in open competition with it. It was a vital element in Scandinavian prosperity.

The movement in Finland was unique in character and extent. There the first coöperatives joined farmers and urban workers in a common organization. The farmers, however, were independent operators, imbued with the philosophy of individualistic capitalism. They built their coöperatives solely for the purpose of saving themselves money on the goods they purchased (or sold). The industrial workers of the cities, on the other hand, saw in the coöperative movement a lever by which the whole social and economic structure might be transformed. This fundamental divergence in point of view led to a split in the movement in 1916, and to the organization by the "reformist" group of Kulutusosuuskuntien Keskuliitto (KK), and its wholesale society (OTK), while the older groups, dominated by farmers and bourgeois, continued as the Yleinen Osuuskauppojen Liitto (YOL), with its wholesale society (SOK). Both groups grew by leaps and bounds.

In 1946 the two organizations, commonly known as KK and SOK, were approximately equal in total membership and annual turnover. Together they enrolled 841,746 and did an annual business of 14,226,000,000 marks (*c.* $14,000,000). They were the two leading business concerns in the country. The membership represented at least 50 per cent of the families of Finland, and the two companies counted 40 per cent of the national trade. These coöperatives ran life insurance companies, restaurants, bakeries, mills, fish-curing establishments, dairies, sausage factories, shops, and farms. Their stores were well-planned, often handsome modernistic structures, and their main office buildings in Helsinki utilized the finest of materials and of architectural skills.

In Norway the consumers' coöperative movement went through many vicissitudes, but in the twentieth century became firmly established, and now one central organization has nearly 600 local societies. Each individual member pays from 60 to 100 kr. for his capital share, but he may "buy-in" for one kr. and accumulate the rest gradually through dividends on purchases. He gets 5 per cent return on the investment. In the Rochdale plan coöperatives the sales are made at regular market prices and the member then receives rebates on the goods he buys. Reductions are first made for reserves and for administrative costs. Since there is no profit on the purchases of members there is also no tax on that business; but the Norwegian coöperatives sell also to non-members and such sales are taxed. Reserve funds, and the factories owned by the Coöperative Union for making cheese, chocolate, flour, shoes, etc., are taxed the same as any business enterprise.

An additional 400 local coöperative societies are not affiliated with the central association. Some of these follow a different principle in sales. They sell not at market prices, but as low as possible, and thus let the purchaser "take his rebate home in his basket." All together the members of the various consumers' societies, with their families, number in Norway about 800,000, or more than one-quarter of the population.

In Denmark the coöperative movement and the folk high schools have been intimately interrelated. The pioneer leaders of coöperative organization came to a considerable extent from folk high school students, and the folk high schools for many years carried on the educational work which is part of the coöperative movement. In town after town, village after village, small groups of workers and farmers got together to buy their foodstuffs, then their clothing and their household goods, attempting to evade the high prices caused by the profits of middlemen and retailers. They fought tense economic battles with the capitalistic interests, but slowly they established themselves on firm footing. The system they built is highly decentralized, yet the 2000 local distributive societies are now all members of the coöperative wholesale. Membership is about 420,000 which, with the total of family members, means a representation and a market of 1,000,000. The business turnover in 1945 was about 600,000,000 kr. (*c.* $130,000,000).

The story of Swedish coöperation has been well told and widely read in Marquis Childs's *Sweden, The Middle Way*, although most of his readers gain an exaggerated impression of both the bigness and the goodness of Swedish coöperation. In its essentials it was the same kind of development as in the other Scandinavian lands; conditions were similar, ideas were interchangeable. Price advantages of large-scale buying and distribution were brought to Sweden by the coöperatives as they were brought to the United States by the chain stores. In the relatively small market of each of these countries organized buying was particularly significant. Social advantages were secured by the working together of people in a great common enterprise. The Swedish consumer coöperatives have grown to about 700 societies and 880,000 members, representing almost one-half of the population. They account, however, for only 2 to 3 per cent of total national production; their field is retail trade, where they handle 12 per cent of the total. (In groceries they do over 25 per cent of the business.) And they are coördinated in a great national federation, Kooperativa Förbundet (KF).

These various "consumers'" coöperatives have extended their activities far beyond mere local buying and selling. Their factories, their production, and their techniques have been influential in a realm wider than figures can indicate. For example, it was in the folk high school coöperative society milieu in Denmark that Mrs. Anine Hansen in 1894 proposed the milk recording societies: farmers began to keep records of production from their different cows. They soon discovered that with a poor cow it might cost 585 øre to produce a kilo of butter, whereas with a good cow it cost only 112 øre. Milk-recording societies spread through Denmark, Scandinavia, Europe, and to the United States. Rapidly the quality of cows improved, and the quality of butter too.

Price dictation by private concerns was broken down by the establishment of coöperative factories for margarine, overshoes, bread, rubber tires. Capitalist operators learned the hard way that if they did not keep their prices reasonable the coöperatives would take their markets from them; they learned too that if they managed efficiently and sold at fair prices the coöperatives would not attempt to supplant them.

Just as the coöperatives grew from local to national organizations, so they developed also a larger Scandinavian organization, not for over-all control, but for servicing the national societies. The Scandinavian Wholesale Society was organized shortly after World War I, and is now the chief foreign purchaser for the societies of Finland, Denmark, Sweden, and Norway. From its central office in Copenhagen it buys (for the national societies) coffee by the thousands of tons, sugar, cottonseed, grain—varied products from all over the world, gaining the advantages of a single large-scale dealer.

It is in connection with an all-Scandinavian venture that there occurred one of the most illuminating examples of coöperative activity. The European electric lamp trust maintained high and irrationally different prices in various countries: the price on the same 25-watt bulb in Sweden was 37 cents (1928), in Denmark 27 cents, England 52 cents, Hungary 18 cents! Anders Hedberg of Sweden's KF thought this way of charging what the market would bear had gone to a ridiculous extreme. Saving 12 cents a lamp on Sweden's use of 12,000,000 per year would mean $1,500,000. That was worth while.

Just then it became possible to hire the dissatisfied manager of the trust's Stockholm factory. KF had the funds and decided to build a new lamp factory. The trust invited Hedberg down to Geneva and told him what a foolish venture this was, and how the trust could cut prices ruinously in Sweden. Hedberg was not in the least impressed. For one thing he knew he had a loyal buying group. More important, as he told the trust people, they were interested in high prices, while his organization was one of consumers, interested in low prices. If the trust wished to lower prices or even to give away lamps in Sweden that was good; it was the people's saving that counted.

By 1931, when the factory began production, its base had been widened. The five coöperative organizations of Finland, Norway, Denmark, and Sweden united for ownership and sales in the North European Luma Coöperative Society. While the plant was still under construction the trust dropped its Swedish price to 27 cents. The Luma lamps were then placed on the market at 22 cents, and the trust had to meet that figure. The resultant savings were shared by the clientele of the five coöperating coöperatives in the four countries. They were shared also by the non-members who bought Luma bulbs, and they were shared by the entire consuming public: one factory had forced down the price of all bulbs, no matter who made them. The other side of the picture was that the shareholders in the trust had to look forward to reduced dividends. Repercussions spread to England where the first talk of a coöperative factory tumbled the price 10 cents. Here was a farsighted and daring venture in consumers' production, and a pilot experiment in international coöperation. And the Luma, much expanded, continues to operate with profit, and now has plants in Oslo and Glasgow.

The story of margarine is similar to that of lamp bulbs—and the stories of overshoes and bread and rubber tires. This is why Sweden has been slow to pass direct anti-monopoly legislation.

The coöperatives have taken over the job of putting the brakes on capitalistic excess in the domestic market.

There is still another side to the picture of coöperatives in Scandinavia, for the consumers (even when they produce) represent only half of the economic interest. People must make money even before they can save it by wise purchasing. Producers' coöperatives are therefore also vitally important; they are for the most part completely separate from the consumers' coöperatives, though of course a man can belong both to a producers' and to a consumers' society.

In Norway, for instance, the price of milk kept dropping lower and lower, due to unorganized production and selling. The farmer-producers were in danger of being ruined. Instead most of them got together in eight district milk pools, or "centrals." Membership represented from 80 per cent to 97 per cent of production, and the eight pools made agreements not to compete with each other, and for the more fortunate pools to share profits with the less fortunate. They brought prices back and maintained them at a profitable level. But is not this itself a dangerous monopoly?

It could be, indeed. To check such a tendency there is called in that peculiar blending of private and government activity. A Marketing Board has been established, composed of representatives of this milk pool and of similar pools for meat and pork, and for eggs; other representatives are from the coöperative organization, the merchants' association, and the three agricultural societies. This Board guides in regulation of market and prices, and is itself responsible to the Minister of Agriculture. Funds are obtained by small fees levied by the Board on the various products, and by government fees on margarine and certain feedstuffs used on farms. Operation includes among other things a mixing of butter (up to 20 per cent) in the manufacture of margarine; the actual amount is regulated and shifted by the Board so as to absorb butter surplus, yet maintain margarine manufacture.

In Denmark agriculture and producers' coöperatives are inseparable: "92 per cent of all Danish farmers were members of coöperative dairies," which produced 94 per cent of the butter; coöperative butter export societies handled about 50 per cent of foreign sales. This is particularly significant because Denmark accounts for about 30 per cent of international trade in butter, as well as 50 per cent of that in bacon and hams, and 15 per cent in eggs. Coöperative bacon factories do 88 per cent of the number of killings of Danish pigs. Large proportions of the business in eggs and cattle are handled through coöperative societies, and likewise the farmers' purchasing of fertilizers and feedstuffs.

The coöperative societies, therefore, as well as the farmers individually, have a large stake in the government agreements for trade with Britain and Russia and other countries. One can almost say that individuals, coöperative societies, and government are in business together, and this of course binds the community together in bonds of common interest for the maintenance of quality, fair price, and sustained production.

This common interest is activated by various forms of state aid for farm finance. In Denmark in the depression years of the 1930's a moratorium on farm mortgages was granted, and a fund of 100,000,000 kr. set up by the state for loans to farmers in distress. The interest rate was made to fluctuate with changes in the business cycle. Similarly in Norway a Loan Bank for Farmers was set up by the Storting to adjust debts, and if necessary to force adjustment when the mortgage on a farm became higher than the actual value of the farm (by the deflationary process). Foreclosures under such circumstances obviously meant loss to creditors as well as to farmers; the Loan Bank tried to save both by forcing new appraisals, reducing mortgages, and by then granting new small loans to help the farmer on the road to recovery. "Support for self-support."

The relationship of the coöperatives with the trade unions on the one hand and with the government on the other implies almost an interlocking directorate. Trade union members and their families are active in the consumers' coöperative movement, and there is a strong ideological sympathy tying unions, coöperatives, and social democrats together. Coöperative officials, like Axel Gjöres, in Sweden, occasionally move over into high government positions. Both consumers' and producers' coöperatives are "big business" in each of these countries, and therefore they play a part, sometimes alongside large private interests, in trade agreements made by government with other governments—as, for example, the Danish trade agreements with England, and the agreements of each of these countries with Russia. But they become themselves vested economic interests, and in that capacity sometimes find themselves allied with private business in opposition to state policy. They are likely to be as much against nationalization as any big capitalist; in Sweden Albin Johanson, able head of the KF, is credited with blocking the government desire to nationalize the oil industry after World War II.

These few illustrations give something of the scope of the coöperative movement throughout Scandinavia. Most of the facts given for one country are in their essentials paralleled in each of the other countries. To round out the picture would require chapter upon chapter on production, sales, architecture, employment policy, reserves, correspondence courses, lecture series, schools, coöperative housing, publishing (Sweden's most widely circulated magazine is the coöperatives' *Vi*), and other matters too numerous to list. The movement is vast and almost all-embracing, a semi-self-sufficient economic structure operating within a still larger economic order.

As a saga of business the story of coöperative expansion is dramatic; it rivals that of Andrew Carnegie or the dreams of Horatio Alger. Here is not one person combining chance and skill in the creation of a great economic structure. Nor is it the use and expansion of invested capital in gambling or the accidental discovery of a new gold mine. Here is the phenomenon of the little people, people without money or credit, strong only in the idea which unites them, acting together and building capital slowly out of savings made from this working together. They gain gradually in financial strength, but their real strength lies in their cohesion as a mass buying force. The great trusts could break small private interlopers by price wars; when challenged by the united coöperators they were fortunate if they could hold what they had. Again and again the coöperators determined the prices at which trusts (such as the electric light and the margarine) could sell their products.

In a way the coöperatives provide the means for spreading the base of investment, and in providing an outlet for the savings of the small investor as is done in the United States by the investment trusts, or in different fashion by the widespread popular shareholding (as for instance in American Telephone and Telegraph and similar corporations). The significant difference is that democratic control comes much closer to realization in the coöperative meetings—general meetings locally, delegate meetings nationally. The purpose of the coöperatives is economic, but the underlying ideal is economic democracy. The broad base of actual participation is their strength.

The coöperative societies cannot be scared, cannot be driven into financial debacle, cannot be lured away from their basic principles. The societies hold and increase both membership and customers because they offer good goods at cheaper prices. They do not rely upon appeals to moral or social idealism. Their appeal is economic, sometimes long-run rather than immediate, but the canny northerners are intelligent enough to understand the "long-run." The leaders have been shrewd enough to venture into only worth-while enterprises, and their management of those enterprises is as able as the membership support is loyal.

The local coöperatives are able to coöperate in large national organizations, and the national organizations are able to coöperate with each other in one great organization to buy on the world market. The success of the movement is not accidental, and it is not dependent on one man. Perhaps it is due fundamentally to two factors: (1) the economic factor, money savings actually achieved, and (2) the psychological factor, the satisfaction to people without individual economic power of controlling their own business, of functioning as directors in a significant enterprise. For such satisfactions the baker and the railway worker and the housewife may spend as many hours planning for a grocery store as does a board of directors in managing a large manufacturing concern.

The success of the coöperative movement has worried many advocates of private business, yet there is surprisingly little outright opposition. It may be that the movement has now attained its full growth. Expansion appears to have leveled off, for the pace of growth is slower than a few years ago.

The coöperative movement has made a place for itself in a mixed economic system; it has not killed off private enterprise. It might or it might not function equally well in another environment; it has gone far in England, comparatively made less progress in the United States. In Scandinavia it is a triumph of economic democracy. This must be said by any fair-minded viewer of the scene whether he personally favors the coöperative idea or condemns it—just as anyone must recognize the success, for example, of John D. Rockefeller.

3. PLANNED SECURITY

As the twentieth century advanced people became less and less satisfied with the natural workings of the economic system and with the limited activities of the state. The well-being of the individual might be enhanced, but could not be assured, by the coöperative societies. The citizenry wanted increasingly to use the state to direct the economy for the benefit of individuals. The new attitude, basis of the Scandinavian "middle way," is stated in a nutshell by David Hinshaw:

The dominant social welfare conception throughout the world has developed from (a) a growing humanitarianism, (b) an emerging sense of social justice, (c) depression-created insecurity, (d) a misconception that the state owes every citizen a living, (e) the assumption that the forces of science, engineering, industry, and commerce (which have magically created so much comfort and opportunity for so many people) can produce the wealth necessary to make realizable the welfare dreams of today's social and political leaders.*

This and following chapters are devoted to an attempt to explain the pragmatic Scandinavian application of the ideas thus stated by Mr. Hinshaw. The northern peoples are building a new social structure, but not by revolution, rather by a guided evolution based on ancient foundations. It looks paternalistic, but it is a far cry from the regimentation of totalitarianism. It stops short of collectivization, but it certainly checks free competition. The purpose is to free the individual, not to bind him, but to free the many sometimes requires restraints on the few. And occasionally over-eager legislators or bureaucrats lay restrictions on everyone, and hinder both security and achievement.

In the attempts to equalize opportunity for all people the Scandinavian countries have acted on the basis of a common ideology, and the results are similar in character though varied in detail in the different lands.

In the old rural society of Scandinavia, as elsewhere, there was security within the family. The farm was a family enterprise, and each family member contributed according to his ability and received according to his need. When a man's days of work were over he was cared for as a matter of right; in his own younger days he had produced more than he had eaten. When he was injured or ill he was cared for because he was a member of the family; no other reason was necessary. If a family was destitute, or an individual alone, he was supported by his neighbors. In Denmark a regular system survived into the nineteenth century which allowed the destitute to make the rounds of their neighbors' farms and receive a meal at each in turn. Similarly the fishing communities of Norway closed ranks and carried on when fathers were lost at sea. So too, when the nazis carried off to prison camp the breadwinner of a family

* David Hinshaw, *Sweden: Champion of Peace*, p. 208.

he could be sure that his children would be housed and fed.

The shift from agriculture to industry and the movement from country to city have weakened family ties and have actually made it impossible for families to assure security to their members. On the European continent and to a lesser extent in the North the Christian church gradually assumed responsibility for relief of poverty and distress. Alms-boxes in the churches collected contributions and the pastors dispensed charity. Such a system, however, was never quite satisfactory either psychologically or economically. With secularization and the growth of population and industry it became less and less satisfactory. Neither pleasant nor sufficient was the contemptuous charity tossed out by rugged individualists who had won their top hats. It was not even good business to produce a weak and bitter laboring proletariat. The problem was, how could the individual be protected, and how could he be made most productive? If neither the family nor the church could find the answer, then the job belonged to the state. Hence the secular government slowly assumed more responsibility. Local communities were required by law to care for their poor people, and the central government offered a helping hand.

In 1837 a committee of the Swedish Riksdag was appointed to investigate the problem of relief. The committee came to no definite conclusion as to whether aid should be centralized in Stockholm or left largely to the communities.* But it recognized that the simple personal methods of the past were no longer adequate. Not everyone could become the pensioner of a wealthy farmer. Nor could all beggars be deprived of legal protection and forced into the army or into "work houses"

* "Mostly it happens that the poorest people in greatest need are taken to the poor-house. Others receive occasionally money or provisions. Children who are in need are distributed among foster parents. In some places in the country where there are no poor-houses, the poor live for certain periods of time with the richer people and there they do as much work as is possible for them. Still there are only few places that do not have begging at all. Most communities take begging for granted." (Quoted in Arthur Montgomery, *Svensk Social Politik*, p. 71.)

which threw the innocent poor into contact with criminals, had a degrading effect, prevented marriage, and threatened loss in the next generation.

From 1840 many of the unemployed were put to work draining marshes, building roads, and later railroads. A law of 1847 began the coöperation between the state, the county, and the commune, which has come to characterize the relief program.

The state at the same time gained two powerful, though unofficial allies: emigration and industrial development. Emigration gained momentum in the 1840's and reached flood tide in the 1880's. Thousands of young men and women left to give their brain and brawn to the New World. Their places at home and the thousands of new places created by factories and railroads created an unprecedented demand for labor. Professor Arthur Montgomery is probably right when he suggests that the building of railroads in the mid-nineteenth century meant more for social development in Sweden than did legislation.

Yet there was still famine and crime, there were still unemployed and poor, there were still the sick and the aged. Emigration and industrialism helped solve some problems; they created also many new ones through breaking-up of families, the growth of cities, the increase in industrial accidents. The state had on its hands a job bigger than ever before. The tasks of government in a new social policy were similar throughout Europe. In countries such as Germany, England, and France the problems were often more acute than in the North. But the Scandinavian governments showed themselves peculiarly responsive to the needs of their people, and it was out of careful study of their own situation and of the methods used by their neighbors to the south and west that they worked out their solutions.

The principle of state regulation of working conditions was established in the eighteenth century both in Denmark-Norway and in Sweden-Finland. Denmark then operated under an autocratic monarch and Sweden under a paternalistic mercantilism. Many of the basic principles underlying programs for workers' welfare date from this period of "Enlightenment" in Europe. Control legislation on such items as child labor and hours of work in mines continued into the early nineteenth century.

In Norway, for example, mercantilists and liberals in the Storting agreed on an act making arrangements for the management of the Röros copper works (1818): The laborer was entitled to a pension at age 65, the amount to depend on family responsibilities and former wages; in case of illness caused by his work he was to get full wages for one month and one half the next month; he might work only 8 hours underground in winter and 9 in summer; he could buy food from the company at cost plus 10 per cent.

In 1842, under the broader human principles of liberalism, these rules were extended to all mines in Norway. Similar acts were passed for shopmen, cotters, and seamen. Attempts to enforce such laws and additional rules requiring safety devices led inevitably to "inspection acts" and supervision.

Steadily there grew a broadening of government interest in the working man. The state was concerned with national production. Then too, its interest was enhanced because the working man himself was playing an increasing role in politics. Mass education, universal suffrage, and social legislation were born of this union of economic and humanitarian motives. The problem of the workers' security came to be seen as a problem of the whole society, not just the concern of one community or one company.

Thus it was that the Scandinavian states began in the late nineteenth century to build up bodies of social legislation that have become models for much of the rest of the world. German and other experience was helpful, but these northerners were never slavish imitators. They examined their own needs and possibilities first, borrowed techniques from outside only insofar as these seemed to fit. In the careful thinking out of every step they improved and invented at many points, and ended with a unique pattern of government-individual relationships.

Insurance against the devastating results of accident, illness, and old age was the first major field of the new activity. S. A. Hedin in Sweden raised the question of social insurance in the Riksdag of 1884, and by 1886 a law on accident insurance was passed. Sickness insurance came next, but haltingly. Norway too began, in 1894, with insurance against industrial accidents of factory workers, and within the next twenty years had broadened the law to include fishermen and seamen. Finland in 1895 started in the same way with an act holding employers responsible for industrial accidents.

Since only the details differ in the different countries Denmark may serve as an example of a carefully integrated scheme of social insurance. "Support for self support" is the basic principle of Danish insurance which covers sickness, permanent invalidity, and old age. It is compulsory and universal, including all citizens below an income limit. It is contributory, except for old age. It is national in regulation, but local in administration and membership.

The Danish system is a typical Scandinavian blend of individual responsibility and social responsibility. The individual contributes toward the insurance premiums and part of his compensation is paid to him directly; the other part to hospital, doctor, or where necessary. The state assumes responsibility in that it requires every one to be insured (since 1933), and it pays a large proportion of the cost for the unpropertied citizenry. The whole system has evolved from the voluntary "sick clubs" which sprang up after the middle of the nineteenth century. These clubs were originally replacements for the self-help gilds, abolished in 1860. Now they are widespread, usually one for each commune (several in the larger cities) and are managed by their own elected boards. They enroll all citizens—farmers, shopkeepers, and workers—who earn a skilled worker's top pay or less. Those who earn or have more than this income are required merely to belong to an "association" wherein they pay only a nominal sum and get slight benefits—but they may be quickly transferred to the full insurance sick club in case need arises (if, for instance, they lose their high income status). The associations are therefore passive organizations, a reserve for the sick clubs.

The year after the Danish National Insurance Act, which in 1933 codified and simplified existing practice, 1609 sick clubs reported 2,100,000 members above fourteen years of age. The sickness insurance associations (also state controlled) had 112,000 members, and the separate State Railway Men's Sick Club had 38,000. Altogether the public health insurance included 2,460,000 or 90 per cent of the people fourteen years of age and older. Membership subscriptions covered about two-thirds of the direct expense of members' illness, the state's contributions about one-fourth and the communes' the remainder. The state assumed much of the responsibility for dealing with special diseases like tuberculosis. However, there was and is a large category of indirect expense where the commune bears the burden: the maintenance of hospitals whose regular charge is thirty cents to $1.00 a day, and half of that to sick club members; provision of ambulance service; and help toward expenses of specially distressed cases.

This system combines insurance and relief, or compensation and assistance, and has great social-psychological advantages. The individual gets what he needs, and even though he may not pay for all of it he has the sense of contributing. He retains the status of an insured person; he is not classed as a pauper.

When a member becomes ill he can expect free medical service from a private physician, hospitalization, up to three-fourths of the cost of medicines (insulin and a few other medicines are specifically mentioned), and a small daily cash compensation. Hospitalization allowances can continue normally for not more than two 13-week periods in twelve months. Actual amounts and services differ somewhat in different communes and clubs. For instance, some include dental work and some do not. The individual has a choice of doctors, but fees are regulated by the clubs according to a locally negotiated schedule. In the hospitals the practice in Denmark is different from that in the United States in that all the work is done by full-time staff physicians; being or not being a sick club member of course has no effect on that.

In addition to regular sickness insurance is disability insurance, to protect against permanent incapacity. For this the insured pays six kroner per year, less than half the cost; employers about 15 per cent, communes about 12 per cent, and the state 22 per cent. Old age is reckoned as a special kind of invalidity, but "Old Age Pensions" come as a right and without payment of any special contribution. This has been true since the act of 1891. These pensions are financed out of general revenues, and the costs divided: four-sevenths by the state, two-sevenths by the communes in general, and one-seventh by the commune in which the recipient resides. Most of the aged receive from 600 to 800 kroner per year, but the actual amount is raised up or down from the base sum according to place of residence, other income, and degree of incapacity— blind people, for instance, receiving an additional sum.* Accident insurance is a smaller item than any of the others, but here the insured pays nothing, the state and the commune only insignificant amounts, the employer over 90 per cent. Industrial accidents are counted a proper charge to include in the expenses of industrial production.

The entire program integrated in the Danish National Insurance Act cost, in 1934–35 (exclusive of hospital maintenance, etc.), 172,000,000 kroner, or 48 kroner (*c.* $10.00) per capita of the entire population. Cheap enough for the security of the individual and the health of the community!

Unemployment insurance in Denmark is a different category, but operates on principles similar to the various forms of

---

* In Sweden since 1948 these amounts are more than double, as a result of postwar legislation; the Swedes differ also in requiring graduated tax contributions of six to 100 kronor from every citizen for the old age pension fund. Everyone is in the system, including the king.

sickness insurance. For unemployment, however, the employer pays only a token amount, the worker pays about half, the state one-third, and the commune one-sixth. The state contributions are based on a percentage of the contributions of the insured, but vary from an even matching of the payments of the lowest-paid workers to only 15 per cent of the payments of highly-paid workers. Benefits are never paid for the first six days of unemployment, and are paid for a maximum of 100 days in a year; they are limited also to about $1.00 per day, a figure considerably below the wage rate. Still further to discourage deliberate idleness a worker is required to accept a job even outside his special training and at the regular rate of pay for that job. In other words, pay is based on the work done, not on the worker's special training. Throughout the country the state operates labor exchanges to facilitate new employment. In case of strikes or other industrial conflict the worker must look to his union's funds. In short, the state will help the individual, but it will not be imposed upon, and the worker who is idle or on strike can never gain as much as the equivalent of his regular wage.

In addition to these various kinds of insurance there is of course public relief for special need. The blind, the mentally ill, paupers—all are cared for, and the basis for all care is *right*, the right of the human being, the right of the member of a society who is less fortunate than his fellows. The person is protected against the indignities of nineteenth-century poor relief.

Through all the variations in detail in Denmark, Norway, and Sweden there is at least enough similarity so that a citizen of one country who needs public assistance in one of the other countries can receive care and the expense be balanced up later between the governments concerned. A worker from Denmark employed in Sweden, for example, will pay his "social security" fees to the Swedish offices. Many of the laws on social aid have been passed after conferences of experts from all Scandinavia. Finland has participated regularly in such conferences. Both the pattern and the underlying philosophy of social insurance are therefore the same throughout the North, and administration is coördinated.

Insurance against distress or tragedy is, however, a negative approach, ameliorative at best. Much is being done on a more positive basis. In Norway, for example, Public Health Boards were established by a law of 1860 and have steadily expanded their usefulness. The country has 378 public health districts in cities, towns, and rural communities. The district health officer occupies a prominent place in his community, and serves on juvenile courts, factory inspection boards, building commissions, and health organizations. He is assisted in each case by a local board which must contain one woman, the public engineer when there is one, and a veterinary if possible. From two to four members are elected for four-year terms. These boards throughout the country have supervision over epidemic diseases, water, cemeteries, public halls, garbage, and housing conditions. Here again is the system of local democratic control, with national coördination and supervision through the Ministry of Health and Social Welfare. Preventive medicine is strongly emphasized.

It is thoroughly understandable that it was in Norway that the "Oslo breakfast" originated. At school any child may receive an invigorating morning meal: orange (when possible), milk, biscuit or bread, cheese, raw carrot or apple. This Oslo breakfast has not only vitamin quality, but the social significance of training in cleanliness and manners. It has been copied widely throughout Europe.

Tuberculosis is still a serious problem, but it is constructively attacked with compulsory X rays, vaccination, and health training. Even the war-born cynicism and brutalization is being treated as one of the problems of public health. Venereal disease has been brought under control by the united efforts of medicine, publicity, and law.

Special problems of health and sanitation arise in these lands of long winters and heavy clothing. The bath is not a universal daily exercise. Yet when the Finns, for example, go to the *sauna* they get gloriously clean. The *sauna* is a family and sometimes a social event, and prudery is at a minimum; the bath is often the occasion for a week-end outing. The bath-house is a special building of logs with shelves around the side walls, a fireplace covered over with a pyramid of stones, and in the roof a small outlet for smoke and steam. When the stones are heated, water is thrown on, and men bask in the steam. They are stripped clean, and lie first on the lower shelves. As they begin to warm up a girl or an older woman comes in and beats and scrubs their perspiring bodies with birch twigs; as they can bear it they crawl up to higher shelves and more intense steam as fresh water is dashed on the hot stones. When their pink bodies can stand no more they jump into the snow outside or perhaps through the thin ice of a near-by lake. Then a rubdown and an evening by the fireplace.

In the cities the public bathhouse is a highly refined institution, and the ritual of the *sauna* is lost. Men and women carry their little suitcases with a change of clothes, make special appointments for the "Class A bath," much as American women make their dates with the beauty parlor. There is no longer excuse for the filthiness of the nineteenth century, of which a famous doctor said: "Most people of the lower classes in Stockholm get their bodies clean only twice—when they are born and when they die."

4. CHILD WELFARE

The modern fear of population decline and the social interest in children, particularly in Sweden, have led to much legislation in recent years. Sweden may serve as the example for a characterization of child welfare programs. The first Swedish child welfare legislation dates from the twelfth century and an institution for orphans was established in 1633. Children are regarded as a social asset and a community responsibility regardless of the accidents of parenthood.

Education, one phase of child welfare, is state regulated and state-supported from the nursery school through the university. For elementary education the state provides about three-fifths of the funds and the localities two-fifths; since 1946 the total costs have included free textbooks for each child. Vocational guidance is systematically organized both in school and in industry.

The most interesting developments, however, have been in the field of health, primarily since legislation passed in 1937. In this program state aid and regulation limits itself to preventive medicine, and is not therefore comparable with the socialized medicine program in England. Every prospective mother in Sweden is entitled to free prophylactic treatment, examination, and advice on prenatal care, and more than 68 per cent take advantage of the system. Every infant is entitled to free examination and preventive treatment, and over 85 per cent receive it. Vitamins and medicines are available free for both mother and children. Later in life vaccination for tuberculosis is both compulsory and free.

All this and more is organized through local Child Welfare Boards, established in every community according to the law of 1924, charged to "follow attentively the prevailing conditions in the commune with reference to the care and training of children and youth," and to help them. These Boards have supervision of matters affecting juvenile delinquency and have introduced many reforms in procedures of dealing with such cases. They also have oversight in the whole broad realm of health facilities.

The state gives subventions for equipment and pays part of the salary of doctors and nurses; the community pays the remainder. The total cost of somewhat over $1,000,000 per year is in practice divided about equally between state and locality. In method the system works similarly to American practice in such things as the high-school teaching of agriculture under the Smith-Hughes Act. Dental clinics are established on a similar pattern, and with a similar distribution of cost.

Here, however, the individual child pays a small fee—$1.25 per year if he is the first child in a family, 90 cents if he is second, 60 cents if he is third! Where these dental clinics exist the participation is practically 100 per cent of the children. These services, dental and medical, emphasize prevention strongly, and use regular private physicians and dentists on a part-time basis in clinics and schools. The result is both improved general health and increased work for the private practitioner.

The services provided for children include day nurseries, playgrounds, summer camps, and careful legal protection.

5. HOUSING AND PUBLIC WORKS

Closely related to questions of health and child welfare is housing. In fact housing is a central factor in social welfare as a whole, influencing family life, children, religion, and the stability of the community. Much emphasis in these self-conscious societies is thus placed on housing, in its technical and its social aspects.

The Stockholm housing exhibition of 1930 was a pioneering and an eye-opening illustration of modern design. The influence of German functionalism was evident, and also the philosophy of Frank Lloyd Wright. The Swedes proceeded, though, to make something of their own, to create new designs in houses and in furniture for Swedish living. They have shown themselves clever in planning apartments for comfortable living in small quarters. Both apartment houses and "villa" homes are constructed to take advantage of all available sunshine and of views across water or valleys. An illustration is a group of octagonal apartment buildings, eight stories high, built on an irregular rocky height in Stockholm; each small apartment has a balcony large enough for two people—three if necessary, and an open view.

The cities of Scandinavia are keenly aware of the need of open space. Stockholm allots about half of its land developments to streets, playgrounds, and parks. And the law requires of individual subdividers that they turn over to the city at least 40 per cent of the tract for such purposes. Stockholm, too, like other larger cities in the North, has extensive colony gardens, where closed-in apartment dwellers can have cottages and little patches of land for flower or vegetable gardens, and for sun-sitting.

Copenhagen has a tradition of municipal landownership dating from 1100 when unfenced farm lands became public property. Once the city purchased an entire adjoining village. Such land was held by the city but rented to individuals. In 1795 a government commission wanted to sell some of the lands to help pay costs of restoration after the great fire, but the city objected in strong terms:

> The property and ground of Copenhagen belong to the city and its inhabitants, those of the future no less than of the present; therefore, any attempt to take away from future generations the opportunity to utilize this property . . . is positively deplorable.*

Oslo, cradled among the mountains at the head of Oslo fjord, is carefully planning future expansion with homes and apartments open to the air, fine highways, and large park areas. In the years just before World War II the municipality of Oslo did Herculean work in clearing out slums. In one the city erected its impressive new city hall. Outside the central district the municipality built many large apartment houses, with modern facilities inside, playgrounds outside, and set a scale of low rents which private enterprise had to match. Homes, like health, are recognized as assets for the community as well as for the person.

Rebuilding of the war-devastated areas of northern Finland and Norway evidences again the combined interest of government and individual. Many homes were destroyed by bombing, then whole towns and vast rural areas were burned and laid waste by the retreating Germans in 1944–45. Over 100,000 people were evacuated from Finnish Lapland. Quite naturally

* As quoted in J. Graham, Jr., *Housing in Scandinavia,* p. 8.

government aid has helped them to rebuild their homes, as well as their power stations, ferries, telephone poles, railways.

Norway curtailed postwar building elsewhere in order to help the people of the far north to reëstablish their homes and their economy. Transportation subsidies were granted and the government assumed general oversight. One of the great worries was that in their haste to rebuild people would construct unsafe and unsightly shacks, poor economy in the long run. Government planners, therefore, agreed upon twelve different types of wooden houses; surveyors and town planners had to give approval before any construction could proceed; seven to twelve thousand carpenters and other skilled laborers from the South were maintained in Finnmark. People were sometimes forced to build homes larger and better than they wanted because the government thought this was the time to raise the standard of living and to build for the future.

The total result of this carefully planned program is a slower and more expensive rebuilding, but an improvement of living conditions on a permanent basis. Financing was organized through the Norwegian State Housing Bank, with 2½ per cent loans on a large portion of the cost and subsidies for part.

The Scandinavians are interested in *homes* even more than in *houses*. They have become worried over declining birthrates and over a divorce rate that has risen everywhere, in Sweden to one divorce for each four marriages. Strenuous efforts have therefore been made to ease the financial burdens of renting or owning homes, and to relieve the expenses of parenthood. This program in Sweden has broadened out from meager beginnings in 1904 until in 1946 the government set up a fund of 400,000,000 kronor ($110,000,000) for housing alone. From this fund municipalities could borrow up to 100 per cent of the cost of housing projects, coöperative organizations could borrow up to 95 per cent, and individuals to 85 per cent.

Government in Sweden did not build homes, but it eased the way for building. It also controlled standards, and insisted upon modern conveniences and good locations. It required that houses be built with children in mind, and be near to schools and playgrounds. When builders and tenants fulfilled the demands their privileges were large. Contractors were occasionally granted subsidies as high as 30 per cent of their building cost; no repayment was expected, but if after ten years economic conditions had so changed that the builders were making excessive profits the subsidy might be reëxamined and interest demanded.

The father of a family could borrow from government funds or government-guaranteed funds most of the cost of a new home; then he could have the payments on the loan postponed until his youngest child had reached working age. If he rented he could have the rent reduced by 30 per cent if he had three children, 40 per cent if he had four—and so on to 70 per cent for eight children. Often the companies for which men work make special grants for home building, too—Boliden mining company will give up to 3000 kronor ($800), with no obligation to repay if the worker stays with the company for ten years. The coöperative housing societies have a large share in well-planned building programs. The general aim is to reduce rents to 20 per cent of the worker's wage. No wonder that slums are practically nonexistent, and that apartments and separate houses are neat and in good repair. If a family is in need its privileges are greater.

Many Swedes think social reform may have gone too far. A banker in Gothenburg frankly said, "the Swedes are living beyond their means, and a sad day of reckoning is coming." An American ECA report of 1949 said the same. But Gustav Möller, the minister of social affairs, thought that after the war Sweden's foreign reputation for social progress was undeserved and it was his ambition to make the facts equal the reputation. The other northern countries have not had the reserves of wealth or production to keep pace with the Swedish example, but again the general policy has been the same. It is state support, local control, family use. It tends to level out differentials in income and it produces greatly improved housing. Demoralization of its beneficiaries is feared and predicted, but so far is not apparent.

This question of the effects of social legislation is a vital one, and the writer has kept it in mind on successive visits to Scandinavia. Some employers complain of a slowing down in the tempo of work, but production statistics do not support their charges. The newly legislated three-week vacation in Norway, especially when taken as "common vacation," certainly slowed down summer business in 1948, when it first became effective; yet the Norwegians have increased total production 150 per cent over 1939. Aid to the indigent seems so generous that it should tempt men to lay down their tools. Yet in Swedish factories, Finnish stores, Danish farms—everywhere, men worked conscientiously and skilfully. There is no leaning on shovels; people work. It reminds one of how the Presbyterians claim to believe in predestination, but strive to be saved just as hard as if they thought they had to. The Scandinavians realize that if they do not work none of them will have anything.

But—can society afford such generosity? What will happen in case of depression? To arrive at favorable solutions of these questions the governments of the North, already started in social and economic planning, are steadily moving farther in more planning to try to avoid depression.

Public works and state-owned enterprises play an important role, but so also do the major private enterprises such as Norwegian shipping and Danish agriculture. These small countries realize the dependence of peoples on one another, the interaction between labor and capital, the dependence of the whole community on the prosperity of the major industries. The same thing is true in larger countries, but there it appears farther away, and the individual cannot easily visualize his own part in the whole. The intimacy of life in these small countries makes quick and effective common action seem more possible.

Taxation policy is directed so as to moderate the business cycle. A company which expands its plant during a period of economic decline is granted a lowered tax on such building.

Thus the government encourages business to lay aside reserves for future construction, and stimulates the labor market in periods when business is slow. The governments try to avoid coercion, but they do have practical means of persuasion!

The governments themselves try to carry out road-making and public building projects in times of threatened emergency. They plan ahead. For example, the Norwegian government-in-exile in London during the war carefully saved the earnings from the fleet for the rebuilding of both the fleet and the country.

Natural resources are held directly by the state or are controlled by it. The water power of Norway until recently has been for the most part privately owned. When a company wishes to develop a power station it first buys the waterfall from the farmer or whoever owns it. Then the company must sign a contract with the state, and agree to state regulations such as to employ only Norwegian labor; it then gets the use of the development for fifty years, after which all rights revert to the state.

Utility companies are ordinarily owned by municipalities, as are all the public services. In Norway even the motion picture theaters are city-owned. Telephone and telegraph service is state-operated, efficient and cheap. In all these lands the radio is state-operated, hence free of advertising—one never hears of soap or soap-opera; expenses are met by license fees on each radio set, not by subsidies from business promotion. So too the main railway lines are state-owned. Thus many state activities are self-supporting or even profit-making enterprises.

The governments have their hands in many business concerns: the Norwegian government owns about half of the stock of the large Norsk Hydro nitrates firm, and the Swedish government has gone still further. Even in Sweden, however, more than 90 per cent of business is private, and such enterprises as the state railways buy rolling stock from private manufacturers. The government's declared principle is to keep hands off as long as private business is doing the job; but if there is an economic or social need that the government thinks it can meet better than private business it steps in to try. This was the case with the interrelated iron-mining and railway-building program in northern Sweden. Usually there is an impelling social cause as well as an economic one for state participation in business enterprise.

A significant illustration of this combined social and economic motivation is the Norrbottens Jernverk in Luleå, Sweden. Again and again private companies had tried to make pig iron in the far north, near the ore supply. Fuel was the great problem for even timber was scarce and slow-growing in those upper latitudes, and charcoal was hard to get; it was much too far to take coal to the ore. There was labor and room for thousands more workers but those who already lived there on the meager returns of arctic agriculture and fishing were discontented and inclined to think that the rest of the country reaped the rewards of the rich iron mines which belonged to the north. Couldn't they have some kind of manufacturing, retain some profits and create a happier society?

When water power was made to produce more electricity and electric smelting was introduced the mining areas had all the fuel resources necessary. Still private capital was not interested. It was easier and safer to keep production in the central area. But the government was interested in people. Careful investigation indicated that pig iron could be produced economically in the area. The government decided to build an up-to-date pig-iron plant at Luleå. In 1948 some 350 workers were erecting the plant and producing pig iron; within a few years they expect to see 1800 workers turning out a superior product, and in a quantity to make Sweden at last self-sufficient in pig iron and steel—though not in steel plate.

The state-organized company subsidizes four-dwelling housing units at 2000 kronor per apartment, and the workers themselves have a mutual society which borrows 70–90 per cent of the cost of construction from the banks. Rentals are about 108 kronor ($30) per month for a four-room apartment.

Wages are the highest in the Swedish iron industry, but costs of living are high too.

Wages are on a piecework basis. The general rates are determined in Stockholm, but the details of adjustment between different classes of workers are made in Luleå. It was a revealing experience to sit in with the committee which elaborated these final arrangements: the engineer-director and three elected worker representatives, two of them communist and one a social democrat. All were able and articulate, and all were convinced of the importance of this plant as a pioneering undertaking. The engineer emphasized the value of competition between three forms of enterprise—private, state, and mixed. Costs here are low because of new equipment and "rationalized" methods, partly learned from the United States where the manager of the plant traveled before the factory was started. Ore and transportation are arranged for on a long-term basis, but at prices at least as high as any company would have to pay. The pig iron is shipped south in private boats and sold to private concerns at competitive rates.

Such plants as the one at Luleå, and a similar one which Norway is building at Mo-i-Rana in northern Norway are straight government-in-business, even if they have a background of social purpose. Other government ventures help more directly in the realization of social goals. In Sweden mothers may travel for ten days free on the state railways if the family income is less than 2500 kronor; their children under 16 may travel for a month. Special family rates are available to all, and all rates are arranged so that travel becomes progressively cheaper with distance, a system which encourages people everywhere to enjoy the far corners of their country. In Denmark the state railways provide favorable annual and monthly ride-where-you-please rates. In Norway, where railroad-building faced the barriers of fjords and sheer rock cliffs and snow slides, it was frankly accepted that construction could not be economically justified. Throughout the North the rail routes are regarded primarily as public service. They are well run by state employees and they are used to overcapacity by the people for whom they are built, whether on the birch-burners of Finland, the smooth electric lines of Sweden, the oil-burning "lightning-trains" of Denmark, or the tunnel-boring coal-driven trains of Norway. In sparsely-settled Iceland there are no railways, but there are horses, cars, and airplanes.

6. TOBACCO AND LIQUOR CONTROL

Goodly revenues for the social programs are obtained by extraordinary taxation on certain luxuries, tobacco and liquor particularly. Tobacco import and manufacture is handled through government-licensed monopolies. When dollar exchange is particularly short it may be, and is, forbidden to import American cigarettes, tobacco, and other substances. The domestic cigarettes sell for forty to sixty cents per pack, and imported American brands for about seventy-five cents. Despite these heavy taxes one country (Sweden) reports a 50 per cent increase in cigarette smoking since the war.

Liquor control is managed differently in each country, but always with a dual purpose: to discourage consumption and to gain revenue. Denmark and Norway rely chiefly on high price. Finland tried the noble experiment of prohibition, but it worked out much as it did in the United States and was abandoned after twelve years. Sweden has a system which is interestingly different.

In 1909, during the general strike in Sweden, prohibition was instituted as a temporary safety measure. It worked, and many people wanted to continue it. More cautious reformers feared that when the emergency was gone uncontrollable smuggling and lawlessness would develop, and advocated a workable limitation rather than an unworkable total prohibition.

Gradually the system which Gothenburg had pioneered and which Dr. Ivan Bratt had developed in the city of Stockholm was adapted for the country as a whole. Basically it permits each adult the right to obtain alcoholic drink, but only in proportion to capacity—capacity to pay and capacity to partake. A young man just married and with a good job might be allowed to buy two liters of strong spirits per month, and what beer and light wine he wished; the basic control is on *akvavit*, whisky, and liqueurs. A prosperous businessman with a family might buy up to four liters per month, but no one more than that. A spinster might have one-half liter per year for seasoning her cakes, or for an occasional cold. For a wedding or other big celebration there could always be a special dispensation. Under the privilege of local option many communities are "dry," but individuals may buy elsewhere and carry the liquor home.

If a person who has been given a ration book for liquor is arrested for drunkenness, or for driving under the influence of liquor, or if he spends too much of his income for alcoholic pleasure, he may have his book taken away, either temporarily or permanently.

The system is organized by parishes, and purchases have to be made at the neighborhood liquor store. Saloons and taverns are taboo; hotels and restaurants must be licensed to sell drinks —but only together with food; their profits are limited in order to discourage consumption.

From the selling side the system works through a national wholesale monopoly and through a number of local retail monopolies. The wholesale company is owned and operated by the government and by ten government-approved shareholders (whose profits are limited to 5½ per cent). This company owns all the producing establishments in the country and imports all alcoholic beverages. The local retail "systems" are set up with private capital and operate like any business, except that their profits are limited to 5 per cent. Thus the pressure of the profit motive is eliminated. All surplus earnings go to the government, and it was the fund created by this surplus which financed Sweden's public works program of the early thirities, and successfully cushioned the depression. Prices, incidentally, are surprisingly close to those in the United States.

Bootlegging? Very little. Opposition to restraint? Some, but on the whole people get nearly enough what they want that there is little complaint against this government-aided self-control. The system is enforced not so much by law as by innate aversion to excess, by a society which is homogeneous and level-headed. Sweden is a drinking community, but a temperate one.

7. LABOR AND SOCIALIZATION

In few places on earth is there less poverty and more evenly distributed wealth. Labor gets a large share of the national income. For the basic organization of labor-employer relationships Denmark and Sweden can serve as fairly typical examples.

Denmark was the first to become significantly industrial. Next door was Germany to furnish examples of labor organization, and Danish labor began to create unions on a wide scale in the 1870's and 1880's. The gilds had been abolished in 1862. It was the employers, however, who first built a national association in 1896. The unions then combined to form the Amalgamated Trade Unions in 1898, and these two organizations of employers and employees have since dominated the scene in industrial relations. By 1943 the Employers' Association represented the employers of about 40 per cent of Danish industrial workers; the Amalgamated Trade Unions represented 563,800 workers—95 per cent of those organized, and 85 per cent of all industrial laborers.

The September Agreement of 1899 defined the relations between the two great Danish associations. Actually it defined the relations between employers and employees as a whole. This agreement recognized the rights of each party to "decree and approve labor stoppages"; declared that a strike or lockout must be voted by at least three-fourths of a "competent assembly"; required two notices to be given, fourteen days and seven days before a stoppage; and specified a three-month notice for cancelation of a labor agreement. The right to organize was stated, but also the right of an individual to refrain from joining. The employer was specifically recognized to have the right to allocate work. One notable passage in the Agreement deserves to be read beyond Denmark's borders:

It is taken for granted that the Amalgamated Trade Unions will be willing to work with all its might together with the Employer's Association for peaceable, stable and good working conditions, first and foremost by ensuring that nothing be done by any organization whatever under any circumstances to prevent any worker from making use of his natural right to do so much and such good work as his abilities and training permit.

Under this September Agreement, which is still in force, a Permanent Court of Arbitration was set up in 1900, and this court was given legal prerogatives. In 1910 it became the Fixed Court of Arbitration. Between 1910 and 1943 it handled 3375 cases. One of its far-reaching decisions was that if an organization remains passive when it should step in to halt an illegal action, then the organization is liable as an accessory. The emphasis in labor relations, however, is not on legal action, but on agreement. Conciliators were set up in 1910 to aid organizations to come to a settlement. A shop stewards' system has been inaugurated to provide liaison between workers and management.

A complicating factor of recent years is the development of state contracts with foreign countries, and to meet this difficulty a Labor and Conciliation Board was established in 1940—three representatives of labor, three of employers, and three of the state, to advise on legislation to promote trade.

In Sweden labor has come a long way from 1770, when an ordinance stated, "If journeymen or other workers unite for the purpose of causing a rise in wages be each one fined . . ." By 1864 the gilds were abolished and in 1872 the first trade union was formed. But labor's position was pitifully weak as was illustrated by the famous Sundsvall strike of 1879. That affair, however, dramatized to labor its need. By vigorous action based on the right of the individual to form associations, labor's "right to organize' was established. In 1899 *Landsorgan-isationen* (LO) was founded through the Social Democratic Party; and in Sweden it was labor which first built a comprehensive national organization of organizations. LO has since that time made itself one of the great powers in the state, perhaps the greatest power. By 1949 the laborers affiliated with LO numbered 1,100,000 out of a total population of less than 7,000,000!

In 1902 the counterpart to LO was established, the Swedish Employer's Association, and soon, as James J. Robbins concisely puts it:

> The associational structure in the labor market had matured into a powerful instrument of *private government* by voluntary groups . . . to the State was reserved but a fraction of disciplinary power in the relations between the organized adversaries, and one of the most important official State organs dealing with labor relations, the Labor Court, was composed of judges, a majority of whom were outright representatives of these organized interests.*

The major pattern of organization in Sweden is the industrial union. The closed shop has not been an issue any more than in Denmark. By a careful statement agreed upon in 1907 between LO and the Employer's Association the employer's right to allot work and to discharge was recognized, also the right to hire regardless of union affiliation. The barbers are the only major group who maintain the closed-shop principle. Yet practically all Swedish industrial and craft labor is unionized; the unaffiliated worker is regarded as a parasite, a man refusing to shoulder common responsibilities; labor is so strong that it does not need artificial compulsions.

The Basic Agreement (or the Saltsjöbaden Agreement) of 1938 is the parallel in Sweden to the September Agreement in Denmark. It is an "instrument of functional self-government." It establishes a Labor Market Board of six members (three representing each group) to provide for settlement of disputes without state interference, limits conflicts affecting essential

* James J. Robbins, *Government of Labor Relations in Sweden*, p. 11.

service, affirms principles and methods of labor-employer relationships, and protects individual rights. It "rests upon the assumption that while the interests of both sides are likely to conflict in many instances, it is to the advantage of each, without attempting to destroy the other, to compromise those interests peaceably." *

Much the same spirit, and even much the same history, characterizes the labor movements in Iceland, Norway, and Finland. In Norway the LO was organized in 1899 and an employer's association in 1900; there is the same privilege of either employer or employee to affiliate or not, but also the same attitude toward the individual who will not join hands with his fellows; and there is the Basic Agreement and the Labor Court. In Finland development was somewhat later. The typesetters formed the first union in 1894, then a generation afterwards the rights of labor were spelled out in the constitution, both the right to organize and the liberty of the individual to abstain from joining.

The wage system varies with companies and tasks, but it leans strongly to a piece-work pattern. In Sweden almost 60 per cent of the industrial workers are on a piece-work basis. Some firms have tried a combination method, giving the workers about half their income as a guaranteed basic wage and half as piecework pay.

One of the recent trends in industrial relations is the shop committee. Considerable attention is paid to American experience with this idea, and shop committees are being instituted throughout the North. But some workers are slow to accept the scheme, for the committees do not discuss wages, and there is uncertainty as to the purpose. As a liaison with management such committees can be useful, but perhaps two things tend to check the introduction of the system in certain plants. One is that Scandinavian labor, operating in comparatively small factories and mines, is not out of touch with management. Another is that labor regards itself as labor. The desire to have

* Robbins, p. 137.

more voice in factory direction is a desire to participate *as labor*.

It is this self-conscious labor which drew up an all-inclusive 27-point labor program for postwar Sweden. It acted through its theorists and political leaders with Minister of Finance Ernst Wigforss as chairman of the committee. The 27 points are divided into three groups. First comes full employment:

That is the principal objective of our economic policy. To achieve this end, our monetary system, state finance, price and wage policy, and private and public undertakings must all combine to provide full employment for labour and material resources.*

The state is expected to regulate prices so as to prevent depression; to assure steady employment by coördinating plans with industry through "a joint public body"; to grant credits to obtain markets and raw materials abroad; to increase housing and cheap consumer goods; and to improve the system of labor exchanges and job training.

On the foundation of this full employment the state must next assure higher wages, higher living standards, and fair distribution of income. It must bring about a leveling of the differences in income between agricultural and industrial workers and between men and women; expand insurance and unemployment benefits; shorten hours; improve public health; equalize educational opportunities; and (in the long run) abolish class distinctions.

The third major category of goals is "greater productive efficiency and increased economic democracy." This is to be attained by national planning of investments; government supervision of foreign trade; rebuilding of crowded areas and gradual transfer of apartment houses to municipal ownership; "rationalization" of agricultural and domestic work; "government support for non-profit production or socialization where private enterprise entails abuses or monopolization"; publication of price agreements; greater support for research; control

* *The Postwar Programme of Swedish Labour*, p. 6.

of the quality of goods; and last but not least, "greater influence on the part of workers over the administration of industry."

This last point is much discussed and little understood. The workers talk about it with proud hope, but seem vague about what they really want, or what is entailed. I asked two workers in a pulp mill, when they mentioned it, if they thought that sharing in the responsibilities of management should bring with it sharing of the risks—in something like profit-sharing (and loss-sharing). These men were dumbfounded that anyone could raise such a question; obviously the thought had never entered their minds. They wanted a larger share in profits, they wanted to help make decisions, but they had not the faintest expectation of sharing losses if their decisions should result in loss. In brief, they and their fellows still think primarily as laborers, employees, and one wonders if they are seriously intent on participating in management.

For labor itself is a career. The laborer's son can become a lawyer or a teacher or a banker as he can in the United States, but he is less likely to do so. He is more likely to accept the status if not the occupation of his father, and to do so with a definite feeling of self-respect. Such attitudes differ in the various parts of Scandinavia, and they differ only in degree between Scandinavia and the United States. But the difference certainly does exist. Scandinavian society is less fluid than that of the United States, labor is less mobile. Industries and cities are growing, however, and the degree of difference is much smaller than it was a generation ago.

Production methods are efficient, but they depend somewhat more on the man, somewhat less on the machine than in the United States. The proportion of handicraft work is considerably greater. This is partly due to deliberate policy, and it results in preservation of skills and in a sense of pride in workmanship. The laborer respects the managerial skill and general economic knowledge of the employer; he expects the employer to respect the skillful eyes and hands which guide a pail of molten metal or construct a table or shape a vase. The laborer therefore can sit down in a wage conference with his employer with a sense of his own dignity and worth. There is little of either humility or resentment. The laborer is simply representing one set of interests, the employer or manager another set of interests. Labor as a whole is a clear-cut functional group, and it has political and social power. But it remains labor. Shareholding by labor leaders is frowned upon, for labor hesitates to compromise its position.

The feeling of difference between labor and management is heightened by the fact that ordinarily plant managers are trained engineers. In the United States the business, promotional, and personnel side of management is emphasized; in Scandinavia the technical aspects are given more prominence. It is for this reason that the great technical schools of Scandinavia train engineers for both the scientific and the management aspects of mining and manufacturing.

Another significant contrast between Scandinavian and American labor history is this: in Scandinavia the first demand of labor was for rights; in the United States the first demand was for specific advantages, wages particularly. Both rights and advantages were demanded simultaneously, of course; yet American labor, having won extraordinary success in wages and other practical matters, still finds itself in the middle of the twentieth century battling for bargaining rights, the closed shop, an assured legal position. Such issues were settled long ago in Scandinavia. Perhaps it is because in Scandinavia labor and management first worked out a basis on which to deal with each other that additional problems have been adjustable without overmuch strife.

But violence and bloodshed have had their day, and disastrous strikes have tested the strength of companies and men. Sundsvall and the great general strike of 1909 in Sweden have been mentioned. In Finland in the postwar period strikes and strike threats have kept the air tense. Denmark used a general-agreement strike during the war as a most effective weapon against the nazis. Worker demonstrations in Iceland have sought to bring pressure on the government. The general spirit of recent times is represented more accurately, however, by the no-strike pledge taken by Norwegian labor after World War II. With this was coupled a wage-stop act in 1947, for the socialist government and the worker-citizen recognized that the upward movement of wages as well as prices must be stopped to avoid runaway inflation.

The sense of national responsibility showed by Scandinavian labor is surprising to many Americans. But it is quite natural: labor is almost completely organized in trade unions; the trade unions control the Social Democratic Party in each country, or as some would put it the directorates of each are interlocking; the Social Democratic Party is in control of the government of the state. Labor is therefore responsible for the maintenance of the total national welfare.

It is probably this attitude which explains why socialization (or nationalization) is carried through only to a moderate extent. In the above program it is mentioned repeatedly as a second alternative, *if and when necessary*. Complete socialization is not necessary. Private ownership under this "middle way" can be forced to serve the public good even when it is tempted to go its own way. Through the yardsticks and the direct competition of the coöperative movement and through direct government legislation it is possible to hold in line private prices and private methods. And what everyone wants is practical results, not the realization of a theory.

Labor has power and is sufficiently mature to see that the national good must come foremost. Both labor and capital recognize each other's importance and they have come close to discovering the place where the functions and the advantages of each are balanced. Leadership has been farsighted as well as strong on both sides, and membership has been intelligent and realistic. Mutual confidence has resulted. A true story told me years ago and confirmed later by one of the participants will illustrate the prevailing attitude.

French labor and capital were, practically speaking, cutting each other's throats with strikes and lockouts and physical violence. They heard that in Sweden labor and employers had learned how to make agreements for mutual advantage. So they invited a delegation of Swedish employers and employees to come to Paris to discuss with French employer and employee representatives the whole problem of industrial relations.

At a long table the French employers sat together toward one end, laborers at the other; across the table sat the two Swedish groups. Before the discussion began a French labor delegate asked where the interpreter was. The Swedish workers did not know French, but the employers did. The Frenchman's question was translated by an employer, and the Swedish employees answered that the employers would be their interpreters. The astonished Frenchman said, "What, can you trust them to translate fairly?"

When this question in turn was translated the answer of the Swedish labor delegates was to get up and throw their arms around their employer-opponents and to shake their fists at the distrustful French workers.

Fight they do, stubbornly and with all the resources at their command. The struggle between labor and capital is often intense, and each denounces the other. Each side works for its own interests, even while recognizing the existence of mutual interests. The communists are often viciously denunciatory. Labor-management relationships are not all sweetness and light. Yet in Scandinavia both workers and employers know that they can depend on each other's integrity. "When two strong men stand face to face . . ."

8. EDUCATION AND THE PRESS

In few places on earth is the poet or the professor held in such high esteem as in Scandinavia—professors are actually welcomed in the legislatures and as cabinet ministers. Literacy is universal; and book publishing and book sales per capita are the highest anywhere.

The whole culture of the North is built on a foundation of general education, broad but disciplined. Thorough teaching is done in the traditional branches, religion is a part of the regular curriculum, and special attention is paid to languages. English is far in the lead as the first foreign language and many students learn to read and speak it fluently, beginning their study in about the fifth grade. After the first four to six years of school, however, pupils are separated according to ability and interest into different curricula. It is recognized early that only a portion will go to the university, and courses are mapped out accordingly.

Economic difficulties make higher education more difficult for some students than for others, as everywhere in this world. But there are no actual barriers. All higher education, in universities, technological institutes, schools of commerce, medicine, etc., is state supported; fees are insignificant and scholarships are available. The able and purposeful youth can usually get the education he wants, but he must be able.

For those taking the "cultural" program the great milestone is the *student examen*, coming at the end of the secondary school training. The ceremonies attendant upon success roll together the emotions involved in graduation from high school and college in the United States. When one gains the privilege, at eighteen or twenty, of wearing a distinctive national student cap, he has demonstrated achievement in a rigorous schooling, and he is then admitted to the university. University work therefore begins at a level corresponding to the sophomore or junior year in an American college, and is specialized from the beginning. The great universities and technological schools of the Scandinavian cities inspire intensive work and produce scholars and engineers of world-recognized stature. The thirst for higher education has overflowed the older schools and has led to the establishment of several new universities added to the long-known institutions at Upsala (1477), Lund (1668), Copenhagen (1479), Oslo (1811), Åbo (1640, transferred to Helsinki, 1827; reinstituted at Åbo in a Finnish and Swedish division

1922 and 1919), and Helsinki (1827). Aarhus is the twentieth-century addition in Denmark, Bergen in Norway, Stockholm and Gothenburg in Sweden, and Reykjavik was established in 1911.

The unique institution of the Scandinavian educational system is its folk high school development—"The talk high schools for adults" as an American student described them. These people's colleges and the spread of adult education for all classes of the population are the features of education significant for social democracy. The regular school system retains a traditional and highly academic flavor; the institutions of adult education, on the other hand, are as uninhibited and as varied as are the facets of modern civilization itself. It is these institutions which to a large degree have given inspiration, self-confidence, and training to the social democratic leaders of present-day economic and political life.

The modern renaissance began with Bishop N. F. S. Grundtvig (1783–1872), the Prophet of the North, who in a period of national disaster and discouragement showed Denmark how to make from "Outward loss, inward gain." He was a Christian reformer in a modern society, and his medium was education; through it he redirected the mind of Denmark. He visited England and felt the heroic spirit of the nineteenth century; he sensed in the great factories the "sound of Thor's mighty victorious hammer." God meant man to achieve. Through poems and hymns and personal inspiration Grundtvig helped Danes to feel that nothing was impossible. But man must know, and he must work. Knowledge must be born not so much through books as through speech, through "the living word." "Dead are letters even if they be written with the fingers of angels, and dead is all knowledge which does not find response in the life of the reader." * Knowledge must be in the people, not just in leaders of government and business offices. How achieve such goals?

Grundtvig emphasized small schools for youth in the upper

* Quoted in Peter Manniche, *Denmark, A Social Laboratory*, p. 83.

teens, schools where personal contact would be influential, and preferably with a farm attached. "The conscious fellowship of a people" made the school as well as the nation. The man to implement the Grundtvigian idea was Kristen Kold (1816–1870), a "rustic blend of Socrates and Pestalozzi," who, as Peter Manniche describes him, as a boy "was so awkward with cobbler's tools that his parents in despair sent him to a teachers' training college." * From seminal schools for peasant boys at Ryslinge and Askov an idea spread from Denmark to Scandinavia and to the world. The emphasis was not on job training, not on educating for a different status in life; it was on development of mind and personality. Farming was taught, and economics, but the major subjects were history and the Danish language. Young people learned to know themselves and to understand their culture. They learned to think, to discuss, and to coöperate.

In 1937–38 there were fifty-seven such schools in Denmark with 5800 students, almost evenly divided between male and female. Most of the students were in the 18–25 age bracket. Over half of the schools were owned by the principals; all were supported by small fees from the students plus state grants covering about 50 per cent of the expenses. They operated in two terms of three or four months each, one in the winter for young men and one in the early summer for young women, with occasional short institutes in addition.

Norway, Finland, and Sweden established similar institutions which have flourished like those in Denmark, and some have been made into Scandinavian rather than national institutions. In a beautiful location at Elsinore in Denmark is the international folk high school directed by Peter Manniche and attended by students from around the planet. The schools in other cities have moved away somewhat from the ethical purposes of Grundtvig. Some, such as Brunnsvik in Sweden, have become workers' institutes, emphasizing studies in unionism and economics.

* Manniche, p. 88.

But in all the North the folk high school has been no sterile institution ending in itself, it has led on to an infinite variety of adult education projects. Many of the veterans of the folk high schools became the nuclei of study circles in their own communities or factories. In 1948 Sweden alone had 325,000 men and women in study circles organized by the Workers' Education Association, coöperative groups, religious groups, and others. Widespread systems of public lectures reach not only women's clubs but large cross sections of the population. Four- to six-week institutes in remote places reach thousands more. Municipal libraries have mushroomed, to serve both study circles and individual borrowers. Norway, under the leadership of American-trained Arne Kildal, has done a particularly notable work in library extension, under difficult conditions of distance and population sparseness. Traveling libraries, like traveling hospitals, are occasionally put on boats. State-operated radio is a powerful influence in general education, though weakened considerably by a political-born timidity in airing controversial questions.

One of the unusual phenomena of adult education is the "people's university" inaugurated by the students of the university in Stockholm. During the depression in 1933 these students desired to do some social work. They picked up the study circle idea and offered themselves as leaders or teachers. The idea took, and widened out to Gothenburg, Lund, and staid Upsala; in 1943 the four formed a kind of union. In Stockholm alone by 1948 this extension university, based on general education, granting neither grades nor credits, enrolled about 7000 students. Some 300 student-teachers got experience in one of the most difficult and inspiring forms of teaching. They taught the gamut of a university curriculum, including psychology, unionism, public speaking, fine arts, dramatics, but the most popular subject of all was English, "the key to the world," which was studied by almost 2000.

This university extension idea too spread throughout Scandinavia. When the students of Copenhagen became interested they went to Stockholm to study the problems, then adapted the idea to their own situation. They held registration in the city hall, and 300 queued-up at the opening hour. Others joined the line just because it was a line, and within three days 7000 had registered. Every class but one was filled to overflowing. The last class was entitled "Jesus as seen from the documents." With several hundred left in line that filled up too, and the instructor was hurriedly telephoned—could he repeat the class for another 200? That he could not do. The secretary handled the situation in a typically Danish way; standing on the city hall steps he called out to the waiting line, "We are sorry, but Jesus cannot be duplicated."

Much of the work in these institutions is begun as foreign language teaching, but expands from language to a study of the foreign country concerned and often to travel in that country —and to actual group tours and classes in Paris, Rome, or London. In 1949 arrangements were being made for some of the young instructors to obtain a year of study and teaching experience in the United States.

Education, in forms tailored to the needs of the people, opens windows to the world. Though the radio avoids controversy the press welcomes it. Newspapers are often owned by political parties, and are usually the mouthpieces of groups with political convictions. They belabor each other with vehemence and sometimes remind one of the old days of personal journalism in the United States. They occupy a place in opinion-forming and popular expression more important than do newspapers in the United States. This is due to the political vacuity of the Scandinavian radio and to the dearth of magazines of opinion and news, like *The Nation*, or *Time*.

Periodicals do exert some influence, however. One of the most significant is the vigorous weekly *Farmand* of Oslo, which enjoys a wide circulation among businessmen. It leans strongly to the West and is outspokenly liberal. There is nowhere in the North a voice more consistently critical of social democracy, but the magazine deals primarily with economic and financial questions and preaches to a clientele already converted.

Conservative dailies such as *Svenska Dagbladet* of Stockholm carry articles of literary and historical value, and statements of opinion written by outstanding men. The other leading conservative papers are *Aftenposten* and *Morgenbladet* of Oslo; *Berlingske Tidende*, 200-year-old veteran of Copenhagen, organ of the conservative party of Denmark; *Uusi Suomi* of Helsinki; and the *Sydsvenska Dagbladet* of Malmö.

Each of the capital cities has a good social democratic paper, such as *Morgontidningen* in Stockholm and *Arbeiderbladet* in Oslo. Numerous papers represent party groups and shades of independent thinking, examples of which are *Hufvudstadsbladet* of the Swedish people's party in Finland; *Nationen* of the Agrarian party in Norway; *Kristeligt Dagblad*, a liberal religious paper in Copenhagen; *Verdens Gang* of Oslo and *Information* of Copenhagen, two interesting outgrowths of wartime underground publishing; and in each country alert local papers in the middle-sized towns.

Each country has also a communist press, but its circulation is surprisingly small. *Ny Dag* of Stockholm strained itself to attain a sale of 30,000 at its peak, and in 1949 was reported to be down to 8000.

It is the liberal press which reaches the high circulation figures. *Dagens Nyheter* (Herbert Tingsten, editor) leads in Swedish distribution (as of 1949) with 252,000, and the liberal *Stockholms Tidningen* reaches 190,000; another in Gothenburg, *Göteborgs Posten*, tallies 217,000. It is strange that the leading organ of the social democrats has but 64,000 followers, fewer than the conservative *Svenska Dagbladet's* 92,000. People vote for the social democrats, then buy the papers which damn them! A similar phenomenon exists in Finland where the *Helsingin Sanomat* leads in popularity, and in Denmark where "almost everybody reads" *Politiken*. The explanation is complex, but these papers are well edited, and they interest people because they express different opinions with vigor and clarity. The "line" of the social democratic papers is the same as that in the labor unions and in official statements, and people seem to want variety of opinion.

If thorough and lifelong education and a vigorous free press are the measures of democracy, the North can be hopeful. Provincial papers are often as outspoken and colorful as the city dailies. Although native northerners complain of the political disinterest of the public, especially its lack of attention to foreign affairs, the outside visitor usually thinks these people as well informed and as much concerned with world problems as are the peoples of other lands.

9. TAX POLICY

Broad social service programs cost money—much money. To pay the costs the government uses two sources: its own productive enterprises and taxation. Taxation pays the lion's share.

If we take Sweden as an example of the tax method and the tax load we find some interesting comparisons with the United States and England. Taxes on salaries and wages run as shown in the accompanying table (as of 1947 and for family with no children; the krona was worth 27.85 cents).

In comparison with the American federal tax the Swedish

COMPARISONS OF TAXES ON SALARIES AND WAGES

Income * in Sweden Kr.	Sweden		England		USA—in state of N. Y.	
	Kr.	%	Kr.	%	Kr.	%
4,000	365	9.1	158	4.	19	0.4
10,000	1,703	17	2,386	23.9	1,057	10.6
20,000	4,837	24.2	6,466	32.3	3,133	15.7
40,000	13,960	34.0	16,660	41.7	9,354	23.4
100,000	47,973	47.9	58,110	58.1	39,825	39.8
200,000	111,328	55.6	143,860	71.9	105,982	53.

* Sven-Ivar Ivarsson, *Skatterna i England Schweiz och U.S.A.*, p. 10.

begins much higher, but is graduated more moderately, so that at an income of 200,000 kronor ($57,500 at pre-1949 rates; as of 1950, about $40,000) the tax is nearly the same. The British tax is graded much more steeply.

The Swedes, however, make a distinction between income from work and income from capital. Whereas with the American and English systems the tax is about the same whether earnings are from labor or from interest, the Swedes tax an income of 4000 kronor from capital at double the rate on wages. By the time they work up to an income of 200,000 kronor (40,000) from interest the tax takes 80 per cent of it. And if income from capital is combined with a good income from salary the Swede can soon find himself paying taxes on the capital income higher than that income. As an illustration, a man earning a salary of 40,000 kronor ($8000) will pay 13,960 kronor tax on that income; if he gets also 20,000 kronor ($4000) in interest he will pay 20,275 kronor tax on that added income—and if he gets 30,000 kronor in interest he will pay a 31,780 kronor tax.

Inheritance taxes are likewise high in Sweden. If one child inherits he pays 840 kronor on an estate of 25,000 kronor, 12,440 kronor on an estate of 100,000 kronor, and 5,406,840 kronor on an estate of 10,000,000 kronor.

Comparisons cannot be made accurately, but generally the American tax is more mild than it appears in the statistics because of the number and the liberality of deductions. There are few deductions in the Swedish system, and still less "hidden income." There are also corporation and excise taxes in both places.

Certain facts stand out from these few illustrations. One is a Swedish prejudice against income from capital. The state is taxing the large coupon-incomes out of existence, with the purpose and result of redistributing that wealth to more and smaller holders. Especially hard hit is the man who has both salary and property income. The other most weighty fact is the size of the tax itself—more than 50 per cent greater than the American tax of 1947 (before reductions) at an income of 20,000 kronor. And Sweden did not have a war to pay for!

What does it mean? Does it mean simply that this is the cost of social democracy, and that therefore neither Sweden nor anyone else can afford it?

If anyone answers "no" glibly he has not understood the preceding pages. The money thus collected in Sweden from taxes is paid out for hospitals, schools, old age pensions, church support—a vast host of social services. All these things cost no more money in Sweden or the other northern countries than they cost in the United States. In the United States people pay for their churches, hospitals, community funds, etc.—only partly by taxes, in large measure by contributions. If the "average American businessman" would total up his taxes, then add to that figure his voluntary contributions and the "quota-contributions" levied on him in various drives he might find that the sum of it all was not much different from what he would pay in taxes if he lived in Gothenburg or Copenhagen.

People never like taxes, and even the good-natured Scandinavians complain about them in colorful language. They do buy valuable services with those taxes. But a basic financial-economic question remains: will the tax-cost burden kill (or discourage) the goose that lays the golden eggs? Will the economy collapse because of the strain?

The answer to that question is an opinion only, and it can be stated here very briefly. The Scandinavians are not wasteful; their ambitious building for the future is done with great care; most of that building, whether in healthy human life or in ships or factories, should be richly productive; granted the possibility of peace and unhampered commerce there is no inherent impossibility in the maintenance of present or improved standards of living in the North. On the individual basis it is true that the present tax-level has brought many a businessman to the point of asking, "What's the use?"—but the fact is, he answers his own question by continuing in vigorous work!

5. The Twentieth Century Economy

A poetic historian has pointed to three lines in which are traced the history of his country, and of the entire North: the furrow of the farmer in the valley, the wake of the ship at sea, and the trail of the ski on the snowy mountains. A fourth may be added: the twin steel rails tying mines, factories, and cities together in productive enterprise.

1. STRUCTURE OF THE ECONOMY

The economy of the twentieth century is a development out of the natural resources and the earlier economic history already surveyed. New techniques and the increase in population presented opportunities for a much fuller utilization of resources than had been possible in earlier centuries, and increased the interdependence of these northern countries on the outside world. As an introduction to this elaboration of the economic structure of the twentieth century the economy of each country will be briefly characterized, then the major segments of economic activity of the five countries together; statistical tables at the end of the volume will illustrate the generalizations.

Denmark's national income in 1929 * amounted to $992,-000,000, or $282 per capita, which compares with an income for the same year of $701 per capita in the United States, $426 in Britain, and $253 in France. In 1948 Denmark's income was $3,230,000,000 or $807 per capita in the inflated dollar

---

* Statistics on national income are given for 1929 because that is for comparative purposes as nearly a "normal" year as can be found.

values of that year. This income was rooted in agriculture, especially as agriculture provided 75 to 80 per cent of the nation's exports; it employed 30 per cent of the workers; but 28 per cent were engaged in industry and handicraft, about one-sixth of whom were occupied in the processing of agricultural products. About 11 per cent were engaged in commerce, seven per cent in shipping, and the remainder were scattered.

Norway's national income of 1929 was $700,000,000, an average of $249 per capita, less than the Danish but higher than the French. For 1948 the income totaled $1,750,000,000 or about $500 per capita. The basis of this income was quite different from that of Denmark and was dependent for its foreign earnings especially upon Norway's enormous merchant marine. Of Norway's workers 20 per cent were engaged in commerce and shipping, and 7 per cent in fishing and whaling. As Denmark's wealth comes from the land, so Norway's wealth comes out of the sea. This is supplemented, however, by diversified activities on land: 27 per cent of the people are engaged in mining, industry, and handicraft, and 30 per cent are in agriculture and forestry—the latter being of great importance in Norway and nonexistent in Denmark. It is Norway's preëminent place in shipping which brings in the foreign exchange needed to buy imports, and which makes Norwegians more international minded than their fellows in the neighboring countries.

Sweden is the most populous and the most prosperous of the northern countries, with a national income of $2,090,000,000 in 1929, a per capita average of $342; an income in 1948 of approximately $6,000,000,000, or $855 per capita. This income is obtained from a wide variety of goods and services, but the major export items are wood and wood pulp, iron ore, and manufactures of iron and steel. Thirty-four per cent of the workers are in agriculture and forestry, 32 per cent in mining, industry, and handicraft. Fishing employs less than 1 per cent, and commerce and shipping 15 per cent. Sweden's importance in industry is largely in shipbuilding and the metal trades, where Swedish steel has become a synonym for quality. Sweden is a major supplier of telephone apparatus and other electrical equipment for Europe, and she makes the finest of ball-bearings.

Finland's national income in 1929 translates into $412,000,000, or $120 per capita, figures which becloud the truth because of the artificiality of exchange rates and the low cost of living in Finland. In 1948 the cost of living had skyrocketed, and the national income was about $1,450,000,000 or $380 per capita. The output of the forests creates most of Finland's income, her railroad engines burn native birch, and her exports are pulp, timber, prefabricated doors and windows, a host of products of wood. Sixty per cent of Finnish workers are in farming and forestry; farming is, however, of the subsistence variety, while forestry furnishes fuel and the surplus for manufacture and sale abroad. The common pattern is to combine agriculture and work in the forests. Most farms have a small patch to plow and a larger section of woodland. Seventeen per cent of the workers are in mining, industry, and handicraft, and 8 per cent in commerce and shipping. This long-existing balance was upset by the Russian demand for reparations in ships and manufactured articles, but the new factories change little the over-all character of the economy.

Iceland as of 1930 had 36 per cent of its workers in agriculture, 21 per cent in fishing, 15 per cent in commerce and shipping. The agriculture, like that in the other northern countries except in Denmark, was food-raising for domestic consumption, while the fishing provided the bulk of export, and therefore paid for imports. Industries employ 14.4 per cent of the laborers, but are largely for domestic production—carpentry, woolen goods, and other common domestic industries. Of recent years factories have increased their processing of fish-oils, fish-meal, canning and freezing. Water power is being harnessed, and the hot water springs have been piped to Reykjavik for heating homes and greenhouses, because Iceland has no coal.

This brief treatment of the five countries emphasizes the

special features of each economy: agricultural Denmark, sailing Norway, wood and iron-land Sweden, timbering Finland, fishing Iceland. It is both truth and distortion. Actually the similarities in the five countries are more imposing than the differences, and a treatment of the larger segments of the economic structure will emphasize these likenesses.

Agriculture. Agriculture is a major aspect of the Scandinavian economy, but most of the countries are only 60–90 per cent self-sufficient. Denmark jumps to 142 per cent of self-sufficiency in food and sells quantities of foodstuffs abroad, but even she must of course import such items as coffee and citrus fruits, as well as fodder and oil cakes. In bread grains these countries can be self-supporting. It is vital for them to have fertilizers, however, and most of these must be imported; when war interrupts trade the land in long-continued and intensive use deteriorates rapidly.

Most of the land which is arable is already under cultivation, but each country is seeking to expand its farmlands. Finland, faced with the need to resettle the refugees from Karelia, is clearing forest land (with the aid of American bulldozers), and is parceling some old holdings. Denmark is reclaiming the heath of Jutland and winning some new acreage each year.

Land used for agriculture		% of total area
Denmark	8,100,000 acres	75
Norway	2,550,000	3
Sweden	12,000,000	11
Finland	8,300,000	9
Iceland	100,000	0.5

Half of the total acreage is in hay or rotated green crops, one-third in cereals, and one-twelfth in root crops. As for centuries past, the cereals are oats, barley, and rye, with wheat recently climbing to 15 per cent of the total. The root crops are one-third potatoes, the rest fodder-beets and sugar-beets. Sweden, aided by government, raises and refines most of her sugar, and exports a small quantity.

The yield per acre is high, due to intensive family style farming on small farms. In Denmark half the farms are less than 25 acres and the average is 38 acres. In Sweden and Finland three-fourths are less than 25 acres and in Norway nine-tenths. Size and other complications make the Norwegian farm least productive per man and per acre. Generally, however, the adaptation to size and circumstance seems satisfactory. Folk high schools and agricultural agents keep farmers constantly alert to the best methods of land utilization.

Ownership is a practical and psychological aspect of agriculture, and the actual operators have with government support gained a high degree of ownership. In Iceland in the mid-nineteenth century only 17 per cent of the farms were freeholds, but by 1940 the figure was 54 per cent. In Finland 70 per cent of the farms are owned by the farmers and in Denmark, Norway, and Sweden they own more than 90 per cent. The great estates have been broken up, often under direct governmental pressure, and the peasants have been helped to buy land by low-interest, long-term loans. Individual incentive is thus stimulated. If the advantages of large-scale operation are in danger, the farmers try to regain them by coöperative use of machinery and coöperative buying and selling.

The typical farm is hard to find, but in Norway it consists of some 20 acres of tillable soil lying on the side of a mountain. A cluster of small buildings encloses three sides of a courtyard, and here the family lives, stores its produce, and houses its animals. There may be a horse, six or eight cows, one or two pigs, ten to fifteen hens, and up on the mountainside a dozen sheep or goats. Far up a winding pathway may be a *saetter*, a simple cottage in a clearing, where the women and children go for a couple of months in summer to weave, make cheese, and pick berries. Near by is sure to be a stream with fish, and a village down the valley.

The Swedish farm in the north will be rather similar, though it and its Finnish counterpart are likely to have also from 20 to 50 acres of woodland. In southern Sweden and in Denmark the fields flatten out, and the livestock increases. The home is clean and comfortable, often picturesque. An automobile is not likely, but there will be a radio, and perhaps a telephone.

Progress is notable and eagerly sought. Government research laboratories test soils and develop seeds for northern climates. Processes of preserving seasonal foods are spreading, though canning and freezing are still not as common as in the United States. The freezing of Norwegian berries for marketing in England and the Low Countries had gone far enough in 1948 to annoy bitterly the residents of the cities who could find no fresh berries for sale. Preserved marmalade is a standard item for the breakfast table, and vegetable packing is growing more important: "Findus" in Sweden, for example, has large numbers of farmers in Skåne raising peas on contract for canning factories. Rural electrification and mechanization are spreading.

The dependence of these small countries of the North on world conditions is illustrated again and again in agriculture. In Denmark, the agricultural revolution of the late nineteenth century was due to external factors. Denmark had been an exporter of grains, but in the 1870's and 1880's the rich fields of North America flooded Europe with cheaper grain. The Danes intelligently reoriented their agriculture to emphasize dairy products and animal husbandry. They developed a powerful "Jutland horse," which they sold to Germany, and in recent years to Poland. They improved their red and Holstein cattle, and increased production of cheese and butter. By-products such as skimmed milk made excellent pig-feed. Hence the Danes learned to know the squealing of pigs, and exported bacon for British breakfast tables. In 1945 Denmark had 170,-000,000 chickens; shiploads of eggs accompanied the bacon to England. The numbers of both pigs and chickens were drastically reduced during the war, and were rebuilt only slowly because of the collapse of old markets, particularly by the British belt-tightening policy. Denmark's agricultural production index at the end of 1947 was but 70 per cent of that in 1939.

During the war itself only Denmark ate plenty; Sweden got along on restricted rations; Norway did not starve, but never did she have quite enough; Iceland was supplied from the United States; in Finland lack of foodstuffs increased tragically the dependence of the country on Germany. After the war production climbed back, but markets and money were difficult. The Danes produced food but they deliberately curbed their appetites. They needed foreign *valuta* to pay for new ships, new industrial equipment, and fertilizer; the only way to get the *valuta* was by selling their butter and cheese and eggs. The land of plenty became a land of scarcity, but it was using agriculture to build its future.

For normal consumption one must look to the future or go to the period of the thirties. At that time each of the Scandinavian countries consumed more milk per capita than Great Britain, France, the Netherlands, or Belgium. Denmark led in meat and sugar consumption. On imported articles the Scandinavians were all low in fruit consumption, average in tobacco, and high in coffee—the Swedes leading with 16 pounds per capita. There was enough everywhere in peacetime.

Fishing and Whaling. The ancient art of fishing is transformed in modern Scandinavia, but it is still vital to life and prosperity. During World War II and since, the Norwegians have averaged only one day a week for meat, but there is always fish. The Icelandic catch of 6000 pounds per capita is the world's record. The chart illustrates the importance of Scandinavian fisheries in a world setting; and indicates too their significance in Scandinavian economy.

The Danes have invented a special seine for flatfish, the Norwegians the purse-seine for herring, and the Norwegians and Icelanders have developed trawling to reduce the seasonal limitations on fishing.

Many peoples fish the Iceland waters where cod migrate by millions from Greenland and back, but the Norwegians send

FISHERIES PRODUCTION, 1947
(in Thousands of Metric Tons)

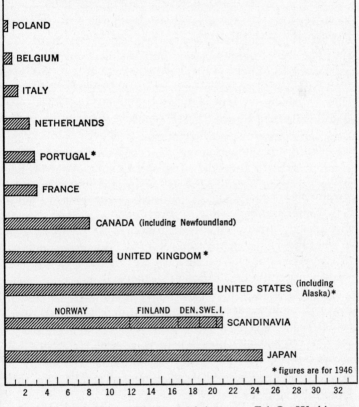

Source: *Yearbook of Fisheries Statistics,* 1947, F.A.O., Washington, D.C., 1948, pp. 250–251.

the most boats and take home the biggest catch. They catch additional tons of cod in the Lofoten fishing of January to April; Norway and Iceland together ship most of that cod-liver oil which is enjoyed by small boys the world over. The Icelanders catch most of the Norway-haddock from which medicinal oil is extracted. After the oil has been taken the remainder of these fish is ground into meal, excellent for animal feeding. Thousands of tons of salted cod (klipfish) are exported.

Even more valuable than cod is herring, which in various forms and sizes is caught from the Baltic to the shores of Iceland. Some 200,000 tons is sold abroad annually—fresh, salted, spiced, frozen, or smoked; the Norwegians do about two-thirds of the business. It is the summer herring catch which is vital to Icelandic prosperity.

Many other species add to the total and vary the local diet: lobster, crabs, eel, salmon from the fresh-water lakes and streams and from the slightly salt water of the Gulf of Bothnia. The two remaining items of large-scale importance are the tiny brisling (sardines) and the great whale. Sardines are sent in tins all over the world from Norway. When war and high prices reduced the supply of olive oil for packing, the Norwegians used fish-oils, carefully deodorized.

After the northern waters were closed (1904), the whalers took their equipment and their skill to the Antarctic. With the aid of the harpoon gun and the great floating factories the Norwegians catch about 15,000 whales per season, and account for 40 per cent of the world catch: in the 1947–48 season whaling operations brought in 1,046,000 barrels of whale oil, worth $76,000,000; in 1948–49 the catch was almost exactly half of the world's catch. Whale steak, whale sausage, and other delicacies give variation to the Norse diet, but this comes from the smaller types of whale still hunted in the near-by northern waters.

New techniques of processing fish and whale are constantly sought. By-products are carefully preserved, and airplanes are being tried to hurry fresh fish to English markets. The freezing of fish is increasing: in Danish Esbjerg, for example, fishermen take out ice, and bring in the fish in a nearly frozen condition; the fish are then made into fillets, frozen, and sent into the continent by huge fish express trucks.

Forest Industry. In summertime the rivers of Norway, Sweden, and Finland are as full of logs as they are of fish. These three countries boast 25 per cent of the coniferous forests of Europe (56 per cent if Russia is omitted). One-half of this is pine and the major part of the other is spruce. Although it takes from one hundred years in the central area, to two hundred in the far north to grow a tree, there is both time and space. Fifty million acres each in Sweden and Finland is forest land and fifteen million in Norway; the forests are the great natural wealth.

Of the 100,000,000 cubic meters of annual forest growth about 90 per cent is utilized. The high degree of exploitation is due largely to the favorable transportation provided by nature. The slow-moving Swedish rivers thaw first in their lower reaches. They thus provide excellent floating transportation for they take first the logs from near their mouths, and as the northern sections are gradually freed of ice the logs come to the mills steadily throughout the summer. Special passages are made for logs around the power stations. For shipping the

MAJOR USES OF ANNUAL CUT OF TIMBER (1938)
(In millions of cubic feet)

	Sweden	Finland	Norway
Sawn Timber	423.6	423.6	70.6
Pulp, paper	423.6	247.	141.2
Pitprops, poles		106.	
Charcoal burning	70.6		
State railways		35.3	
Household fuel, etc. ...	388.3	530.	106

processed product many of the ports can be kept open throughout the winter, sometimes by the use of icebreakers.

The vast unclaimed tracts of forests in Finland and Sweden were decreed by Gustav Vasa in 1542 to be government property, and in Finland the state has retained control of a large portion. In Sweden much was allowed to pass into private and corporate ownership in the nineteenth century, but the state later repurchased some tracts. In Norway the greatest amount has remained in the hands of the individual farm-owners.

In each country a large share of the cutting is done during the winter season by the small farmer, either for his own account or as a hired worker of the large companies. Timber-felling fits into a seasonal pattern of labor for the northern farmer. Many industrial firms, especially in Sweden, own their own forests, but they need additional wood. They buy it from individual owners and from the state forests, by auction or agreement, and then have it cut and floated to the sawmills or the pulp mills, or burned in the charcoal ovens.

OWNERSHIP OF FORESTS

	Sweden	Finland	Norway
State	18.7%	39.8%	10 %
Companies	27.1%	7.5% *	9 %
Individuals	49.1%	51. %	70.7%
Parishes and Communities .	5.1%	1.7%	10.3%

* State shares in ownership of one-third of this figure.

In the old days poles and tar were the chief forest products and Norway the chief exporter. When steam sawmills brought the vaster forests of Sweden and Finland into commercial importance, quantities of sawn timber for construction were exported. Swedish match kings built their fortunes on the aspen of Finland and Sweden. The rapid development of new processes and products has transformed the scene.

The Northerners have been eager to refine their raw products themselves and thus retain the profits of manufacture. Mechanical wood pulp began to be used in paper manufacture in the mid-nineteenth century just when the increasing newspaper demand surpassed the supply of rag paper. The new possibilities thus opened for the northern forests were augmented by the discovery of the chemical processes for making sulphate pulp (and strong wrapping papers) and sulphite pulp (and soft fine papers). The manufacture of plywood opened market possibilities for Finnish birch; before World War II Finland was providing 30 per cent of the world's exported plywood.

Both Swedish and Finnish companies have gone into prefabricated housing on a large scale, though production has been retarded by shortages of interior fittings for new homes. For the plywood in the houses themselves glue must be imported from the United States, but most of the other materials are at hand. Finland sends ready-made doors and windows to South Africa, and to the Balkans; Sweden sends prefabricated houses to England, Holland, and France; the rapid rebuilding of war-devastated Norwegian towns owed much to these quickly constructed homes and shops from Sweden.

New mills and factories and research laboratories have been built and populous industrial communities have grown at the mouths of the floating-streams. Chemists estimate that half the materials from the wood still flow wastefully into the sea, but they are ceaselessly trying to capture everything of value, to use everything but the knothole. The Swedish Cellulose company, for example, ships around the world pulp for paper-making, but it can first extract 9,000,000 quarts of alcohol—when it is sober sense to do so.

Mining and Minerals. Minerals have created both wealth and problems for Scandinavia. Particularly is this true of the iron ore found in rich abundance in the "ore mountains" at Gällivare and Kiruna in northern Sweden. Germany needed that ore in World War II, and it is a prize for anyone.

Sweden's earlier exports of iron had come from the central

area, especially Grängesberg. The northern deposits attained importance only after the state built a modern electrified railway at the beginning of the twentieth century. Norway built a continuation from the border to Narvik, and most of the ore, 6,000,000–9,000,000 tons annually, goes out from Narvik to Britain, Belgium, Germany, and even to the United States. Another 2,000,000–4,000,000 tons go down to Luleå in Sweden to be processed or shipped through the Gulf of Bothnia.

This ore is exceptionally rich, assaying from 58 to 70 per cent pure iron; it contains also phosphorus, which makes it especially valuable to the German Ruhr, where the ore can be used for iron and steel production and the phosphorus for fertilizer. Sweden herself uses the better but less abundant ore of the central area for her tool and munitions manufacture.

Other minerals have been recently discovered. Norway and Finland have nickel and zinc, though Finland's richest nickel deposits were lost when the U.S.S.R. annexed the Petsamo district. Copper and pyrites are mined at Outukumpo in Finland.

The most valuable producing complex is in northern Sweden, where the Boliden Company works both its own mines and some of the government holdings. The company began scientific electro-prospecting in 1918, searching under the mountains and the swamps for copper. They found copper, but they found also gold, silver, lead, zinc, and more arsenic than the world can use. The excess is buried in huge blocks in the Baltic, but much is used for plant sprays and other products. One of the most interesting by-products is an impregnation material which lengthens the life of wood in railway ties, silos, and telephone poles. And the search of laboratory explorers for by-products continues to parallel the year-round search for new ores and new processes.

Norway has extensive quantities of molybdenum and pyrites. Greenland has the world's one great cryolite mine and newly discovered uranium. Denmark, deficient in the harder minerals, has valuable limes and clays, and silicon.

Scandinavia has variety and wealth in her rocky subsoil, but she suffers also great lacks, notably oil and coal. Weak "brown coal" is found in Skåne, but the only first-class coal is in distant Svalbard (Spitsbergen), now Norwegian, where an American company began exploitation in 1905. Now the Russians work the largest deposits, but the Norwegians get about 400,000 tons per year. Peat is found and used in all the northern countries, on a large scale in Iceland, and as an important extra fuel in Denmark. But its high water content (30 per cent and more) exasperates the industrial engineers, and they use it only in dire emergency. The lack of coal and oil is serious, but is partially compensated by the rich "white coal" of the waterfalls.

Water. In all the North, except Denmark, there is a wealth of water power, and in Iceland a uniquely valuable supply of hot water. Finland's power is used for mills and factories. In Sweden the waterfalls are being harnessed and are tied into an integrated system; they provide electricity for city lighting and power for the country's industry and the electrified railway system. Years of drought put too great a strain on the supply, but this should be greatly relieved when the mighty Hårsprånget station is completed (about 1950). Norway has so far realized about one-sixth of the 80,000,000 kilowatt power available from her "white coal." Her magnificent abundance of waterfalls gives her the greatest potential resources in Europe, and could provide vastly more power for domestic use as well as for export to Sweden and even by land or under-sea cables to Denmark. Definite plans for this export of power were drawn up in 1949–50. Norway produces also the rare "heavy water," which they, and for a time the Germans, used for research in atomic fission.

Industry. Scandinavian industry is based on the raw materials supplied by her own farms and fisheries, forests and mines. The industries are closely related to resources, as illustrated by the fact that in Sweden *akvavit* is made from sulphite as a by-product of cellulose manufacture, while in Denmark it is made from potatoes, which grow there more easily than do pine trees.

Fishing and fish-industries are even more closely related. Much of the fish and whale processing actually takes place on the "floating factories" of the trawlers and the whaling fleet, but freezing and tinning are done on land.

A company like the Sandviken Iron Works utilizes a combination of resources. The company owns vast forests in central Sweden, iron mines, and a sprawling factory. It burns its own charcoal, uses it to make steel, and rolls out the steel into powerful bands or razor blades or springs for Swiss watches. This vertical type of organization is frequent, particularly in Sweden. The Swedish Cellulose Corporation, a 1929 amalgamation of a score of separate companies, takes a log from its own forests down river and through its mills into finished products, be it alcohol, rayon, or a prefabricated house. The Korsnäs Company of Gävle operates in similar fashion, and has such extensive and yet scattered forest holdings that it does not feel the need to insure them. This is partly because the state safeguards the forests.

Such large companies reach out horizontally too. For example, they become owners of power stations which produce more power than they need, and which enables them to sell power as well as sulphite and alcohol.

The rule that industry is built upon native resources has certain exceptions. Among these exceptions are the processing of tobacco, chocolate, orange marmalade, and cotton for local consumption. Another is the electro-metallurgical industry of Norway, which is founded on Norway's supply of water power, and on the deep fjords which permit ocean freighters to bring the raw materials directly to the power stations. Hence Norway receives bauxite and other ores, processes them and exports them again. Many industries use a combination of local and imported materials, e.g., the automobile industry (Volvo) of Gothenburg, and the shipbuilding concerns.

Shipbuilding is an appropriate industry for Scandinavia, and in 1948 Sweden ranked second only to Britain in output. Her largest producers are Götaverken of Gothenburg and Kockums of Malmö. Götaverken launched in 1948 the beautiful new *Stockholm* for the Swedish-American Line. In Denmark the big company is Burmeister and Wain, which has long produced fine ships and which in 1948 completed a huge floating factory for Norwegian whaling. Norway gets her larger vessels from these countries and from Britain, the Netherlands, and the United States, and builds the smaller ships herself in many private yards. Her luxury liner, the *Oslofjord,* was launched in Amsterdam in 1949. Finland likewise builds smaller ships for herself, and for the Russian reparation account.

Machines and precision instruments of all kinds call upon the inventive and manufacturing skill of the Scandinavians—telephones, separators, vacuum cleaners, tractors, arms, ball-bearings, bicycles, cameras. Denmark builds about half the world supply of marine Diesel engines. Northern engineers plan and build for themselves, and for others throughout the world, bridges, cement plants, power stations. Their technical skill is an export item almost as important as their products.

Scientific acumen is applied with equal success to chemistry. The Swedes have isolated, alone or in coöperation with others, one-third of the known chemical elements. And they have used their knowledge directly in industry. A Norwegian invention served as the beginning for the development of a large industry for making nitrogen fertilizers.

Products that develop from chemistry, the instruments and machines made from iron and steel, and forest products are the important and typical contributions of Scandinavia. But there is also widespread handicraft and small-scale industry.

Crafts. The Scandinavians express themselves through craft work; they create things of beauty, and supply an eager export market. Danish silver, Swedish glass, Finnish ceramics, all are in wide demand. When the industrial revolution began to affect the North at the end of the nineteenth century, and in the early twentieth century, a few far-seeing men and women urged that the traditional crafts be maintained. Museums were built and developed into places of both inspiration and play, at Bygdø and Lillehammer in Norway, at Aarhus in Denmark. In Stockholm's *Skansen* typical provincial homes and shops were bought up and moved into an open-air park where people could gather and actually use the old surroundings to celebrate holidays, or for weddings or dinner parties. Home craft societies (Hemslöjd) continue to produce toy wooden horses, artistic weaving, and the dozens of symbols of a beloved past.

In some of the crafts the twentieth-century products have far surpassed those of the past. Glass has been made for centuries, but in simplest form. About 1918 two artists, Simon Gate and Edvard Hald, were invited to take over a soda glass factory on a small estate in Småland; within a few years the glass they made at Orrefors was cherished art, richly engraved and delicately shaped. It was both an artistic and a business success. And life in this rural industrial community should delight any prophet of decentralization. "Swedish modern" in furniture, home decoration, and architecture illustrates the functional blending of arts and engineering techniques.

The Finnish "Arabia" plant is reputed to make the finest ceramics to be found today. Silversmithing is beautifully done in Norway, Sweden, and Denmark, with the late Georg Jensen of Copenhagen, and Erik Fleming of Stockholm as two of its outstanding artists.

More significant socially than the output of the famous plants is the widespread appreciation of such arts, and the everyday practice of wood-carving, pewter-pounding, book-binding, weaving, and the making of the "beautiful things for everyday" which give pleasure both in making and in use, and which preserve the traditions of peasant art in a mass-production age.

Banking and Finance. Banking and currency have long been controlled by central banks. Sweden's Riksbank dates from 1656, and the others from the nineteenth century. In each case the central bank is a government institution, and carries out government policy through semi-private channels. Private commercial banks, often with nation-wide branches, make industrial loans and receive deposits. Banks and mortgage companies coöperate through government guarantees in loaning funds for home building and allied purposes. Personal checking accounts are much less common than in the United States; instead payments of dues and small bills are frequently made through an efficient and extensive system of postal banking, merely by a signed request to the Post Office to transfer a certain sum from the depositor's account to another specified numbered account.

The major problems of finance for the northern countries are maintenance of stable currencies on the world market, and the acquisition of a usable, freely circulating, foreign exchange, or *valuta*. In such problems these lands were in positions similar to those of Belgium, the Netherlands, and many others. In 1931, when Britain abandoned the gold standard, they were forced to follow suit. Their currencies sought equilibrium with the pound sterling. In the period since 1945 the dollar has been the dominating influence. The combination of the dollar influence and the dependence of the Scandinavian countries on Britain and western Europe caused them again in 1949 to follow the British pound into devaluation. Finland's currency had already suffered severe inflation, and the government in June 1949 had devalued it by an additional 17 per cent, but the Finns felt it necessary to follow the further devaluation by the full amount in September.

The new problem has been not only to maintain a proper exchange ratio, but to acquire dollars for trading purposes. The need for dollars is not simply the common need for money; these countries have money of some sort or can get it by trade, but they cannot buy what they need with French francs or even with British pounds. They want machinery and other goods from the United States, and they must have dollars. Since the United States does not buy from them enough to give them the dollars they need they are forced to buy in other markets. Even in these other markets they could often buy more advantageously in dollars. What they need is a currency convertible into goods wherever they need to purchase. The character of their exports is such that their markets are best in certain countries, formerly England and Germany, now England. The character of their required imports is such that they must come from many different lands, and in the years since World War II far too many of their needs are produced best in the United States itself or in countries of the dollar area.

The effects of the lack of dollars and the working of the foreign exchange control can be illustrated by the case of Direktör K., a Scandinavian manufacturer. He had bought in 1945 some satisfactory machines from the United States. In 1949 he needed more. But to spend dollars he had to get permission from his government, and the government said he could use pounds sterling, but not dollars. He therefore had to buy the machines in England. In this particular case the machines were less satisfactory and the price was much higher than for the American products. Prices are not often so unfavorable, but the restrictions are galling and prevent free trade.

All these countries are associated with the World Bank and the International Monetary Fund, and the currency of each has an agreed value, but that does not mean it will buy goods! Most of the currencies were pegged at figures which they had attained in normal economic processes, but other countries were not eager to trade in them. Their value declined (1946–1948) in the little free financial trading which existed.

Sweden, long an exponent of managed currency, attempted to run counter to the trend, and by governmental decree raised the value of her krona by about 16 per cent, in July 1946. She did this because her government planners foresaw severe inflation in the United States and wanted to establish a high price for Swedish goods. The high price was indeed fixed, but the American economy did not get out of hand. As soon as the pent-up demand of the first postwar years was satisfied, Sweden found it difficult to sell her products at this inflated level. Most difficult of all was to sell in the dollar market. Exports of wood pulp declined disastrously. Prices were lowered repeatedly, but often too late to win back the market. Imports of dollar purchases therefore had to be curtailed still further, for Sweden's 1945 reserve in dollars had vanished in 1947. Private business and financial circles condemned the government policy, but to no avail. Managed money was having trouble, but its sponsors hung on determinedly.

After 1918 the foreign indebtedness of the Scandinavian lands was small. Foreign capital had helped build the railroads and large industrial enterprises, but World War I gave most of the companies an opportunity to pay off these debts. Finland borrowed heavily for her new national development, but developed a reputation for financial integrity by her prompt payments. Internal government debts were not burdensome. Then World War II struck, producing inflation, worst of all in Finland and Iceland. Denmark and Norway had inflation forced upon them by the Germans and were left with huge and worthless "German accounts" on their books. For these countries the ERP (Marshall Plan) was a breath of hope to their gasping financial machines.

Transportation. Transportation is of utmost importance to the Scandinavian economy. These five countries, with less than 1 per cent of the world's population, operate 11 per cent of the ocean shipping. It must be reiterated that they are essentially islands. Norway's fleet in 1950 was again approaching 5,000,000 tons, half of this in new vessels, and half of the total fleet in tankers. Norwegian sailors are found in every port, and Norwegian ships sail the sea lanes as if on a continuous conveyor belt, carrying goods from everywhere to everywhere.

Scandinavian ships carry the trade of the Far East and of South America; they represent 10 per cent to 16 per cent of the total tonnage entering the harbors of the United States, of England, of Chile, Belgium, and Canada. By this shipping service all earn foreign *valuta* (in the case of Norway earnings amount to 10 per cent of her national income), and to a large extent gain the foreign exchange with which to buy their imports. Shipping likewise extends their cultural contacts and enhances their realization of interdependence.

The merchant fleets of the North are privately owned, but are also of public interest. They were of vital importance in the allied cause in World War I and in World War II, and their tax payments are important items especially in the national budget of Norway. Partly because of purposeful farsightedness and partly because of wartime losses and replacements, these fleets are highly modern in equipment; about half are motor-driven (the first motor-driven ocean vessel was constructed in Denmark in 1912). The intelligent interest in free commerce is illustrated by the establishment of "free ports" for goods in transit in Copenhagen, Malmö, Gothenburg, and Stockholm. (See tables on Merchant Marine and Shipbuilding in Appendix I.)

An amazing amount of the internal traffic of the area, both freight and passenger, also goes by boat. Sweden has her picturesque cross-country Göta Canal, her coastal vessels and skerry steamers, and the big train-ferries across to Denmark and Germany. Denmark uses ferries for taking trains across the Great Belt, and her complex of islands is tied together primarily by ships. Norway depends upon ships for both local and long-distance traffic along her thousand-mile coast, and Finnish and Icelandic traffic with the outside world is primarily by boat.

The railroad lines, largely state-owned, give excellent service. In Norway the engineering problems are particularly severe, but the result for the tourist is correspondingly breath-taking, as on the magnificent mountain-and-tunnel route from Oslo to Bergen. The line north of Trondheim does not yet reach to Narvik, and passengers often cross into Sweden and go northward on the Swedish route and then back into Norway; the Norwegian army finds it ten times cheaper to use the Swedish rail route for soldiers from north Norway rather than to send naval vessels for them. The Swedish railways are electrified for all the main lines, and electrification is steadily being extended. In 1948 a fast train was installed on the Gothenburg-Stockholm run, a luxury express which makes the trip in less than five hours. In 1949 a similar stream-lined Scandia Arrow began speedy service from Copenhagen via Malmö to Oslo. Denmark's close network of railroads, and especially her Diesel "lightning trains" (the name is exaggerated), Finland's woodburners, the main-line trains of all these countries are crowded but run on reasonable schedule and provide cheap and comfortable travel.

The Scandinavians have been eager to keep pace with air transportation also. Iceland has lines flying to Copenhagen and Oslo. The privately organized airlines of other countries have joined in the Scandinavian Airlines System and operate balanced schedules both within Scandinavia and to the main centers of the European continent and the Americas.

Bus service is growing rapidly in Scandinavia, both in the cities and in country routes. Private companies operate long-distance luxury buses for tourist traffic to France and Switzerland and Italy. Buses are especially important in Iceland where railroads are lacking, and there is scheduled bus service to the railless north of Norway. Private automobiles, mostly of American make, are almost as numerous as in countries like France and Britain, though not as common as in the United States. Railroads, particularly in Sweden, are tending to use Diesel railbuses on short, light runs.

Communications are on a high level of efficiency within and between the Scandinavian countries, only Iceland being distant and somewhat isolated. The others maintain between themselves postal letter rates identical with their national rates; telephone and telegraph are cheap and good. Stockholm, incidentally, has more telephones per capita than any other city outside the United States. Radio is government-owned as in England, and is supported by license fees of the users of sets.

A minor but respectable item in the economy of these countries is the tourist traffic. Finns trade in Sweden; Swedes enjoy themselves in Copenhagen or see the grandeur of nature in Norway; Danes do business in Sweden and ski in the Norwegian mountains; Norwegians study in Denmark and buy luxury goods in Sweden. Occasionally a few of them get to Iceland and sometimes Icelanders visit them. Englishmen and Americans crowd the tourist agencies, the hotels, trains and shops during the summer months. Before the war Germans also came in large numbers and a few French, Dutch, and Belgians. They found good eating, clean countries, quality goods, cool weather, and long light nights on up to the Land of the Midnight Sun and the North Cape. In the good years of the middle thirties the tourist trade brought annually $650,000 to Iceland, $6,500,000 to Finland, and about the same to Denmark, $12,000,000 to Norway and upwards of $13,000,000 to Sweden. About one-third of this money was Scandinavian, two-thirds from outside.

These then are some of the important sectors of the economy. What now are the bases and characteristics of that economy as a whole, and its relation to world economy and politics?

Characteristics of the Economy. Preëminent is the position of Scandinavia in international commerce: these 17,000,000 people, less than 1 per cent of the earth's population, carry on 5 per cent of world commerce. Norway with 3,000,000 people has as much foreign trade as the U.S.S.R.; Sweden with less than 7,000,000 people has as much foreign trade as India; Denmark with 4,000,000 people has as much foreign trade as China. If we exclude the intra-Scandinavian trade these five northern countries have about the same amount of foreign trade as France. To the economy of the world this means something, to the economy and the politics of these small countries it means everything. The Scandinavian countries are profoundly dependent on international trade.

This emphasis on foreign trade grows out of the narrow base of resources: Scandinavia has wood and iron in quantity, but it lacks much. It has soil which can produce, but which must have imported fertilizers. It has water power for electrometallurgical industries, but must import the bauxite and other ores for processing. Scandinavia can prosper only if her economy can be closely intermeshed with the economy of the wider world.

The limited variety of salable resources is illustrated by the character of the export trade: Sweden's exports are two-fifths forest products and two-fifths the products of mines and factories; Norway's are over four-fifths forest products; Denmark's are four-fifths agricultural products; and Iceland's are six-sevenths fish.

With these few products the Scandinavians must buy the things needed for well-rounded living. They therefore import raw cotton, spin their own yarn and make their own cloth, enough to satisfy from 50 to 80 per cent of the domestic requirements. Similarly they try to buy other goods in the cheapest form and do the processing themselves: tobacco which they make into cigarettes, chocolate which they make into candy. They must import direct oranges and bananas and nylons and automobiles (at least 85 per cent of their automobiles normally come from the United States). They must also buy production goods: machines for the textile factories, fertilizer for the soil, fodder for the livestock, hemp for fishnets, coal and oil for the fishing boats, equipment for their ocean-going vessels.

In wartime the serious problem is supply, in peacetime it is markets and foreign exchange. If the British tighten their belts and buy less butter, the Danes have lost business; if the British take Canadian bacon instead of Danish then farmers in Jutland can't sell pigs, and ships do not sail from Esbjerg. If the Swedes cannot sell their pulp in America or for United States dollars they have nothing with which to buy oranges or automobiles.

The importance to other countries of the Scandinavian trade is almost as great as the importance to Scandinavia. In "the good old days" Germany got from the North 8,000,000–10,000,000 tons of iron ore (40 per cent of her imports), 56 per cent of her butter imports, 50 per cent of her fish, 86 per cent of her pulp, 90 per cent of her cod-liver oil. Of her total imports of all commodities 10 per cent came from these northern neighbors. Great Britain likewise obtained there 10 per cent of her imports. Britain in turn sold to the North textiles, coal, and machinery, and Germany sold coal, manufactured goods, chemicals, and structural steel. It is clear that the devastation and dislocations of war on Britain and Germany, the two chief suppliers and markets of Scandinavia, had an immense impact on the Scandinavian economy.

Inter-Scandinavian trade is large, but it does not and cannot provide self-sufficiency. The resources of these countries are too much alike for them to sell extensively to each other. Iceland and Norway are the great exporters of fish, but Sweden, Denmark, and Finland do not need to buy much fish, since they catch their own. Sweden, Norway, and Finland do sell pulp and lumber to Denmark and Iceland, and Norway sells sulphur to Sweden. Cultural and geographic affinities make for interchanges and coöperation.

Finland and Sweden, for example, though competing for markets in forest products, exchange information and protect themselves against being played against one another in foreign trade. In 1930 the Oslo Convention attempted to go farther, and to guarantee against sudden changes in tariffs and trade policy not only in Denmark, Norway, Sweden, and Finland, but also in Belgium, Holland, and Luxemburg. This agreement was no customs union, but it crumbled to pieces under British opposition. More long-lasting was the Scandinavian Monetary Convention of 1874 which until 1914 provided common names and common values for Scandinavian coinage. Since 1890 many common laws have been passed by Denmark, Norway, and Sweden on trademarks, exchange, checks, and other financial and economic matters. The method is for experts from the different countries to meet in conference, agree on principles and even phraseology, and then for the national parliaments to legislate separately.

The habit of coöperation is deep-seated, and its advantages obvious. Many would like to see it carried further than voluntary agreements and common action can reach. Since 1863 the idea of a northern customs union has been discussed. Since World War II C. V. Bramsnaes, Danish minister of finance, has advocated it energetically. In 1948 a Joint Economic Commission began consultations, and its advocates are hopeful of success, later if not soon.

At the opening of 1950, however, this group admitted failure; the chief stumbling block appeared to be Norwegian fear of Swedish industrial competition. A somewhat different approach was attempted when the British, in December 1949, initiated conversations in Stockholm with representatives of Denmark, Norway, and Sweden. Here the goal was closer integration of the Scandinavian economies with the British. All the northern countries were already coöperating in the Council of Europe, which sought a still larger coördination. One thing only was certain: repeated and varied projects would continue to seek for a basis of union until perhaps a "DaNorSwe" or a "Uniscan" would be born to parallel "Benelux," or until western Europe as a whole could attain economic integration.

From instances cited in the preceding pages it is plain that government and business are in close alliance. In relation to foreign trade three groups, government, labor, and business management, are consciously allied. In few places can one find such an intelligent appreciation as in Scandinavia that workers and employers, producers and consumers, the nation and its neighbors, all have strong common interests, interests which transcend the temporary advantages and disadvantages of any one group.

The workers of these small countries know that if they do not maintain production and quality the whole community loses; the employers know that if wages and working conditions and health are not good their own production and profits will suffer. Labor and management fight stubbornly ofttimes, but with intelligence. The strike is used sparingly and wages are negotiated with a minimum of wasteful controversy. In Finland a war-born government wage board increased wages about 5 ½ per cent for each 5 per cent increase in the cost of living index —a national system comparable to the General Motors Company plan. The Finns abolished this system in February 1950, but similar adjustment devices were used throughout the North.

Against the background of history and pragmatic philosophy it seems a natural phenomenon to see the coöperation of government and a private company in the development of the northern Swedish iron mines. The problem was how best to do the job of construction, administration, and production in the difficult northern wilds. Hence the governments of Sweden and Norway built the servicing railways, and the board of the mining company became half governmental and half private, with the private company chairman holding a theoretical balance of power. Government also joins with private enterprise in selling by auction or agreement the product of the national forests for private processing, and in leasing mines for private development. Through various methods governments and private management work together in the development and utilization of water power, notably in the extensive interlocking power plants of Sweden. Occasionally the state and private enterprise are partners in share-holding and management, as in Norway's largest individual industry, Norsk Hydro, which processes nitrates and heavy water. The government, since taking over from the Germans after World War II, owns 44 per cent of the stock, and other Norwegian interests 8 per cent; of the remainder the French own 36 per cent. Government also works closely with the coöperatives and other enterprises as described in the chapters on coöperatives and public works.

Government plays a direct part in economic as well as in social affairs: government is the representative of competing yet combined economic interests, the agent of compromise and adjustment. In government the diverse interests meet to create and stabilize the welfare of the entire society. Hence government follows the principle that public planning is necessary, but that well-working free enterprise should be left untouched. Policy is practical, not doctrinaire, yet government is always there ready to act. The total economy, in the broadest sense, is coöperative.

A final basic characteristic of the Scandinavian economic structure is inherited investment. In America only a few generations ago there was nothing but unexploited resources; factories, cities, property, have been born under our eyes. But the ancestors of twentieth-century Scandinavians began construction of their social and economic order many hundreds of years ago. Copenhagen was a great trading center before Columbus crossed the Atlantic, and Gustavus Adolphus was leading conquering armies through Germany while the Pilgrims were settling the wilderness.

Buildings from the seventeenth century are still in use in the cities of Scandinavia, and will last for years to come. New homes, modern furniture—but also well-built old homes, substantial old furniture from generations back. The men of the past built for the future, and the men of the present have the use of that inheritance. Not many productive enterprises can boast of the 600 years of the *Stora Kopparbergs Bergslag*, but many farms and factories and business houses are established on beginnings made a century or two centuries ago. The investment built up through the years is a solid foundation for the modern economy.

Intelligent work is the key to Scandinavian prosperity. There are patches of good soil, but they require special fertilizers. There is timber, but it has to be cut and processed and transported. There is iron ore, but the big mines are north of the Arctic Circle. There are fish, but the life of the men of Lofoten or of the whalers is not easy nor guaranteed long. There are neither palms nor banana trees.

Well-being can be had, but only at the price of planning and hard work.

It is therefore this basic economic structure, combined with the planning described in the following section, which have produced in Scandinavia an unusually high material standard of living and a sense of security for the individual and the family.

2. ECONOMIC PLANNING: BACKGROUND AND CURRENT PRACTICE

Planning in Scandinavia began early. The land policy of the city of Copenhagen dating from the twelfth century, the public ownership of forests and mines in Sweden dating from the decrees of Gustav Vasa in the sixteenth century, are merely illustrative preliminaries for the managed currencies and the long-term programs of development of the mid-twentieth century. The scope of planning has been widened, but the psychology of planning was deep-rooted.

The purpose of governmental planning is to organize the utilization of resources so as to obtain for the entire community the largest possible economic and social advantages. Planning involves restraints on individual action in some cases, special stimuli in others. It tends to channel production and consumption in certain directions. For example, planning for child welfare will encourage manufacture and distribution of children's shoes and clothing; planning for export will give special privileges to certain manufacturers. Other production inevitably feels discriminated against. Hence the pressures of social reformers and of special business interests play strongly on the responsible planners. Always in vigorous opposition will be the persons who for selfish or ideological reasons favor competition and free enterprise. And the endemic diseases of bureaucratic power must be watched constantly. In democratic societies like those of Scandinavia planning is therefore subject to constant scrutiny and to compromise; there it is not at all the complete regulation which is found under a totalitarian regime. It is just the democratic processes involved which give to Scandinavian planning its particular interest.

Private business furnishes many examples of planning: long-term investment, research programs, rationalization of production, community planning for workers. This kind of planning has been more conscious and more careful in Scandinavia than in some other countries. Economic stringencies have impelled it, the temperament of the people and the stability of society have made it possible.

As business-planning enlarges its field of operations it impinges more and more on the interests and the functions of the state. Business attempts to use government for its own benefit in relation to labor, markets, supplies, both at home and abroad. Government has a natural concern for these businesses and for the general economic interests of its citizens. Certain private enterprises, such as shipping in Norway or mining in Sweden, loom large in the national economy. The resources they control and the markets they use weigh heavily in the national prosperity and in questions of war and peace. The intervention of the state becomes inevitable. The question becomes one of the extent of this intervention: (1) shall it be only in the realm of tariffs, subsidies, credit control and taxation? or (2) must it involve participation in management, as with the Kiruna Mining Company in Sweden? or (3) should it proceed to monopolistic control, as with the army, the post office system, and the railways, and eventuate in socialization? The Scandinavian countries use all three methods of state intervention, and therefore have not gone to complete socialization. But the public interest is recognized in not only the giant industries, but in the total agglomeration of economic enterprises.

Government has become interested in the planning of all important businesses and in the integration of these plans for the national welfare. Until recently government action usually confined itself to dealing with problems presented by internal or external crises, as in the case of the Swedish gold exclusions order during World War I, the rationing of scarce commodities in both recent wars, restrictions on imports, and limited control of wages and prices. But increasingly, private economic interests and government have come together in common attempts to meet their problems in more far-sighted planning. They have begun to try to solve not only *ad hoc* difficulties, but to formulate a planned and controlled future.

An interesting illustration of a program much broader than those of the *ad hoc* variety, yet less consciously projected into the future than the four- and five-year plans, was the Danish land reform. It illustrates well the pragmatic and farsighted approach of the Scandinavians to planning for the nation.

The Danish Land Reform. The reformation of Danish agriculture carried through in the late nineteenth and early twentieth centuries is now a completed program. It was a revolution, increasing productivity, changing agriculture from grain raising to animal husbandry, and shifting ownership of the land from the large landholders to the mass of men and women who worked the land. The long-time development was only partly envisaged in the early stages, but planning was nevertheless real and farsighted. As with most planning it was forced by circumstances.

The Danish peasant began to be released from feudalism in the 1780's, and he was encouraged by government leadership to become an independent proprietor. It was, however, two factors of the mid-nineteenth century which really placed him on the road to his twentieth-century freedom. One of these was the liberal constitution of 1849, the other was the teaching of Grundtvig which created a faith in political and economic progress. At first the movement from communal to capitalist agriculture was steady though slow, but it was aided by government and by private societies, and by the folk high schools. By the middle of the nineteenth century 58 per cent of Danish farms were held as freeholds.

External factors accelerated the programs of the social planners in the late nineteenth century. Cheap grain from the fresh overseas fields came to destroy Denmark's market in Britain. The great landowners and the rural proletariat alike faced impoverishment. Many of the able-bodied moved to the industrial centers or emigrated to America. Rural prosperity could be restored only by revamping the agricultural system. The new agricultural schools pointed the way and the discouraged squires followed their lead. Intensive farming of individualized plots with raising of livestock instead of grain for export seemed to offer salvation. The holders of the large estates were willing to let their workers have five-acre plots of their own if they would also work part time in the larger fields and thus maintain something of the old economic structure.

Therefore the Rigsdag passed an Act in 1899 offering state loans of 90 per cent of the cost of such small holdings. Within twenty years the government put 58,000,000 kroner into this program, and 9263 new small holdings were established. In 1919 the program was broadened, and more money was provided. In the first years the peasants had to buy land from the owners. The great estates were parceled out, but only partially. Increasingly it was realized that the old system of both agriculture and of landholding was obsolete, and that Danish prosperity must depend upon individualized farming. This required small holdings not of five acres, but of 15 to 35 acres, with each family earning its living entirely off its own land. The government, therefore, bought private lands for redivision, and used the old glebe lands also. At the same time the government laid a heavy tax on the landed estates unless they would surrender one-third of their land, for compensation, to the state. Thus the private estates were diminished and small holdings further extended. Between 1920 and 1932 the government provided an additional 100,000,000 kroner in smallholder grants, and 6200 new holdings were established.

The state continued to give loans to qualified smallholders for 90 per cent of the cost of land, buildings, and equipment. It also introduced a different system, based on Henry George's ideas: the holder paid no purchase price for his land, but an annual "ground-rent" of 4 per cent of the value of the land as reappraised at periodic intervals. Rents were at first made to fluctuate with farm commodity prices, but this worked out unfortunately, for it caused rents to rise during hard times when grain supply prices rose, increasing the costs of animal feeding. Hence the method of determining rent was changed to follow a sliding scale calculated each year by the Bureau of Agricultural Economics, and based on the earning capacity of small farms. Detailed regulations and controls were worked out in legislation of 1933, 1938, and 1943.

Altogether the state has invested 300,000,000 kroner in the small holdings. About 18,000 holdings were started under the terms of the 1899 Act and 7000 under the ground-rent provisions of 1919. Of this total of 25,000 state-aided small holdings about 5000 have become completely independent by repayment of the loans. About one-fifth of the 110,000 smallholders of Denmark still hold from the state. And about 95 per cent of all the farmers of Denmark are individual proprietors.

The early five- to ten-acre farms were gradually expanded, the later parcels were carefully sized to family needs, so that the present small holdings average about 25 acres. It should be borne in mind that three-quarters of the small holdings were established without state aid both before and since 1899. Many of these, however, were built under the guidance of enabling legislation, and were stimulated by the social ideals and planning of the coöperative societies, the smallholders' schools, and the state agricultural schools. In the nineteenth century the smallholders formed societies and became a political force, fighting vigorously for their privileges. From an early stage the revolution demanded by social reformers for human reasons became merged with the agricultural-economic revolution demanded by world market changes. This coincidence unquestionably eased the conflict inherent in both the social and the economic revolution. The most significant item remains: that private leadership, group pressures, and state action joined in an adaptable, progressive planning which rebuilt Danish agriculture and prosperity. Direct state intervention was used to make more complete a socio-economic change already decided upon by society as a whole, and viewed in its total setting—economic, social, and personal.

Early Swedish Planning. The preliminary phases of twentieth-century over-all planning in Sweden were caused by World War I and by the depression. At first they were financial in nature, for the government thought that through money, the key of the economy, it might avert disastrous shifts in the price level and the cost of living. The details of monetary controls need not detain us, but the method is significant.

In Sweden the goals of monetary policy were outlined by the government, and the implementation was left to the directors of the Riksbank. They in turn consulted with financial theorists such as Professor Knut Wicksell, Professor David Davidson, and Professor Gustav Cassel, for

the professional economist . . . commands an honored place in the scheme of things, in marked contrast to the scepticism or the polite indifference with which he is regarded in this country (England) and in the United States.*

However, the theorists did not wholly agree, and the bankers would not follow any one consistent theory. When during World War I gold began to flow to Sweden from the belligerent countries, the bankers were worried about inflation; they could not accept Wicksell's idea that "economically we could do nothing better than exchange our barren reserve of 100 million kronor of metal for useful goods abroad." †

The Riksbank did forbid further importation of gold, yet because of the established monetary agreement could not stop its influx from Norway and Denmark, and contradictorily lowered the discount rate. The measures taken slowed the progress of inflation, and it never got out of hand as in Germany, but inflation came in a degree slightly greater than in the United States and Britain.

* Brinley Thomas, *Monetary Policies and Crises,* p. xx.
† *Ibid.,* p. 4.

When the world depression enfolded Sweden in 1930, monetary policy concentrated on maintenance of internal purchasing power. The real purpose was to "stabilize the cost of living," and to avoid labor unrest by maintaining jobs and prices. Sweden was fortunate to have a reserve to throw into public works and relief. The government borrowed heavily, and happily demand for iron ore and timber remained relatively strong. Export prices rose, 1931–1933, while import prices were held low.

Finland profited too by the continued demand for her timber products, but her internal purchasing power suffered severely. Norway was at the mercy of autarchic policies elsewhere which deprived her ships of cargo and curtailed her markets for fish. But in Sweden, by 1933,

the monetary policy had brought the economic decline to a standstill, and in the favourable situation which thus arose the recovery in export trade started a general business revival.*

By the combination of guidance and good luck Sweden weathered the storm remarkably well. Belief in planned controls was strengthened. In succeeding years exports were encouraged by keeping the krona below its normal free market value. In 1937 monetary authorities, in order to check the influence of high prices abroad, considered "raising the value of the Swedish krona in relation to sterling and tightening up domestic credit," but conditions changed and these policies were not effected.

Such experiences and attitudes form the background for the more sweeping plans of the 1940's. The early short-term calculations were adjustments to circumstances. With World War II the Swedes decided to do more than adapt themselves to conditions. As Gunnar Myrdal stated the new concept, "the problem is to try here and now to guide developments in the right direction."

* Arthur Montgomery, *How Sweden Overcame the Depression*, p. 66.

One of the first steps in the new activist policy was the appreciation of the value of the krona in July 1946. The scheme of 1937 was now carried out, but in 1946 it was directed at the dollar instead of at the pound sterling. The Swedes reasoned that the krona was undervalued, and that inflation was coming in the United States. By increasing the value of the krona they hoped to minimize the reaction of that inflation on the Swedish economy. They expected demand for Swedish pulp and other products to remain strong regardless of this price increase, a price increase which would affect goods sold to other countries also, including the U.S.S.R. under the trade agreement then being negotiated. They expected to be able to buy goods abroad more advantageously. One result, Myrdal wrote a few months later, was that "price control had a less restrictive effect on imports than would otherwise have been the case." * But Sweden imported so much that she soon spent her dollar reserves and had to restrict imports drastically in 1948 and 1949 (cf. p. 294). And she priced many of her own goods out of the American market.

For planning in its broader aspects, however, the story must go back to the war period.

Wartime Planning. In the early months and years of World War II the Scandinavian countries could follow only the catch-as-catch-can policy. They stock-piled foreign goods as much as possible and rationed scarce items of importance. Finland's war and postwar plans were channeled very definitely by immediate needs and by the imposed program of reparations, which necessitated industrial reorganization. The Finns themselves had to plan for the resettlement of their dispossessed people from the ceded areas in the east and north. From 1940 to 1945 planning in Denmark and Norway was controlled by the nazis, yet some worth-while and permanent projects of roadbuilding, and construction of railways, airfields, and factories was undertaken. Devastated homes and industries provided the great common

---

* Svenska Handelsbankens *Index*, Supplement, Dec. 1946, p. 10.

problem, and plans to meet it were formulated both at home and by the Norwegian government in exile in London.

In January 1943 the Danish minister of finance appointed a commission to study the danger of inflation and allied problems. The membership included representatives of government and banking, and professors from Aarhus and Copenhagen. In March the commission recommended price ceilings and a price-wage policy. In 1945 it produced a two volume report, and recommended wide government intervention in economic activity: government orders to stimulate export and investment industry, including purchase of durable consumption goods such as furniture; government subsidy of repair to buildings and of shipbuilding; possible reduction of the interest rate on housing loans. Public works were to be a second alternative. Imports should be restricted on account of the shortage of foreign exchange. Possible unemployment should be distributed by staggering workers' time off. Unemployment benefits should be increased to encourage buying and thus to offset a decline in production. Taxes should be reduced on short notice before a depression could get out of control, and should be raised on short notice to control a boom. Much of this program was made law. In fact, partial steps of a similar nature had been tried in the depression of the thirties through subsidies and discount cards for children of low income families. Denmark was geared for her stringent postwar controls.

The Swedes had the best opportunity to show the natural Scandinavian method of operation: they established a planning commission in February 1944. Chairman of the commission was Gunnar Myrdal, minister of commerce, a trained social scientist and professor. The twenty-one members of the commission represented the main political parties, industry, trade unions, the employers' association, chambers of commerce, the coöperatives, agriculture, and women's organizations. The commission had no authority to act, but was charged to formulate principles.

This Swedish commission had almost completed its work by

September 1945. It took for its starting point that exports and investment were "the active force behind changes in the business cycle." The commission expressed aversion to manipulation of exchange rates, subsidies of exports, "or similar measures." But it recognized a need for state encouragement to industry to produce and store goods for future export. It foresaw some of the difficulties which would follow when Swedish exports would be demanded by countries with "weak" currencies, and Sweden would wish to buy from countries with "hard" currencies. A period of government control was therefore essential, but control should be applied only as necessary. Investment should be evened out between depression and boom; special tax policies could encourage this, and an Investment Planning Commission was established. Industrial construction and public building were to be aided by an "investment reserve" with new projects available to be put in motion at the start of a depression. Housing construction was to be stabilized at a high level. Consumption was to be promoted in depression periods by increases of relief allotments, and by subsidies to families with several children to encourage them to purchase durable consumers' goods. The importance of free competition was emphasized, and price control was to be held in the background, but lowering of the price level and stabilization of incomes was to be sought. The labor exchanges were to be improved, and industry further rationalized.

The commission's program might be labeled "reluctant semi-socialism." It represented what government, management, and labor could agree upon. Much more definite was the postwar program of Swedish labor, referred to earlier (pp. 134–135), but it too stayed within the broad path of the "middle way."

In all these countries the qualms of the business community and the opposition of advocates of laissez faire were overruled. The governments of Scandinavia were prepared to attempt to control the economy, *but only insofar as circumstances seemed to them to require control.*

*   *   *

Postwar Planning: Norway. At the close of World War II Norway was one of the countries which swung most thoroughly to state economic planning. Almost 20 per cent of the national wealth had been destroyed, the entire northern section lay waste, and half the fleet was gone. Replacements of machinery and ships and other goods had to come largely from abroad. Purchase of these items involved not only the individual buyer, but it created a problem of currency exchange and affected national finance. There would be inevitably a competition for scarce materials and manpower. Rationing and a whole series of wartime controls had established a basis for state action and prepared people psychologically for government intervention. Like war, reconstruction was a concern of the whole people, of the government.

The government grasped the reins and in the budget for 1946 laid out a program for the restoration of productive capacity to prewar levels. In the budget for 1947 the bases of planned reconstruction were elaborated in a comprehensive document allocating income and expenditure not only for the government but for the nation as a whole. It was an integration of many smaller budgets, but it was more than that. It was not only a diagnosis of circumstances and a prognosis of probable developments. It was a program of action for the year ahead, an outline of work for all Norway.

The 1947 budget was divided into a series of sub-budgets. 1. *The manpower budget* estimated a 1 per cent increase in the labor force, to be used primarily in forestry, manufacturing, shipping, and whaling; while agriculture, building and construction, and public administration were to use fewer workers. An increase in efficiency was counted upon. 2. *The commodity budget* was concerned especially with materials for building and construction—bricks, cement, lumber. Production of these items was up from prewar, but was to be pushed further. Housing was emphasized, and materials were allocated to aid essential building and rationalization. 3. *The budget for trading goods and services with foreign countries* provided for an increase in 1947 of both imports and exports, with a still greater unfavorable gap between them than in 1946. But Norway was to import the means of new production, and a minimum of consumer goods. Special efforts were to be made to increase exports for dollars, Swedish kronor, and other hard currencies. 4. *The foreign exchange budget* provided for "balance of payments classified by main currencies." The disposable foreign reserves of 1,500,000,000 kroner were to be used for goods, interest, and dividends totaling 950,000,000 kroner and for payments to the International Monetary Fund, and installments on ships under construction. 5. *The production budget* classified carefully the total national product of 8,600,000,000 kronor, an increase of 9.6 per cent over 1946 (quantity increase of 6 per cent, and price increase of 3.6 per cent). This was greater than prewar production, but because of the increase in population and the demands for restoration it would leave per capita consumption below prewar levels. 6. *The budget of consumption* estimated private consumption of 6,500,000,000 kroner and public consumption of 1,000,000,000 kroner—the latter down from 1946 by 100,000,000 kroner because of decreased expenditures for defense. The quality of consumer goods was reckoned better than prewar, but many items were not available, and individual consumption was to be not much above the 91 per cent of prewar which was the figure of 1946. And the people got "movies in place of meat, radios in place of fuel, vacation trips instead of clothing." 7. *The investment budget* for both private and public capital formation was set at 2,000,000,000 kroner, 54 per cent above 1946. Shipping and whaling equipment accounted for 550,000,000 kroner and the manufacturing and electrical industries for 410,000,000 kroner. Housing and inland transportation were also items of importance. 8. *The budget for the public sector*, which restated certain of the above items.

Norway's truly *national* budget of 1947 has been summarized as an example of detailed governmental planning for the community. In 1948 the budget document was simplified and abbreviated; it eliminated the special budget for the public sector, and consolidated the production budget and the manpower budget. The whole plan naturally was based on assumptions and was inexact. Changes in prices or wages or taxes, shifts in international conditions, delay or speed-up in delivery of ships—many factors could influence the realization of the program.

It was, however, a definite program integrating the entire national economy. It was supported by the powerful sanctions of government. It extended rationing to the raw materials for factories, to foreign exchange and to credit for old firms or new, to lumber and building materials and to manpower. It involved import and export licensing, control of interest rates, manipulation of taxes. It granted subsidies amounting to 28 per cent of total state expenditures in 1947–48, the money going chiefly to agriculture, coming chiefly from industry. It laid out a plan for each producing sector of the economy. It kept prices and wages controlled, and checked the progress of the inflationary spiral. It protected the real income of workers, and brought about a more even distribution of income among farmers and fishers, capitalists and laborers. It enabled the government to stimulate the rationalization of industry, with better machinery and larger producing units. Under this plan the state increased its own investment to one-fourth of the total budget. The state was able to restrain private consumption and to direct the increasing output into export channels and into investment in ships and production goods. Shipping, however, was privately owned, and it showed probably the best reconstruction record.

The budget-plan overshot the mark on housing, and set goals for export higher than were attained in 1947 or 1948. Implementation lagged at a number of points. But austerity and control, under the guidance of the successive annual plans, achieved steady increases in production. The cost was heavy, almost 2,500,000,000 kroner in taxes in 1947–48 and 1948–49 (not including about 900,000,000 kroner in local taxes), amounting to nearly one-third of national production. The ECA analysts questioned whether the progressive and profits taxes and even the general tax level might not seriously restrict initiative and output.

The European Recovery Program and Long-term Planning. Norway's budgets of 1946 to 1948 were actually one-year plans, though they implied commitments of policy and expenditure over several years. The Marshall Plan, or European Recovery Program (ERP), forced Norway and all sixteen of the participating European countries to think and plan for longer terms. The whole ERP was predicated upon heavy investment over a period of a few years to produce ultimately balanced economies. Careful planning was essential, no matter how ironic it might seem that the United States was leading European governments along this road.

Norway's long-range program, submitted in the fall of 1948 to the Organization for European Economic Coöperation (OEEC) and for ERP aid, is a projection of the earlier plans on to 1952–53. The deficit in international payments, accumulating at the rate of $200,000,000 in 1948, was to be wiped out by 1952–53. This meant a maintenance of consumption at minimum level along with sharp increases in production for export and in shipping services. Shipping was to be increased to 5,600,000 gross tons, 16 per cent above the 1938 figure, and an excellent means of acquiring foreign exchange, if world conditions developed satisfactorily and if other shipping did not expand out of proportion. Production in agriculture and the other major fields—forestry, construction, fishing, mining, and manufacturing—was to be raised from 10 per cent to 25 per cent over 1948 levels. Exports were to be raised in the four-year period from $420,000,000 to $537,000,000. Since Norway could not expect to expand her exports to the dollar area she planned to obtain her imports to a larger extent from countries which would buy her products. She would sell fats, aluminum, and fish to Russia in exchange for grain. In general Norwegian optimism exceeded that of the Economic Coöperation Admin-

AMERICAN ASSISTANCE UNDER ERP TO NORWAY
(In millions of dollars)

	1948–49				1949–50
	Total	Loan	Grant	Conditional Aid	Total
Norwegian request (fiscal year)	104				131.8
OEEC recommendations (fiscal year)..	84				94.
ECA allotment, net (fiscal year)	81.1 *				—
Allotments in fifteen-month period, April 1948 to June 1949 ..	101.1	35	49.6	16.5	

* Reduction from OEEC figures of 3.4 per cent for reserve.

istration, which warned that it might be impossible to find suffi-cient funds to finance the entire ambitious program.

The Swedish recovery program, drawn up for the OEEC in the fall of 1948, was of a different tenor from the high hopes of 1945. Miscalculations about economic trends in the United States, sanguine imports in 1946 and 1947, and loss of markets for her exports had combined to deplete Sweden's dollar re-serve and to imperil her stabilization program. The apprecia-tion of the krona (July 1946) was partly responsible for the high prices which made it difficult to sell Swedish pulp and other goods in the dollar area. The social reform program was expensive, and domestic consumption was maintained at high levels. The requirement that foreign exchange be turned over to the Riksbank discouraged export. Dollar imports had been slashed to half earlier in 1948, but drastic operations were still necessary.

The Swedish report to the OEEC emphasized the achieve-ments of the government and of the private economy in the

1930's and in the period after the war, the rapid expansion of water-power facilities, and of the iron and steel industry, the overbalancing of the domestic budget, reduction of income taxes and elimination of the sales tax, price controls and agreements reached with labor, management, and agriculture for wage stabilization. It recognized also that a serious situation existed. The deficit in Sweden's balance of payments for 1947 was $400,000,000. This amount equaled one-fourth of imports, one-third of exports, and was too large to be counterbalanced by either a raise in exports or a cut in imports; it would require action from both ends. Sweden therefore suggested a program for both.

Labor supply was a problem, especially as Sweden could not expect continuance of the immigration of some 25,000 workers per year which had aided her expansion in the first postwar years. The country must be careful that the new workers coming of age be located in the activities most useful to the national economy, that is, in mining, export manufacturing industries, and forestry. The depletion of the virgin forests was another problem, causing a structural change in the economy. For hereafter Sweden must depend on the annual growth of the forests, and by research, product development, and commercial organization augment the income from this, her richest natural resource. The American ECA experts seemed to think the Swedes were very cautious in their plans for future exports of forest products, and emphasized the need of present use of all available export resources.

Sweden suffered severely from the bilateralism of postwar trade; her economy was based on a few export items and imports of a variety of materials from many lands. Two-thirds of her raw material had to be imported. If Sweden could obtain freely circulating currency she could reduce her adjustments to bilateral trade. But for that she needed dollars, and it was just with the United States that she had her huge trade deficit in the postwar era. Of Sweden's trade and payments unbalance of $400,000,000 (1947), $358,000,000 was with the dollar area.

The decline in German production was one root of the difficulty. Britain remained the pivotal point for Sweden's multilateral trade, but Britain's own recovery program precluded her from absorbing Swedish exports on the old scale.

These were some of the chief problems Sweden's planners had to face in the attempt to restore the country's viability by 1952. The solution demanded a great reduction in imports, but not such a reduction as to destroy morale or productive capacity. There was also required an upsurge of exports, a matter which involved both the ability and willingness of Sweden to sell, and the ability and willingness of others to buy.

The Swedish plan outlined and extended the development program already under way. Agriculture would be able to increase production over the four-year period by 8.5 per cent, through the increased use of fertilizer and improved techniques. Self-sufficiency in bread grains was to be attained by 1952. Ten thousand new tractors would be needed annually and Sweden would produce seven thousand of these. Forest products would decline in total, but by measures of limiting the use of paper and timber it was hoped that exports of forest products could be increased by $50,000,000 over 1947 levels. Expansion of export of prefabricated houses could be a further item of increase, if tariffs and other trade barriers abroad were relaxed. Production of hydroelectric power was expected to double, and to reach 21,000,000,000 kwh by 1953; this would indicate utilization of about half the country's water-power potential. The iron and steel industries, already under rapid expansion, were expected to double exports and to cut imports two-thirds by 1952–53, and this would save $100,000,000 per year in foreign currency. Iron ore export might reach prewar standards in 1949, and surpass them slightly thereafter. Certain engineering industries exported only 20 per cent of their product in 1947; before the war they had exported 37 per cent and it was hoped to restore this figure while also increasing total production. The merchant fleet had already expanded 20 per cent over prewar, and would continue to grow. Shipbuilding was at an increased level and had orders on hand for several years' full employment.

By reducing imports $96,000,000 from 1947, by increasing exports $227,000,000, and by earnings from shipping and other items of $56,000,000 Sweden looked forward to eliminating the unfavorable balance of 1947 in the course of four years.

AMERICAN ASSISTANCE UNDER ERP TO SWEDEN
(In millions of dollars)

	1948–49				1949–50
	Total	Loan	Grant	Conditional Aid	Total
Swedish request (fiscal year)	109.				70.7
OEEC recommendation (fiscal year) .	47.				48.
ECA allotment (fiscal year)	45.4 *				——
Allotments in fifteen-month period, April 1948 to June 1949 ..	45.4	20.4		25.	

* Reduction from OEEC figures of 3.4 per cent for reserve.

There was no indication in the Swedish plan of an intent to devalue the krona. The ECA experts insisted upon a downward adjustment of prices to make Swedish products competitive, and pointed to a lowering of the artificial value of the krona as one way to attain this. This came at last in September 1949, forced by the British devaluation, and at the same rate of 30.5 per cent. The ECA observers considered also that Sweden could reduce imports more than proposed. They pointed out that Sweden's exports in 1947 were only 12.6 per cent of total production, although in 1938–39 they were 14.9 per cent. Consumption would have to be curtailed and export increased in order to attain the desired goal.

Denmark's situation and plan both were rather different from those of her neighbor. Sweden had been optimistic in 1945 and had allowed consumption to expand at a high rate. Denmark realized that war had left her economically weakened, and the people entered the postwar epoch under a spartan regime of self-denial. Despite this fact direct government controls were less far-reaching than in Sweden. The Danish agricultural and industrial structure was more individualistic, less controllable. Denmark's plan was a statement of hope rather than a commitment to action.

Denmark nevertheless made a plan. It was predicated on a continuance of low consumption to 1952, and on increased production and export. The people had already proved themselves able to adjust to the meager level of consumer goods. Production in industry could doubtless be increased considerably, and the Danes planned to emphasize those goods in which they already had wide markets and reputation: shipbuilding, Diesel engines, slaughterhouse and dairy equipment, cement-manufacturing machinery, articles of skilled craftsmanship. Increase in agricultural production might be more difficult, for Denmark had already reached the highest per-acre grain production in the world. The rebuilding of the livestock census began immediately after the war, but was temporarily set back by the drought of 1947. Supplies of feedstuffs were short the world over, and Denmark's former sources (for example, in Africa) were often selling to other markets. Shortage of tinplate restricted the Danish potential for canning fish and farm products for export. But Denmark hoped to increase exports from $494,-000,000 in 1947 to $898,000,000 in 1952–53, a jump of 82 per cent.

Plans could be made only on the assumption that the worst of the difficulties of supply and of market could be overcome. The Danes optimistically reckoned on an increase of exports to the western hemisphere from 3 per cent prewar to 11 per cent by 1952. Even such an increase would leave them with a dollar deficit of $50,000,000. Since they counted on a favorable balance with England of $146,000,000 they hoped to convert sterling into the necessary dollars—which might prove difficult. Even more perhaps than the brother countries of the North, Denmark was dependent on multilateral trade, and her whole industrious attempt to reach viability by 1952 was conditional upon obtaining fertilizer and other raw materials and selling the product of land and factories. In 1948 ECA aid had been translated quickly into greater production. The Danes were obviously ready to do their part, if only world conditions would coöperate.

In connection with Denmark's position among the planners it should be added that the government in Denmark is less involved in economic enterprise than are the other governments of Scandinavia. The housing program, for instance, is carried on by individuals and coöperative societies with small government assistance. There are no great power plants, because there are no waterfalls. Only 85,000 of the 2,000,000 workers of Denmark are in government service, and the government use of resources

AMERICAN ASSISTANCE UNDER ERP TO DENMARK
(In millions of dollars)

	1948–49				1949–50
	Total	Loan	Grant	Conditional Aid	Total
Danish request (fiscal year)	149.9				110.
OEEC recommendation (fiscal year) ..	110.				91.
ECA allotment (fiscal year)	106.2 *				
Allotments in fifteen-month period, April 1948 to June 1949..	126.2	31.	90.1	1.5	

* Reduction from OEEC figure of 3.4 per cent for reserve.

was only 10 per cent in 1948 of the disposable product (in Norway it was over 25 per cent).

Iceland faced major economic readjustments both during and after World War II. The war and allied occupation brought inflated prosperity and shifted economic relationships toward the United States. After the war much of the unexpected monetary supply was used to reëquip the fishing and fish-processing industry. But the cost of living had increased more than three times over, and wages, geared to the official cost of living index, had soared. Unskilled labor was paid 1.45 kronur per hour in 1939, 8.40 kronur per hour in 1948. In 1947, after the exhaustion of the accumulated reserves, the government took drastic steps to curb imports, and granted licenses for only essential goods. Trade relations fluctuated after the war, evidently *not* based on any Icelandic plan. Russia stepped in as a buyer second only to Britain in 1946 and 1947, perhaps for political reasons. But in 1948 the Soviet state almost dropped out of the scene, and Iceland sold her record winter herring catch to countries in the OEEC and to Poland and Czechoslovakia.

AMERICAN ASSISTANCE UNDER ERP TO ICELAND
(In millions of dollars)

	1948–49				1949–50
	Total	Loan	Grant	Conditional Aid	Total
Icelandic request (fiscal year)	11.				10.
OEEC recommendation (fiscal year) ..	11.				7.3
ECA allotments	7.7 *				
Allotments in fifteen-month period, April 1948 to June 1949..	8.3	2.3	2.5	3.5	

* Reduction from OEEC figures is for "specific adjustments."

Iceland's long-term program is to expand fish production and export, to modernize and rationalize her fisheries and fish-processing, and to diversify the economy. She had more than thirty new trawlers by 1949, and the government ordered ten additional. Increase in production and export of fish-oil, meal, and frozen fillets was to be attained by new machinery; the merchant marine was to be expanded; two new hydroelectric stations and a thermal station were projected, as were plants to make fertilizer, cement, and flour. The state hoped to increase total receipts from $57,800,000 in 1947 to $93,100,000 in 1952–53, and to attain balance at that figure.

But unfortunately one must question the exactitude of any plan for a country which is dependent upon the double uncertainties of catching fish and then of marketing the catch.

Scandinavian Planning: an Evaluation. To some planning is an abomination, to others it is the hope of the future. In the Scandinavian countries it is a natural development out of past experience and a necessary means of adjustment to current difficulties. The mid-century problems of Scandinavia were due to three related factors: 1. reconstruction; 2. the collapse of Germany and the weakening of Britain, the two historically important economic partners of the northern countries; 3. the resultant overwhelming trade unbalance with the western hemisphere, the United States especially. To meet such problems farsighted planning was essential. The only question was the extent to which that planning would be done by private sectors of the economy and to what extent it would be guided by government.

Social Democratic government in each of the countries under consideration assumed a directing role in the integration of economic plans for the nation. It entered upon the work with caution during the war, widened its activities in the first post-war years, and embarked upon long-term planning under the stimulus of the ERP. The method of planning and the degree of governmental control differed considerably in the various countries, yet common characteristics are clear.

In the first place none of these countries undertook the complete and rigid control of the national economy practiced in the USSR or the smaller communist lands, nor did any of them attempt the degree of socialization tried in Great Britain. Direct nationalization of industry was hotly debated, but little practiced.

Centralization of direction was, however, the rule. Denmark went least far in this, yet even in Denmark powerful controls were exercised in quick and democratic fashion through the government and the coöperatives. In the other countries government became involved increasingly in direct economic activity—witness the Swedish and Norwegian pig-iron and steel plants. To a large extent, however, it made no difference whether the government owned and operated plants itself; by control of credit, of foreign exchange, of imports and exports, of manpower and prices and wages, the government could easily direct the economic activity of private industry. Leaders in banking, commerce, industry, labor, were in constant consultation with government. This centralization of direction was one of the things vigorously attacked by the Norwegian economist Wilhelm Keilhau, who insisted that in a new war the first necessity for self-preservation would be decentralization, for central direction like concentrated industry was most vulnerable before atomic weapons. Professor Keilhau also condemned the inefficiency of control by bureaucrats without practical knowledge.

The shift from short-term to long-term planning was itself a revolutionary development. It represented the attempt, already discussed, to depart from mere adjustment to conditions, and to formulate programs which would carry through and beyond the normal trade cycle. It therefore implied an attempt to override and avoid the fluctuations of boom and depression, to eliminate business cycles. Whether this could be done anywhere remained a question, and above all in small countries peculiarly dependent on international trade and world economic conditions.

The matter of the size of the Scandinavian countries bears also another and more favorable relationship to planning. For the homogeneous and comparatively simply-structured nature of these countries made planning in one of them comparable to organizing the economy of a single state in the United States, and quite a different thing from integrating the economic forces of a large country like the United States or Britain.

In general the Scandinavian plans made the same mistake as those of most of the OEEC countries. They overemphasized investment. They provided, for instance, for the rapid rebuilding and expansion of the Norwegian merchant fleet. Yet in 1948, before that fleet had been restored to prewar size, part of it was already idle. The nation as a whole was doing without consumer goods to build up the national earning power. Laudable in itself, but worse than useless if that power could not be employed.

Possible overinvestment was induced by an optimistic prognosis of world conditions, and specifically on the expectation of steadily increasing export to the United States. The planners evidenced a tendency to overestimate production and to allocate more materials than were available. In order to keep the workers happy and hopeful they felt the necessity of making handsome promises for the future, and of constantly expanding the social services. But the fulfillment of these grand hopes depended on many uncertainties. In the first place would America buy the increased production offered to the western market by Denmark and Norway and Sweden and Iceland and Finland? Additional influential and possibly disastrous incalculables included the effect of weather on agriculture, the perennial uncertainties of fishing, and man-made difficulties such as strikes. National planning on a four-year basis was far from a certain thing.

Along with increasing exports each of these countries arrived at a higher degree of self-sufficiency; for example, the Swedes hoped to raise all their own bread grains and to increase their production of sugar. This decline in buying from abroad and increase of selling abroad could produce domestic prosperity only if world conditions improved greatly and a vigorous multilateral trade could be reëstablished. Attempts at special bilateral trade such as that between Iceland and Russia and the famous Russian-Swedish trade agreement had shown themselves incapable of producing even much temporary advantage.

Despite the grand projects a sad but unexpressed fact was obvious in most of the plans: a lowered standard of living, at least in the next decade. Norway, Denmark, and Finland had already accepted stringent limitations on their ambitions; Sweden and Iceland might have to do so. The plans looked forward to balance in the economies by 1952–53; they did not provide for the overbalance which would provide repayment for the assistance given during reconstruction. Only over a longer period of time, with considerably increased production, and in a world at peace and in friendly economic intercourse, could the Scandinavian countries attain their economic and social goals.

If such goals could be realized anywhere the Scandinavians had a right to think that their region might be the place. For these peoples were willing to work and able to plan. They had achieved in the prewar epoch a high degree of economic and social well-being. Perhaps most important of all, they had evidenced the possibilities of planned work through the intelligently combined efforts of the academic, the economically productive, and the political groups in society.

3. WHAT IS THE MIDDLE WAY?

To a group of American students in Oslo in 1948 the Norwegian minister of commerce, Erik Brofoss, gave a brilliant and persuasive statement of social democratic policy. The state and society, said Brofoss, are perpetually revaluing old concepts, seeking the consummation of a better society. Twentieth-century private business has come to be characterized by trusts and cartels; production is organized for private advantage. But the state desires to gain advantage for all consumers. Private inheritance or wealth by itself should not entitle one to a privileged position. Wealth is really a possession of society, a social inheritance or a social product, and the proprietor is only entrusted with its administration. Workers should be treated as equals in a common productive effort; they should participate in management, share in the responsibility for the national economy. They deserve that incentive. Workers must feel the meaning of their work.

The need for initiative applies to workers as much as to capitalist entrepreneurs; the efficiency of workers depends upon their conviction that efficiency redounds to their advantage as well as to that of the capitalists. But the interest of small industrial groups and the interest of the country as a whole are not always synonymous.

Brofoss reminded his attentive listeners from west of the Atlantic that universal suffrage was once regarded as revolutionary, but that it came to be looked upon as a fundamental right. Similarly the right of worker participation should now be regarded as fundamental. Society should determine what is to happen, not merely adjust to what does happen. The difficulties of any economic system are due not to nature but to man, so man should attempt to make himself the master . . . Brofoss was giving voice to the attitude of Scandinavian social democracy as a whole. His basic philosophy was in complete accord with the 27-point postwar program of Swedish labor, of Danish and Finnish and Icelandic practice.

How revolutionary is such a program? Is it a "middle way," a separate path between the right-hand path of capitalism, democracy, and individual freedom, and the left-hand path of communism, dictatorship, and mass thinking? Or is the so-called middle way merely a diagonal lane beginning in the right-hand lane, but veering inevitably across into the left-hand lane?

The final answer to these questions must be left to the future. Now one can say only that the planners in Scandinavia intend to drive straight down an independent center lane. They are not on "the road to serfdom." They are concerned not with theories but with immediate problems and practical solutions.

The essential difference between the socio-economic program in the Scandinavian countries and in the United States lies in the role played by government. In Scandinavia the government tries to avoid coercion, but it does frankly assume leadership. It plans for basic facilities and the use of natural resources, though usually leaving private business to effectuate the plans. It sets efficiency, stability of employment, and income equalization as definite goals. It therefore controls and limits the profits of the entrepreneur and emphasizes security for the worker, who is least able to assure it for himself. It seeks to raise the standard of living, measured in terms of health, education, and material conveniences. And it bases this whole program on a combination of the rights of every person as a human being and the responsibility of the community for all its members. What does the balance sheet show as the results of this program?

On the debit side there are complaints because of restrictions on employers, because of regulation of wage rates, because more power is given to labor unions and more authority to government. In Scandinavia as in the United States even successful businessmen complain bitterly of the government and object to the increased expense of government and to the high taxes. Some warn of the danger of paternalism and a weakening of the individual's "lust for work."

On the credit side there are better living conditions, a sense of security, improved education, hospitals, and insurance, and in industry sustained production. There is pride in work and skill, and in the achievements of social democracy. There is group action through coöperatives, the church, unions, and government. But these associations are not ends in themselves. Everything is for the sake of the person. The Scandinavians never lose sight of the persistent individualism which is their heritage and their character.

Has Scandinavia read Karl Marx? Scandinavia read him before Russia did. His materialistic emphasis was congenial, but the idea of mass revolution of the proletariat was not—was not every Viking a chieftain? Scandinavia was far on the road toward its own moderate pattern of social and economic reform before the Communist Revolution in Russia. The influence from the East has been only incidental; the real roots of Scandinavian social philosophy are in the West. This fact is often forgotten in Scandinavia itself because of the present overshadowing importance of Russia, and because of the concept of the middle way. Only in Finland has Russian influence been significant, and even there it has not attained ideological predominance. The North has developed a socialist modification of western democratic capitalism, pragmatic and moderate rather than doctrinaire or extreme.

There is some reason to question, as did an engineer in north Sweden in 1948, how different in actual result are the systems of Scandinavia and of the United States. In the United States one thinks of the "American Way" as quite different from the middle way. Yet this engineer pointed out that the working of the American income tax gives the lower-income groups more than they get in Sweden, through liberal exemptions which leave the American worker with a larger income both absolutely and proportionally. Therefore, he said, the United States is more socialized (or more "equalized") than Sweden even though the American worker is left with more choices to make in spending his money. Many of the differences one sees on the surface are indeed differences in technique rather than in social effect.

"Control of the few, freedom for the many"—is the essence of the Scandinavian program. It is a "mixed" system, capitalist in form, yet directed by governments imbued with socialist philosophy. It aims at the central ideal of western thought, and simultaneously at the basic goal of communist principle; it seeks both political democracy and economic security. If it can hold to its course it is a real middle way, a central lane in the twentieth-century highway of an engineered society.

6. Neutrality: Tradition, Policy, and Practice (to 1939)

The Scandinavians learned generations back that war "does not regard the neutral powers," that a state which would keep out of war must take care of herself. From the sixteenth to the eighteenth century, as the concept of neutrality evolved, the problem was mainly to gain rights for peoples not participating in war. In the nineteenth and twentieth centuries warring states insisted that obligations must accompany rights, and that states claiming neutral privileges must also obey certain rules. In the evolution of treaties and practices concerning these rights and obligations of neutrality the Scandinavian states have played a prominent part.

It must be emphasized from the beginning, however, that neutrals were not always pious proponents of international law, and not necessarily pacifist. They were pursuing their special interests through neutrality while others were striving for their interests through war. They might fight at another time, and they usually stood ready to fight if their interests were seriously challenged. Neutrality was expediency.

Whatever consistency developed, it came only as relative power and diplomatic and economic position assumed a static character. Through the eighteenth century the Scandinavian states were still unconvinced of their peaceful destiny; they were alternately belligerents and neutrals, and their policies alternated accordingly. Opportunism remained a characteristic of neutrality, however, even after peace became a permanent goal.

The opportunistic, catch-as-catch-can aspect of neutrality was clearly stated by Christian Günther, Sweden's foreign minister, in 1943:

A policy which does not take account of the actual situation of the moment, but stands on a preconceived doctrine without asking where it leads *then*—such is no policy at all, but pure bravado at a time when the whole world is rocking. Sweden's neutrality policy has been formed by world events in these fateful years, there is no reason to hide the fact under the bed and it needs no excuses.*

Günther's statement explains why Sweden's policy shifted like a weather vane during World War II, and was a better indication than the stock market of how the fortunes of war were treating the warring powers. This policy was the product of experience deep-rooted in the past, and the story of that experience is important for an understanding of twentieth-century policy and attitude.

1. SEARCHING FOR A POLICY, 1600–1814

Far back in history the Scandinavian states were trying to adjust themselves to changing circumstances of war and peace. Sweden, for example, fighting in the early seventeenth century against Poland in the eastern Baltic, tried to prohibit all trade with Riga. This exclusion hurt Danish commerce. So Denmark protested and soon was at war with Sweden. Denmark then did to others what had been done to her; she forbade all shipping into Swedish ports. This in turn roused Holland and Lübeck to agree to defend their commerce by force of arms. This agreement, joined by Sweden in 1614, never came into force, otherwise it might have been the first modern "armed neutrality." But the northern states continued to frame regulations on siege and contraband, and to seek for rules which would safeguard them when at war, yet which would permit trade.

* *Svensk neutralitetspolitik under stormaktskriget* (pamphlet); May 7, 1943.

During the Thirty Years' War both Denmark and Sweden still issued general interdictions of commerce. But as their relative power declined the interests of trade grew paramount over the interests of military advantage. The Baltic trade was a thing of importance to all northern and western Europe, so important that on one occasion it caused the western naval powers to intervene to end a Danish-Swedish war which obstructed commerce.

When a new phase of great power war began in 1689, Holland and Great Britain sought to strangle France by a total blockade. French privateers retaliated against the Dutch and English from Danish territorial waters. The Danes and the Swedes began action to defend their trade. A Swedish suggestion of 1672 was acted upon, and when the Dutch seized Danish ships sailing to France the Danes confiscated Dutch ships in Denmark. Joint Danish-Swedish convoys were established. The Dutch at once began to come around, first offering to let forty-five Danish ships trade with France, then suggesting money compensation for ships seized. Perhaps the innocent bystander had found the means to defend himself.

Sweden and Denmark were encouraged, and in 1691 made an agreement for the first active armed neutrality. They insisted upon freedom of navigation, retaliation, joint convoys, and joint action if warfare resulted. Within three months Holland and England persuaded Denmark to modify her demands, but the armed neutrality treaty was reinstated in 1693.

For a moment it appeared that the Scandinavian combination might win respect: English privateers against France were instructed to capture ships attempting to enter blockaded ports, *except* that ships of Denmark and Sweden were not to be molested unless, after warning, they made a second attempt to enter. This concession to the united neutrals, however, endured for only three years.

When Denmark and Sweden were at war against each other, and it happened again and again in those days, they issued decrees that sounded just like those decrees of the western powers which they denounced in periods of their own neutrality. They also coöperated occasionally, as during the Seven Years' War after France had induced them to rebuild an Armed Neutrality. Sweden tried to insist that "free ships make free goods," but this clause was omitted from the treaty, for the wily Danish Minister Bernstorff (J. H. E.) wanted his own freedom either to insist on restitutions or to remain inactive "as existing contingencies and the national interests should require." The following year France inveigled Sweden into war and thus ended Swedish-Danish collaboration.

During the wars of the mid-eighteenth century both Sweden and Denmark-Norway tested the policy of opening their ports to captors of both sides: "neutrality consisted in impartiality alone." Actually this worked out to help the French and not the British, for the French used Norwegian ports as bases for attacking British commerce and bringing in British prizes. But the British could not capture French ships in those waters for the simple reason that French commerce did not use those routes. The British argued that impartiality should mean total exclusion of all ships, and retaliated by violations of Danish territorial waters. Bernstorff insisted that the British were wrong legally, and eventually the British admitted it (to themselves!) but not until they awoke to the fact that they were doing from Mediterranean ports exactly what they objected to the French doing from Norwegian ports.

The goddess of neutrality was not only fickle, she was acquisitive. In the latter part of the eighteenth century the northern countries plied a vigorous trade with the Far East, and were keenly aware of opportunities for commercial advantage, particularly the advantages which opened to them when the imperialist powers went to war with one another. At the same time the Scandinavians began to feel a vague fear of American competition in their iron and other trade. During the American Revolution a Swedish statesman wrote in his diary,

What future may this greatest field of Swedish commerce expect if the English colonies win their independence and they, in peace and with liberty's stimulus, carry all such undertakings to that height to which their country with so much advantages seems to entice them? *

Bernstorff gave a more thorough analysis of the same fears in his Memorial to the King of Denmark, March 1780.

Britain was the most important customer for northern goods, and her prosperity was therefore vital even to those who defied her overweening naval power. They could not live happily with her, but their trade could not live at all without her. Hence the small countries of the North, like the big countries of the East and the West, made strong statements of policy, but were ready quickly to reverse themselves. All were seeking immediate advantage.

The Armed Neutrality of 1780 followed the pattern. It was born out of a temporary community of interests between Denmark, Sweden, and Russia, with some stimulation from France; it was in force briefly; it disintegrated, and soon every one of its members was applying principles contrary to those of the treaty. For the moment the allies wanted a vigorous neutral commerce, and each had separate ambitions as well: Russia was annoyed by American attacks on British commerce to Archangel, and both Denmark and Sweden had territorial ambitions in the western hemisphere.

The neutral league was built on a plan outlined by Count A. P. Bernstorff, the Danish foreign minister, in 1778, and restated by the Empress Catherine of Russia. Denmark and Sweden agreed in 1779 to convoy their merchantmen, Russia was ready to act in the waters north of Norway, and in 1780 they all got together. The principles of the Armed Neutrality of 1780 can be summed up as:

1. Neutral vessels may navigate freely port to port and on coasts of the powers at war.
2. Property of belligerents on neutral vessels is to be free, except contraband.

* *Dagboksanteckningar förda vid Gustaf III's Hof af Friherre Gustaf Johan Ehrensvärd* . . . (2 v., Stockholm, 1878, II, 115).

3. Contraband is that which is so listed in treaties of Sweden and Russia with Great Britain.
4. Blockade is to be recognized only if it is effective.

Benjamin Franklin had been aware of the negotiations regarding the neutral league since 1778. In October 1780 the United States Congress passed a resolution agreeing to the principles of the Armed Neutrality, and in December Francis Dana was authorized to sign treaties on such bases with any neutral nation. Dana then discovered to his embarrassment that the alliance was for neutrals only, and for the duration of the war only. The United States was still willing to negotiate a peacetime treaty, but not to pledge armed support. The first American treaty with Sweden, April 3, 1783, did incorporate the principle of "free ships free goods," and thus opened the path of official Scandinavian American relations.

Early in the period of the French Revolution Sweden and Denmark-Norway combined again to protect their neutral commerce. France was issuing restrictive decrees, but also appealed to the Scandinavian countries, to the United States, to Turkey and Poland and Genoa to form a neutral league. Sweden and Denmark actually concluded an agreement in 1794, providing for armed support of their shipping and the closing of the Baltic to belligerent vessels. The Swedes approached the United States about acceding to the agreement, but the Danes thought America would be more of a liability than an asset for action in the North.

Meantime Greville played the British cards cleverly. He was helped by the fact that American statesmen were working at cross purposes: Alexander Hamilton informed the British that the United States would not join the Scandinavian alliance in any case, while Thomas Jefferson was doing everything possible to frighten the lords of the sea. Russia now stood with Britain instead of with Scandinavia, and the Empress Catherine threatened to station her fleet in the Baltic to prevent Scandinavian ships from sailing for France. The Armed Neutrality could get no subsidies, and soon died. As Gouverneur Morris said, it was "a demonstration of a force and a temper which do not exist."

No issues were settled. In the late 1790's the northern neutrals resumed their struggle for free trade. For them it was primarily a conflict with Britain, while the United States was fighting a naval war against France for the same rights. The mad Czar Paul took vigorous action against British ships and proposed a new Armed Neutrality. The Scandinavians, with some trepidation, accepted in December 1800, and Prussia also. For a few months there was a war of decrees, but the death of Paul (March 1801) and the British attack on Copenhagen brought the neutrals quickly to book.

The treaties provided a British compromise: ships might navigate freely to the coasts of the enemy, and a port was to be considered blockaded only if there was real danger in entering; provisions and ordinary naval stores were not contraband; "honest purchase" made goods neutral; search was proper, but only by regular naval vessels; neutrals could resist privateers but only privateers; on a neutral ship the captain and one-half his crew must be natives of the neutral country; and neutrals could not carry colonial goods from colony to enemy mother country (except that they were to enjoy most favored nation status).

In the years which followed, Denmark-Norway became of less political and economic importance, but Sweden's commerce fattened rapidly, especially in the period 1808–1813. Imports of cotton, wine, sugar, and tobacco increased astronomically; total goods in bond in Sweden grew from 511,000 Riksdalers in 1807 to 10,200,000 Riksdalers in 1813. Much of this goods found its way to Europe, through holes in the back fence of Napoleon's Continental System. This was the major reason for that extraordinary massing of 1200 merchant ships in the harbor of Gothenburg in 1812 (see pp. 76–77). Forty were American sailing, ironically enough, in British convoy at the moment the War of 1812 was declared. But Sweden's neutrality and her illicit commerce ended in 1813, as she fought her "war to end all wars," won Norway, and gave up her continental holdings.

Two centuries of neutral striving proved that effective neutrality must be armed neutrality. They proved also that the neutral purpose was to preserve commerce while others fought. The purpose was wholly reasonable, but it did not involve pacifism nor any other "higher morality." Rules were gradually formulated which established limits for both neutrality and war.

2. A CENTURY OF SUCCESS, 1814–1914

With 1814 began a new phase in Scandinavian neutrality. Up to that time the Scandinavian governments had attempted to make the most out of their occasional nonbelligerent status, but a change to war status was easy if advantages appeared, such as subsidies from France or Britain or a chance to win territory. Abstention from diplomatic bargaining and the international tug-of-war was not considered. But when Bernadotte became Crown Prince Carl Johan of Sweden he conceived of a new system: Finland, taken by the Russians in 1809, would be forgotten; the German territory of Pomerania would be renounced; Norway would be added to the Swedish kingdom in what looked to a French general like a natural geographical unit; and Sweden-Norway would withdraw forever from the quarrels of Europe. Denmark, beaten and deprived of her co-kingdom of Norway, was at the nadir of her fortunes and could think only of nursing her wounds and preserving what was left. Norway wanted only peace and as much of independence as she could get. The whole of Scandinavia was neutrality-minded, though the people did not indulge in much theorizing about it. The nineteenth and twentieth centuries spelled out the methods and developed the principles. Not only commerce but national existence was now at stake.

It was not always easy to sit back and let the rest of the world go its way, but the great powers helped. They said to themselves and to the world that the small states could not participate as equals in international affairs, and that the maintenance of the Concert of Europe was the job of the four (later five) chief military states. Even before the Congress of Vienna the lesser states were excluded from important councils. The kings of the Scandinavian lands and their foreign ministers looked on with interest at the diplomatic and military maneuvering to the south, and occasionally they were almost ready for trouble or for adventure. But the Greek Revolution and then the Near Eastern crisis of 1839–1841 passed without Scandinavian complications.

In the British-Russian tension of 1833–34 Sweden first approached Denmark for a joint declaration of neutrality, then issued her declaration alone. In 1840 King Carl Johan was ready to join Britain and Russia in war against France but Denmark refused coöperation and the King's Swedish advisers forced him to modify his position. Sweden was in a new position since the loss of Finland (1809), the separation of Denmark-Norway, and the creation of Sweden-Norway (1814). Now Russian territory reached far across the barren stretches north of Sweden, and Russian fortifications in the Åland Islands were eyed with fear.

In the Crimean War Denmark and Sweden-Norway declared neutrality in similar but independent announcements. Then Sweden in 1855 signed the November Treaty with Britain and France, pledging herself not to cede to Russia even so much as fishing or pasture rights in the Lapp lands of the Far North. The neutrality bases of 1834–1856 emphasized the right to trade with both Britain and Russia and the right to receive in port the naval vessels of both, a right which meant much more to Britain than it did to Russia. English vessels used the harbor of Fårösund on Gotland for two years during the war.

In general the descendants of the Vikings restrained themselves, outsiders let them alone, and luck was with them. At the close of the Crimean War Sweden got a guarantee of nonfortification in the Åland Islands, but she had antagonized Russia anew. At the same time there was rousing talk of a real

Scandinavian union. King Oscar I of Sweden-Norway, at a student festival, said that not only was war impossible between the Scandinavian states, but that "Our swords stand ready for our mutual defense." The next step was to invite Denmark into an alliance, including a guarantee for Slesvig. Sweden-Norway was pushing a more vigorous policy. But King Frederick of Denmark rejected the alliance and guarantee, and the shrewd Swedish foreign minister Ludvig Manderström soon led policy in calmer paths.

Karl XV, new king of Sweden, was for a bold support of cultural and political Pan-Scandinavianism, but he could not override the united opposition of his ministers, nor could he supply a strong military force, for both army and navy had fallen far behind in the past decade of rapid change elsewhere, especially in the use of steam in warships.

Militarily, the great threat and perhaps the great opportunity of the nineteenth century came in 1864 when Germanic aggression gobbled up Slesvig and Holstein, the two duchies which had been under the Danish crown. The Danes fought valiantly, but against hopeless odds. Karl XV's glib promises of Swedish aid yielded nothing, and France and Britain raised not a finger. Ibsen attacked passionately what he saw as the craven and calculating selfishness of the men in power. The Danes died alone; Pan-Scandinavianism and the dreams of a united State of the North died with them. Bismarck was on the march, and the contrast between large states and small was accentuated by the unification of Germany. The Swedes and the Norwegians and the Danes knew that the odds were against them more than ever. With a mixture of satisfaction and resignation they turned their energies into building up their internal economy and culture.

In the century and a quarter between 1814 and 1940 the only actual outbreaks of war in Scandinavia were in 1848–49 and in 1864, both in Denmark. But there were other threats, and there was constant attention to the problems of defense and of neutrality, particularly in Sweden. The Swedish minister Manderström is a good mirror and mouthpiece of the perennial principles of neutrality: "In political things it is not permissible to entertain sympathies and antipathies, at least not when one has no possibility to make his attitudes valid."

This was in 1866. The lack of power worried Manderström much—or did it merely give him an excuse not to act? When the Franco-Prussian war was threatening, Manderström told the French Minister that his hearty sympathies were with the French, but "what can we give them?" The Frenchman thereupon read Manderström a political sermon:

No European state [he said] can reasonably leave it to others to play the game of European politics without itself taking part and being prepared to take part. Sweden has no army and no fleet. Neutrality can be a great advantage for the moment, but is it so in the long run for a state like Sweden which lies isolated between two unscrupulous neighbors?

Manderström merely listened with resignation; within a week he learned that Russia would remain neutral, and he could heave a great sigh of relief—for the moment.

Meantime Sweden's notes to Prussia urging a plebiscite in Slesvig were brushed aside because Prussia saw in Sweden neither the force nor the will to act. A frank renunciation of influence abroad was written into the Swedish King's speech from the throne in January, 1867:

Without any desire to participate in the solution of the problems which disturb or threaten to disturb other parts of Europe, I have well-founded hope that the united kingdoms, surrounded on all sides by natural frontiers, shall continuingly be able to enjoy the blessings of peace.

Could isolationist neutrality be more bluntly or more complacently stated?

In later years the Rigsdag in Denmark passed various resolutions in favor of neutrality on a permanent legalized basis, but the government did nothing to implement the resolutions. Norway, after 1907, strove to obtain an international guarantee of her integrity and her neutrality. She obtained a guarantee only of integrity.

Of all the talk and all the hope the most practical neutrality act came after the separation of Norway from Sweden in 1905. Tempers had been strained by long tension, and the wounded sensibility of the Swedes was as inflammable as the nationalistic pride of the Norwegians. Yet the Swedes swallowed hard and then formulated some sensible demands; the Norwegians had the good sense and courage to accept them. The result was that Norway went in peace out of the union with Sweden; the boundary in the long mountains between them was neutralized; all forts on the border were demolished, and perpetual friendship was pledged. The Swedish-Norwegian frontier, the boundaries of Switzerland, and the frontiers between the United States and Canada (since 1817) stand as examples to the world of effective neutralization.

3. THE TESTING OF NEUTRALITY, 1914–1918

During the years of calm after 1905 the Scandinavian states issued joint regulations on neutrality (1912), but the effective coöperation between them began after the storm broke in 1914. The holocaust on the continent was an immediate threat to the whole of Scandinavia. The people showed their fears by runs on banks, and by hoarding of foods. Banks and governments reacted differently at first, but all recognized the existence of an overwhelming outside force over whose actions they had no control. The Scandinavian peoples became imbued with a sense of weakness in their innocence, of uncertainty from day to day, of want through no fault of their own, and of a deep disillusionment in the good faith and intelligence of men.

Declarations of neutrality were issued independently by the three governments, Norway, Sweden, and Denmark, but they were similarly phrased. (Finland was still a Russian archduchy, and Iceland was subordinate to Denmark.) Supplementary declarations by Norway and Sweden, agreed on in the last days of July 1914 on the suggestion of the Swedish foreign minister, gave mutual pledges that Norway and Sweden would under no circumstances attack each other—declarations considered necessary because of the bitter feelings and suspicions surviving from the separation of 1905. By the twelfth of November the first joint note of protest was sent to the warring powers by the three Scandinavian states, and a practice was instituted which continued to annoy the belligerents throughout the war. The United States was also sending its notes and several times the various governments of the North suggested coöperation in this work with the United States. But the United States never accepted the proposals.

The Scandinavian states could act in unison because many of their complaints were similar, and many of their needs. After they had begun to work together it was easy to continue, and the old ill feeling rapidly disappeared. King Gustav V of Sweden took the initiative in calling a meeting of the sovereigns of the three countries in Malmö (December 1914), his first meeting with King Haakon of Norway since the incidents of 1905. The foreign ministers met several times during the war and established firmer and firmer bonds. The very differences in personalities and interests helped; for example, Minister Ihlen of Norway was a businessman and was concerned primarily with practical ways of getting things done. Hjalmar Hammarskiöld, Swedish prime minister, was trained and experienced in international law, and interested in doing things in the correct way. Hence it was mutually agreeable that the Swedish chancery compose the official protests which were signed by all.

The Declaration of Paris of 1856 concerning blockade and other aspects of international law during war, the Declaration of London of 1909, and the whole accumulation of custom on neutrality was assumed to be fundamental and dependable. In the first few weeks of war both Britain and Germany acted in accordance with these recognized principles, and for practical purposes it was only these two states with whom Scandinavia was concerned until the United States entered the war in 1917. The Scandinavians maintained, as did the Americans (1914–1917) that neutrals had a right to trade whatever they would, except contraband, with whomever they would. This meant that the neutrals of the North might become important suppliers of Germany, both directly and indirectly, and the British could not tolerate this aid to the enemy, if they could prevent it.

By the twentieth of August 1914, the British restrictions on neutral trade were tightened, and there began the process by which the old maritime laws of war were torn to shreds. "Conditional contraband" lists were extended time after time. When iron ore was first put on the list, September 21, the Swedes got it removed by direct negotiation, but the British found other ways to check its shipment to Germany. In October Germany began to seize neutral ships in the Baltic and to take them to German ports for search, instead of conducting the search at the point of hail. The Scandinavian states became worried not only over export trade, but particularly over their ability to import food and raw materials. Denmark needed fodder and coal, Norway normally obtained all her coal from England, Sweden imported one-third of her cereals: all Scandinavia was dependent on foreign trade.

It was this combination of circumstances which led to the joint Scandinavian note of November 12, 1914, sent to Britain, Russia, France, and Germany. The note protested against the closing of shipping lanes by mines, against the extensions of the right of search, and against the wide interpretation given to conditional contraband. One immediate gain was that the trade route north of Scotland was not completely closed. But as the conflict grew more tense the belligerents paid less attention to the innocent bystanders. Ships with food and necessary raw materials were delayed in English ports, blown up by mines, torpedoed by German submarines; factories had to be closed because raw materials could not cross the oceans. Prices rose to an index figure of 300–400 compared with 1913. Fishermen sold their catch at fantastic prices, sometimes thirty times the prewar price, and without even taking the cargo into port. Wages rose too, but there was little to buy. Housing construction ceased. "Coffee" was stewed from roots; the brew was brown and warm, but bitter. Scandinavia was at peace, but her life was debased by war.

SHIPPING LOSSES 1914–1918
(In gross tonnage)

Year	Denmark	Norway	Sweden
1914	11,176	11,902	9,875
1915	20,621	94,206	32,863
1916	59,321	276,861	42,844
1917	123,600	659,949	65,976
1918	28,989	137,398	49,808
	243,707	1,180,316	201,366

Shipping had a double importance for the Scandinavian countries: the carrying trade as a business, and the import-export of goods. Norway's huge fleet was the chief means of earning foreign exchange for the country as a whole. Some 150 Norwegian boats, for example, were engaged in carrying coal from Britain to France, and the importance of their activity can be seen from the statistics of January and February 1916, when at Cardiff ships from the following countries loaded:

Japan	3	Sweden	36
Uruguay	4	Greece	40
Portugal	4	Italy	45
Russia	9	Spain	61
Netherlands	11	Britain	120
Belgium	14	France	124
Denmark	21	Norway	242

The Germans were understandably eager to destroy this neutral aid to the enemy, and they succeeded to a tragic extent. In the last months of 1916, as Germany stepped up her submarine war, Norway lost 143 ships amounting to 201,000 tons. Despite the frenzied attacks of 1917 the Norwegians sailed on, but in March they lost 106,000 tons and in April 102,000, and the War Insurance Organization had to make a levy on its members to pay a deficit of 118,000,000 kroner. All in all Norway lost 49.3 per cent of her 1914 tonnage and 1162 lives (really one must add 67 ships and 943 men that "disappeared"). Denmark had a smaller fleet and lost fewer ships, but the problem became serious for her in 1917. Sweden, with a fleet about one-third as large as Norway's, lost proportionately, including some 800 lives. To these direct losses must of course be added the loss of markets for fish and timber and ore, the enforced idleness of ships and crews in foreign ports, and of factories at home. Oceans had ceased to be paths of commerce; they were preëmpted as the playing fields of belligerent powers. Both coal and food became short enough to cause real if minor suffering (Swedish supplies of wheat and rye were 55 per cent lower in 1917–18 than in 1913). To alleviate these war-borne difficulties many devices were improvised. Diplomatic protests sometimes gained petty concessions, but in the main the warring powers were ready to attack whatever came in their way. Convoys were tried, but did not succeed very well, and there developed no "armed neutrality league" on the old pattern.

In the latter part of the war Britain furnished armed escort for commerce of interest to her, for she grew worried that neutral shipping might be driven from the seas. She tried to force ships to stay in service by making them promise to return with cargoes to English ports, and she would release from port one neutral ship only when a compatriot ship arrived.

The Scandinavian countries too were concerned to maintain supply routes. To protect her harbors Denmark mined her own waters in the first days of the war, and Sweden mined some passages in 1916. Both Norway and Sweden issued new and drastic regulations on the use of their waters by submarines. The Scandinavian governments set up or aided the setting up of special war insurance boards: the Danish government underwrote 35 per cent of ship losses; the Norwegian 40 per cent of losses of cargo, while the shipowners arranged their own tonnage insurance. Export prohibitions attempted to keep at home dwindling stocks of foods and other necessities.

Most interesting of the devices for neutral living in that chaotic world were the agreements negotiated by the Northern countries for "compensation trade." Here the Scandinavian hope of self-preservation joined with the self-interest of the warring powers. Both Germany and Britain obtained important goods and services from these neutral neighbors and were therefore interested in letting them live. These goods and services could not continue unless the Scandinavians in turn obtained necessary supplies.

Agreements were made for carefully balancing trade, for "compensations" each way in return for concessions. In Sweden this was arranged partly through "Transito," a private joint-stock company, supposedly Swedish, but actually controlled through the British Legation in Stockholm; Transito effected a partial reconciliation between the interests of Sweden and the Allies, permitting imports to Sweden, but forcing Swedish merchants to agree not to reëxport to Britain's enemies. By agreements begun in March 1915 Sweden allowed the export of dairy products, meat, and horses to Germany, in return for which Germany agreed to send to Sweden coal, potash, fertilizers, salt, drugs, and some iron and steel (processed from Swedish ore). The need for a strict balance resulted in some drastic changes. For example, in peacetime Sweden had bought about 90 per cent of her coal from Britain, but during the war about 47 per cent (down to 27 per cent in 1917), while 53 per cent was obtained from Germany. By 1917 Sweden had to permit 90,000 tons of timber to go to Britain in order to obtain safe passage for 19 shiploads of grain from Halifax. Sweden also had to limit her iron ore export to Germany to 3,500,000 tons, and to charter 400,000 tons of her shipping to the Allies.

Such agreements with Britain placed a neutral state's entire shipping in the "enemy" category in German eyes (after April 1918); but Germany was willing to make exceptions and to issue letters of safe-conduct to neutral vessels which pledged that they were only supplying their own people. Most Scandinavian ships which were not under charter to the Allies used this safe-conduct system.

Early in the war Denmark and Norway began more general agreements with the Allies. The governments were of course interested, but the agreements were made by private business organizations in Denmark and Norway on the one hand, with the British government on the other. Norwegian fishermen had to obtain their coal, salt, and hemp from Britain and the British objected to supplying this equipment for the Norwegians to catch and sell fish to the Germans. In January 1916 the British government set aside £10,000,000 for "blockade buying" of the fish-catch; in July they arranged to take 85 per cent of the catch, at a fixed price in a rising market. On Norwegian insistence they permitted 15 per cent to be freely exported to Germany.

This agreement for a meager 15 per cent incensed the Germans and led to a period of submarine retaliation against the Norwegians. At this stage Britain and France permitted Norway to make some additional concessions to Germany; they did not want to have Norway forced into war even on their side, for the extension of their defense zone would have been a heavy burden. But Britain held a firm grip, and in December 1916 prohibited the export of coal to Norway until the Norwegians settled the fish and pyrites question to their satisfaction; it was the use of "economic sanctions." By June of 1917 Britain chartered most of the remaining Norwegian merchant fleet, sent it to distant and safer waters, and with her own armed vessels took over commercial operations in the North Sea. In May 1918 the Norwegians signed an agreement with the United States further limiting their shipments to Germany, guaranteeing certain products to the Allies, and getting permission for food and raw material imports.

Denmark agreed to the British demand not to reëxport contraband to Germany, but insisted that she could sell noncontraband. In general Denmark is, however, the best example of the mutual tolerance showed by the belligerents, and for a simple reason. She sold food to Germany, but in order to produce food she had to import animal fodder from Britain; to get this fodder she must obviously also sell food to Britain. The Germans, in order to get some food from Denmark, tacitly allowed this trade, and in one case captured and then deliberately released two ships bound with food for Britain.

The Danes knew that they must play a careful game and a scrupulously fair one. When they found that a higher price in Germany was attracting an abnormal export of pork to the south they quickly set up a Home Office board which fixed prices and established export quotas on the basis of prewar trade. Thus 75 per cent of the pork exports went to Britain, most of the rest to Germany. In 1915 butter was treated in the same way, and in 1916 eggs, too. In 1917 butter and pork were put on a 50-50 basis, because Denmark had to obtain additional supplies from Germany—Britain had cut down drastically on her exports to Denmark, and the United States had begun to clamp down on fodder. In September Denmark too was forced to put half her fleet at the service of the Allies.

Keeping pace with the increasing tempo of the war the Scandinavian countries had to adapt themselves increasingly to belligerent demands. They struggled for freedom of action, but became more and more circumscribed, and yielded to force of necessity. Both Britain and Germany permitted or aided these countries to obtain supplies, but on a basis which limited those goods to domestic needs. In essence Britain and Germany, at war with one another, determined rations of coal and grain and coffee and raw materials for the "independent" neutrals of the North.

Did the neutrality of 1914–1918 profit the Scandinavian lands? It is a question which cannot be answered. Granted the original fact of war it is obvious that the Scandinavian countries were fortunate not to be drawn in. They avoided destruction and bloodshed and a part of the social disruption that comes with war. But it would be untenable to suggest that these peoples earned a positive profit because there was war around them. Prices rose to levels three to five times as high as those of 1913, and a few individuals reaped rich rewards. Governments, because of the early profits from trade and commerce, were enabled to pay off up to two-thirds of their foreign debts and their citizens became owners of many foreign-built enterprises. But markets were disrupted, wartime trade was often artificial and temporary, destruction of shipping was tremendous, wage rates and currencies were thrown out of balance, and the Scandinavian monetary union was destroyed. New agricultural crops were stimulated, but did not last. And the devastation and unrest in neighboring lands became a serious burden for Scandinavia.

Only two territorial changes affected the North directly: the Danish acquisition of North Slesvig and the independence of Finland. Prussia had in 1864 promised a plebiscite in North Slesvig, but had never held it. German defeat brought it at last after World War I. The voting showed a considerable penetration of German people and influence since the 1860's but brought to Denmark by clear popular choice 184,000 people and 984 square miles of territory in the fertile Jutland peninsula. Here was a satisfying example of historical rectification.

Another factor which can be recorded on the positive side of the ledger was the wartime impetus to Scandinavian coöperation. From July 29, 1914 on to the end of the war this coöperation grew and spread, diminishing old antagonisms and building new foundations for useful working together. This might have happened anyway but the war and the common problems and practice of neutrality hastened the process.

In trade the first effect of the war was to diminish intra-Scandinavian business, because of the concessions demanded from the individual countries by the belligerents. In March 1917 a Scandinavian trade representatives' meeting in Stockholm reversed this trend and thereafter private and official committees worked successfully to expand the internal trade. In 1917 Denmark sold to Sweden 50,000,000 kr. worth of butter, pork, cheese, and eggs, and in 1918 doubled the amount; Norway sent to Sweden 54,000 tons of salt herring in 1918, "which met all the requirements of Sweden in this foodstuff"; Sweden sold to her neighbors iron and steel, lumber, paper, and glassware. This trade, entered into without precise contracts, showed the value of mutual interest and understanding, and laid the basis for later expansion.

Governmental activity was greatly stimulated by the needs of war. In many cases private associations of businessmen and shippers in the three Scandinavian countries dealt as groups with foreign governments, indicating the preservation of "free enterprise" even in a wartime emergency. Yet the shadow of government overcast the deliberations of these private groups, and by the end of the war the governments had assumed vastly increased powers. A government commission in Denmark allocated export quotas, and levied an embargo against certain exports; government fixed prices on food and underwrote shipping insurance. In Norway the government was authorized to forbid the laying-up of privately owned ships, local councils were empowered to fix maximum prices, agriculture was made compulsory, and various commissions and ministries were established: Fish Department, Fat Board, Food Ministry, and Ministry of Industrial Supplies. In Sweden the same things happened, including export prohibitions and licenses, a State Commerce Commission, and an Import Regulation Board. Centralization and the direction of economic activities by the state became a wartime habit and was never entirely discarded.

In short, despite neutrality, the Scandinavian lands experienced many of the same forces and tendencies as did the nations at war.

4. AN ERA OF WIDENED COÖPERATION, 1918–1939

Scandinavia relaxed in November 1918 and settled down to work on a philosophy of *"as if* we shall be left in peace." Serious soul-searching preceded the decisions to join the League of Nations. Independent neutrality had been strengthened by regional coöperation from 1914 to 1918 and had kept the North out of battle. Why should these peoples, who had no aggressive ambitions, get involved in the sanctions system of the League? The Covenant appeared to outlaw neutrality, and when a Dane asked about it Lord Robert Cecil replied that a member of the League had three obligations: 1. To stop commercial relations with a state breaking the peace; 2. To authorize passage of League forces across its territory; 3. To participate in military and naval action.

The Danes and the Swiss agreed that a neutral could break commercial relations, but that it could not take the other steps. The League insisted that all must be prepared to defend the right and quell the wrong. The Scandinavians remained skeptical, and they debated anxiously the whole problem of their international position. The Norwegian Labor Party voted *no* because of its distrust of great power idealism. In the end the Scandinavians all joined the League, but they considered that they were abandoning neutrality in doing so. Once in, they acted energetically and intelligently.

One of the little known but significant chapters of League success was the settlement of the Åland Islands controversy. The islands between Sweden and Finland had been settled by Swedes and had remained Swedish in culture and speech. In 1809 Russia had included them in her annexation of Finland. When Finland gained her independence at the end of World War I the Ålands were thus legally a part of Finland. The Swedes hoped, however, that the principle of self-determination might be applied there as in Slesvig and other areas which were changing hands. Niney-five per cent of the people of

Åland voted for reunion with Sweden. The League Council heard the question debated, and its *rapporteurs* then took the legalistic position that Finnish sovereignty was incontestable. The decision involved a closely related people eager to join Sweden, and it also involved a vital security problem for Sweden, for the islands are a perfect base for attack against Stockholm by sea or air. Nevertheless Sweden accepted the situation with good grace, and did her part toward strengthening international law and the authority of the League in its infant years.

These small states were often useful in avoiding open clashes in the League between the great powers. At one time the British opposed a French proposal in the Council, but dared not say so because of public opinion on the issue. The British delegation wired home for instructions, and got the cryptic reply: "Britain expects every Swede to do his duty." The Swede blocked the proposal and Britain was saved from taking a public stand.

The jealousies of the great powers, the absence of the United States, and the shortsightedness of weak statesmen, however, soon made the League a feeble instrument. No one could find a formula for disarmament; Britain and Germany went off by themselves in a naval agreement of 1935; and the League could only issue a report on the Japanese invasion of Manchuria. The Scandinavians became irritated at the failure to apply effective sanctions in the Ethiopian affair. In July 1936 they joined with the Netherlands, Switzerland, and Spain in a note claiming the right to determine when and how to apply sanctions, a right which the great powers were in practice exercising.

Norway debated complete independence of action and Ludwig Mowinckel, minister of commerce, held out for unconditional neutrality. Halvdan Koht and the Labor Party, however, thinking of the possibility of League action against Nazi Germany, secured approval of a resolution which provided that "absolute neutrality" did not have to apply in case of a war recognized by the Storting as a League of Nations action (May 31, 1938).

Self-interest as well as idealism led the Scandinavians toward international collaboration. Yet the collaboration must include the great powers as well as the small, to be useful or acceptable. As a Frenchman said at the time, European statesmen could depend on the North "if we do not oblige these peoples to despair of our power and of our ability to realize our ideals." But despair was growing, and with it a renewed tendency to look inward.

"Our frontier is within our boundaries, not at the border-lines," a Swedish scholar-statesman wrote for an American audience. He went farther: "Our modest claim is that we are uninteresting nations from the point of view of foreign relations." This smug boast reminds one of Benjamin Franklin's comment that there could not be a really modest man, for if there were such a one he would be proud of his modesty.

In 1938 and 1939 the Scandinavians felt anxious, but also superior and self-satisfied, and it was in this frame of mind that they proceeded in 1938, in the months between January and July, to withdraw completely from the sanctions system. Chamberlain admitted that the League could not offer collective security, and that Britain should not lead the small states to think they were protected. Halvdan Koht, then foreign minister of Norway, was one of the leaders in the series of moves which led to a formal joint declaration in Copenhagen, July 1938, by the seven states of the Oslo Group: "The system of sanctions under the present conditions and by the practice of recent years, has acquired a non-obligatory character."

The Scandinavian states, disappointed in the League, were going to go their own way, but characteristically they thought they should tell the world so in legal fashion.

Since 1856 the Åland Islands had been demilitarized, and in 1921 the agreement had been strengthened. But in 1938, with the powers flexing their steel muscles, Sweden and Finland thought they should relax the "extremely rigorous neutrality requirements," and permit fortification on the Åland Islands. A German geographer had been studying the islands, just as others were active in the fjords of Norway. The ten states signatory to the Åland Agreement were willing to approve the Swedish-Finnish plan, but Russia objected, and nothing was accomplished before the general war broke out in 1939.

The temperature of diplomacy continued to rise; the nazis "Anschlussed" Austria and absorbed Czechoslovakia. It began to look as if Munich might not even bring "peace in our time." President Roosevelt in the spring of 1939 asked if Germany's other neighbors were safe, and Hitler replied in a direct question to each: did it feel threatened? Each quivered and replied "Of course not." When Hitler offered to each a nonaggression pact Denmark felt it impossible to refuse. Finland had a pact of friendship since 1932 with Russia and begged off. Sweden discussed the question with Germany and avoided entanglement. Norway said no as politely as she could.

None of the Scandinavian states in 1939 had any military commitments, nor any military security. The League was powerless, neutrality had been compromised, and armaments were not impressive. Finland had a vigorous military tradition and a sense of danger; she had her forests and she had her Mannerheim Line of fortifications and an intense nationalistic spirit, but less than four million people. Sweden had excellent munitions factories. Norway had the natural fortifications of her fjords. Denmark had nothing. Iceland was all but forgotten.

Was there a common line of action among these states allied by geography and culture? In 1927 they had signed a series of mutual arbitration pacts among themselves. In 1930 Denmark, Norway, and Sweden had got together with Belgium, the Netherlands and Luxemburg in the Oslo Group. In 1932 Finland was added to the society. These small and democratic states of western Europe attempted to combat depression and increase their mutual trade by a mild form of tariff coöperation. But the British saw visions of a powerful bloc which might destroy Britain's trade advantages, and claimed the agreement was contrary to the "most-favored-nation" clauses in treaties between these states and Britain, and thus the Oslo Group was frightened and weakened before it accomplished anything significant. Meetings of the Group were held and pronouncements made as late as 1938. Certainly it could not have developed any military or naval collaboration.

Closer coöperation was attained by Denmark, Finland, Norway, and Sweden, whose foreign ministers met repeatedly in the years of the League and the "long Armistice." Agreement among themselves made it possible for the Scandinavians to have one member regularly on the Council of the League. At one of the foreign ministers' conclaves in April 1938 it was unanimously agreed that the Scandinavian states should stand outside all power combinations, refuse to be drawn into war, and aid each other economically. The Finnish foreign minister, Eljas Erkko, expressed the sentiments of all when he said, "No one can convince us that in the name of peace we could be drawn into the schemes of the great powers to any advantage to the world or ourselves."

All five Northern states signed (May 1938) a set of neutrality rules, revising and bringing up to date the regulations agreed upon in 1912. These rules were in harmony with the Hague regulations and added little besides details, with small variations among the five signatories. The one new item was a prohibition of military plane flights over the air territory of the northern countries. There were no regulations on transport or export of war material. This pact, like most of the other agreements, indicated independence in passive neutrality rather than any common positive action.

Estonia, Latvia, and Lithuania had sought a Baltic military pact, but their neighbors held aloof. Finland was eager for an agreement with Sweden, but the nearest to realization reached in this combination was the abortive plan for joint fortification of the Åland Islands. Discussions among the foreign ministers doubtless touched on the possibilities of Scandinavian action in common, but the inequalities in armament, the differences in geographical position, and the failure to envision future dangers were factors too strong to overcome.

The history of neutrality in the North is the story of the more or less innocent bystanders attempting to protect their own interests. They tried by neutrality to avoid the horrors of war itself, to escape the direct costs of war, and to make what profits they could out of the needs of the belligerents. Consistency in neutrality policy they never attained. The very concept is negative, and the practice must be opportunistic. The neutrals refuse to take part, the participants shape events. But the neutrals can remain a little more calm, and they can see a little more clearly the advantages to all of law and order. The Scandinavians sincerely did their best to promote international stability and coöperation.

7. World War II: Scandinavia Rent Asunder

Neutrality had worked fairly well from 1814 on into the twentieth century. It had saved lives and property through one war after another. Its success gave the Scandinavians a sense of righteous superiority over peoples involved in wars. A little self-restraint, a willingness to accept losses without getting angry about "national honor," a careful attention to one's own business, and a gentle firmness about justice—this was the Scandinavian recipe for longevity and happiness. If a state threatened no one why need it worry that another would threaten it?

Or had the North simply been playing in luck? Munich, the fall pogroms of 1938, and the taking over of Czechoslovakia in the spring of 1939 worried Scandinavian statesmen. Was the rest of the world headed for war again? There was always the possibility that someone might make a mistake and Scandinavia become involved, but that danger was hardly taken seriously. The May meeting of the Scandinavian foreign ministers in Stockholm only reiterated the old determination to remain neutral and to have nothing to do with power groups.

1. FINLAND THE FIRST VICTIM

The most realistic—in the new sense of realism in world politics—were the Finns. They were accustomed to trouble and acquainted with war. The forests and the centuries had hardened them. They had few illusions about their fellow men, and their only illusion about themselves was that four million Finns could dare stand up against 180,000,000 Russians. When Germany concluded an agreement with the Soviet state in August 1939 and the panzers and the planes swept over Poland in September, the Finns knew that danger for themselves was imminent. The Scandinavian foreign ministers had met again in Oslo on August 30, and when Britain and France declared war on Nazi Germany the Northerners each declared neutrality.

Estonia, Latvia, and Lithuania were powerless to resist and one by one they agreed to the Soviet demands. By the summer of 1940 they were completely absorbed as republics of the U.S.S.R. On October 5, 1939, while discussions were proceeding with the neighboring states, the Russians approached the Finns, suggesting negotiations which would yield military and naval bases to the Soviet Union in return for cession to Finland of a large segment of forest land in Karelia. The Kremlin was willing to pay Finland a price, and a few Finns thought the country should make the best out of obvious necessity. Foreign Minister Eljas Erkko, however, pointed then and later to the fate of Estonia and her sister states and said that it was suicide to begin making concessions. The Finnish people were in overwhelming agreement.

Scandinavia was concerned. The diplomats of the North sprang to action, at first individually, then on October 12 in a combined Danish-Norwegian-Swedish statement in Moscow affirming Finland's close association with the other Northern countries. "A blow against Finland is a blow against the North." By repeated steps Sweden made clear her interest in anything which affected Finland's position. On October 18 the president of Finland, the kings of Denmark, Norway, and Sweden and their ministers met in Stockholm in what was both conference and demonstration. The popular reaction showed an unexpectedly strong inter-Nordic feeling. It was clear at the same time that however strong sentiment might be, there was no government ready to ally itself with Finland. Humanitarian aid and supplies were promised, but the Finns were told, as they had been told earlier, that they could not expect military support. The Finns nevertheless stood upon their rights and refused to open the door even for Russia's foot. On November 30 the Russian bear lumbered into action, and the Finnish tiger counterattacked in full fury.

The story of the Scandinavian neutrals in World War II went like the children's game of "The Ten Little Indians." Down went one, and then there were nine . . . until all were gone. The game of "The Little Neutrals" began with five and ended with one. Finland was first.

Denmark and Norway declared their neutrality in the Russo-Finnish conflict; Sweden, with closer ties of geography and sentiment and a vitally direct strategic concern, carefully did not declare neutrality and pointed this out in a note to Russia. The Swedish, Danish, and Norwegian foreign ministers met in Oslo on December 7 and strongly supported Finland's appeal to the League of Nations. The League took its boldest step and its last, and excluded the Soviet Union from membership. But this did not stop the Red armies. When the Assembly suggested the application of sanctions, it was Sweden's Östen Undén who spoke for the three northern countries, expressing the shock and the sympathy of the peoples, but refusing to take a stand on the proposal. Sweden was both profoundly worried and supremely cautious.

"Finland's affair is ours" became the slogan of the day in Sweden, and among the masses of the people there was a surge of anti-Russian feeling and a mighty movement of aid to Finland. Over $100,000,000 in gifts and loans from government and people was sent to Finland, 84,000 rifles and 50,000,000 rounds of ammunition, 300 cannon and 300,000 cannon-shells (all the heavy artillery came from Sweden), 25 airplanes, and quantities of clothing and other goods. Over 12,000 volunteers offered themselves for service to Finland and 8260 were enrolled. The people felt threatened and to a certain extent seemed to feel obligated to help. Some agitated for direct Swedish intervention.

The Swedish government was extraordinarily firm in the well-studied position it had taken. When the Russians protested against Swedish partisanship the government replied without mincing words: There is strong pro-Finnish sentiment in Sweden and a free press; volunteers are recruited privately, in accordance with international custom in Europe and America; commerce is continuing freely as is customary among the Scandinavian countries, and the Swedish government sees no reason for complaint; Sweden, like the Soviet Union, wishes to avoid all complications.

The government was just as firm with its own people. The king, on February 19, 1940, acknowledged that he had taken a leading part in the relations with Finland, and declared it was with sorrow in his heart that he judged that Sweden must not go militarily with Finland. In such a case, he said, Sweden would almost certainly find herself involved in the general war, and then could do still less for Finland's sake. Sweden's vital interests, her honor and her peace were the goals he kept before his eyes. He concluded with an appeal for understanding and support.

Finland fought like a nation of heroes. The concrete pillboxes of the Mannerheim Line held at bay the southern attack from Leningrad; the "Molotov breadbasket" bombs did not frighten Helsinki; and the Finnish armies made steady progress on the central front. The organized women's corps, the Lottas, helped at the front and behind the lines. The nation was united as in the days of storied Ensign Stål against the threat from the East. Many Finns were communists, and deep bitterness survived from the civil war of 1917–18 and from the crisis of 1930. But people faced a decision; which were they *first*, Finns or communists? The answer from the thousands was the answer of Finnish patriots. Otto Kuusinen, a Finnish communist emigré, was set up as president of a communist republic. His followers were a pitiful handful. If the Russians really expected Finland to crack from within they got the surprise of their lives.

Through weeks of bitter cold, filled with stories that remind an American of the tales of Valley Forge, the Finns more than held their own. Russian losses were tremendous. When the men in Moscow decided they could no longer leave the fighting to the troops of their northern army, they sent to Finland their best in men and planes and guns. They rocked the Mannerheim forts on their foundations, they drove with overpowering mass and limitless reserves against the thin Finnish lines. The Finns had neither men nor women left to stem the tide. Four million was not enough against 180,000,000.

Finland's resistance aroused world-wide sympathy. Volunteers joined up from many countries and contributions came from many, including the United States. Most effective aid was difficult to send. The nazis and the communists were hand in glove, and Germany controlled the southern Baltic and Russia reached north to the Polar Sea. The only route by which troops and supplies could reach Finland was across Norway and Sweden. Britain and France were eager to send such forces, but in February 1940 Norway and Sweden refused passage. They feared the aid would be insufficient, and they knew that if they granted such a privilege they would find their lands a theater of war between the great powers. Britain and France hesitated to demand a free transit of troops unless Finland herself would issue a clear and public request for it; Finland was so informed and given until March 5 to issue the appeal.

The Finns did nothing, but they thought long and seriously, and asked about the Swedish attitude as late as March 11. The British raised the question in Stockholm for the last time on March 12. The Finns were skeptical. A Finnish delegation was already in Moscow. Finnish defenses were breaking before the newly massed strength of Russia and unless aid could come quickly and in great force the agony and destruction would only be prolonged.

Could French and British aid be effective? Germany and Russia were close and Britain and France far away from this northern forest bastion. As Finnish military and statesmen analyzed the situation they could see no hope. The only alternative was to make peace with the U.S.S.R. on the best terms possible, and live, perhaps to fight another day. Finland did not issue the plea for aid, but signed a treaty with Russia on March 12. Norway and Sweden did not have to make the final difficult decision with which France and Britain would have confronted them.

In the days of cavalry and sailing ships Scandinavia was on the edge of Europe and had a chance to stand aside. But by 1940 the age of submarines and airplanes was far advanced. Industries, such as those of Germany, were increasingly dependent on iron ore from the North. Total war required not only the total support of a nation's own citizens and all their industry and agriculture, but it demanded also a vast supply system from abroad.

If a route of trade or a product was of importance for one power to have, it was important too that its opponent be stopped from taking it. And if fish and iron ore had been crucial articles in World War I they were much more so in World War II. In World War I it had taken many months for the powers to decide to override the sovereignty of neutral states; but World War II started where World War I left off. In a struggle between giants the little fellows could be let alone only if they did not get in the way. Necessity knows no law, and when nations are desperate in war they make their own law.

For Scandinavia the tragedy of World War II was in her wealth of iron ore and in her geographic position, the same geographic position which had given her security once, but whose significance had changed with the changing technology of war. Germany needed the iron ore of Sweden which came out through Narvik and down the protected Norwegian coast. Britain needed to stop that traffic. Germany needed northern bases from which her submarines might attack British shipping. Britain needed to prevent Germany from getting them. And any of the Scandinavian countries could provide useful air bases for a flank attack on either Germany or Britain—good for each to have, and good for each to prevent the other from having. Scandinavia was in the maelstrom of the new geopolitik.

2. NORWAY FIGHTS

The Norwegians knew the facts as well as anyone, but they deluded themselves in their own correctness and moral innocence. They had worried, but they told themselves there was really no cause to worry. "It can't happen here."

The army was a token force. The navy, with 2100 miles of coast to defend, consisted of fifty-seven obsolete craft and a few antiquated coastal fortifications. Only meager preparedness was made when war broke out on the continent-road building in the north, a few orders of equipment, and in March 1940 the addition of an extra class in the military academy. When troublesome people urged action their suggestions were met with official calm. The social democratic party had long preached pacifism, and it had been the governing party since 1935.

Prime Minister Nygaardsvold saw the danger. He announced in October 1939 that the government could not refuse requests from the military. But the military were hesitant in drawing up plans and requests. To only a small extent did they activate the defense they had. Behind the somnolent military was a somnolent Storting and a somnolent people.

Norway was nonetheless in the war area. In the fall of 1939 Norwegian shipowners contracted to put 2,000,000 tons of shipping at the service of the British. Germany did not protest verbally, but before the ninth of April some fifty-four Norwegian ships had been sunk and 377 sailors killed. The Germans used Norwegian territorial waters for all kinds of traffic. They brought the American captive, *City of Flint*, down from the north through coastal waters and as far as Haugesund. There the Norwegians considered her anchoring a violation of neutrality and released her. Other vessels wrecked along the coast were victims of either mines or submarines, and the British said they would have to disregard the neutrality of those waters if the Germans continued to do so. The Norwegians attempted to tighten their guard, but the task was tremendous on their rugged coast.

Then the German transport *Altmark* came through Norwegian waters with 299 British prisoners in the hold, on their way to Germany. The German captain lied to the officers of the two accompanying Norwegian warships, and said that there were no prisoners on board. The Norwegians accepted his word. The *Altmark* also violated "international law" by using her radio in Norwegian waters. The British were angry and suspicious and with a small fleet intercepted and captured the *Altmark* in Jössing Fjord on February 16, 1940. They found the prisoners and also a spectacular example of the ineffectiveness of the Norwegian neutrality watch. Norwegian protests were brushed aside. The British resented more and more the ore transport down the Norwegian coast.

Ore from the Swedish mines of Kiruna and Gällivare came out from the Norwegian port of Narvik and down the coast. The British could not touch the ships which carried this raw material for bombs and guns and torpedoes. In the final dash across the Skagerrak the Germans could easily mass the protection of submarines and planes while for the long haul from Narvik to southern Norway they covered themselves by the rules of neutrality. These rules they used to their advantage and violated at their pleasure. British patience broke.

On April 8, 1940 the British announced that they would lay mines at three points in Norwegian territorial waters. The result would be that all vessels would be forced into the open sea at those points, and the British navy could then have a chance to capture. The mines were actually laid at one point near Narvik, and the Norwegians were in a furore over this deliberate affront to their neutral rights. While Foreign Minister Halvdan Koht was drawing up a note of protest the Germans made notes superfluous.

Rumors of nazi action in the North had increased in the previous week, and definite reports had come since the fifth of April from responsible sources in Berlin. Foreign Minister Koht asked his friend the German Minister, Dr. Kurt Bräuer, what the reports could mean and Dr. Bräuer denied them. Dr. Koht was himself dubious and feared popular hysteria; he kept the reports secret. The minister of defense, Colonel Birger Ljungberg, got similar reports and was also unbelieving.

In the evening of April 8 the cabinet was called in emergency session. News piled on top of news: a German transport was sunk off southern Norway, hundreds of German soldiers were drowning, others coming to land. The Norwegian legation in London passed on information from the British Admiralty that German naval units and a transport were approaching Narvik. By 9:15 the government decided on partial mobilization, and on the mining of Oslo Fjord. Two hours later they heard that the fortifications in Oslo Fjord were already under fire. Rumors had become realities.

Nygaardsvold called together the ministry at 1:30 in the morning of the ninth. Reports kept coming of German landings at Kristiansand, Stavanger, Bergen, Trondheim, Narvik. Ports and airfields succumbed to a carefully planned, long-prepared attack, carried out with overwhelming power. Norway's natural advantages had no chance to be used, for men and guns were not at hand to use them. The old minelayer with the proud name *Olav Trygvason* sank a German transport and a destroyer, and damaged the cruiser *Emden;* at the fortress of Oskarsborg the German fleet was unexpectedly checked, the big cruiser *Blücher* and another ship were sunk, and some 1600 men shot and drowned. But soon the fort was pounded to bits from sea and air and the heroic Norwegian air force was overwhelmed. Airborne troops dropped on Fornebu airport, soldiers occupied Moss, and by two o'clock in the afternoon the German army was in the streets of Oslo.

At 4 that morning (April 9) the German minister had presented to Professor Koht an ultimatum nineteen pages long. The

Germans made specific demands: immediate surrender, giving over of transportation and communication, coöperation of Norwegian troops, and breaking off relations with the western powers. Without a dissenting voice the government rejected the ultimatum. King and government took a special train at 9:30 A.M. for Hamar, and there the Storting gathered that same afternoon. The sacrificial resistance of Oskarsborg and the ships in Oslo Fjord had given the government time to think and act. The German plan to capture the king and all his men had failed.

The people of Oslo were stunned. The stolid Norwegians were totally unprepared for total war. They gaped in amazement at the German soldiers marching down Karl Johan street. Hysteria? No! Rather a deep bitterness and a profound disillusionment in human nature. A deep and angry determination hardened in the minds and hearts of the people. Young men from Oslo and Bergen and the other captured ports put on their knapsacks and escaped from the captured towns along the hiking routes and over the mountains. Drivers picked up trucks and farm women became army cooks. The men gathered into companies and chose commanders, and the companies joined to make battalions. Partially they were welded into a common fighting force under the able leadership of General Otto Ruge, appointed by the king to head the wartime army.

Was there treachery? Some, as at Narvik, where Colonel Konrad Sundlo, friend of Quisling, gave over the city to the invaders. There was Major Vidkun Quisling himself, former assistant to Nansen in Russia, once minister of war in Norway, but since 1933 out of office. In 1940 he was nothing but a political leader without a single party representative in the Storting. His *Nasjonal Samling* was a party strictly on the nazi model, and it did not appeal to the democratic Norwegians. Quisling was a sincere but disgruntled man. The people did not share his belief that he was their savior. His request to the king on April 10 that he be made prime minister reacted negatively. The instinctive reaction of people in disaster was to cling to known and trusted leadership. His treason acted as a catalyst; people suddenly saw the invasion for what it was. Treachery was insignificant. The tragedy of Norway was the unpreparedness of the rightminded.

The government was hounded from place to place. The meeting at Hamar, where 145 out of 150 members of the Storting had gathered, heard that German forces were nearing, and it adjourned to Elverum. The conservative C. J. Hambro, president of the Storting, took the lead in laying plans for the future. The social democratic government was not allowed to resign, but was broadened by the addition of delegates from the opposition parties. The government was voted full powers to act as necessary for the good of the country, and to transfer its seat out of the country in case of emergency. Everything was legal. The Supreme Court had been given no orders on that hectic morning of April 9, and under the wise guidance of Paal Berg, chief justice, it stayed in Oslo and became a potent factor on the home front.

Meantime the king and his government were driven from Elverum on to Nybergsund. Here the Germans who had received the king's flat rejection of Quisling as his prime minister attempted to destroy king, crown prince, and ministers by bombing, machine-gunning and incendiaries. A captured Luftwaffe diary reported, "April 11. Nybergsund. Oslo Regierung. Alles vernichtet." But the king was sitting in the deep snow of the woods with ministers and villagers, consoling and encouraging them for the struggle against barbarity. Two weeks later the government was at Molde on Romsdalsfjord, retreating steadily northward from the advancing German forces. On April 29 Molde was burned and the governmental group boarded the British cruiser *Glasgow* and sailed north to Tromsö, hoping to hold the northern section of the country.

Immediately after the German attack began, the British informed the Norwegian government that they would aid and coöperate with Norway to the limit. Both British and French sent troops, but they were "too little and too late." Even in places like Aandalsnes and Namsos where the Allies established toeholds the German air attack was too deadly. The British and French had to give up, and the Norwegians had to surrender southern and central Norway (May 1 and 2).

Far north around Narvik the fighting was intense. The defenders had courage, but they had no armored cars, no anti-aircraft guns, no fighter planes. One British squadron of eighteen Gladiators fought briefly, but with no airfield except an ice-covered lake, where thirteen planes were destroyed at once by German guns. Naval engagements of April 10 and 13 left two Norwegian battleships, seventeen German vessels, and sixteen British warships at the bottom of the fjord. Scots Guards, detachments of French Alpine chasseurs and of the Foreign Legion, and finally some Polish mountain troops aided the Norwegian army. After sharp fighting they retook the town of Narvik on May 28, and they held the country to the north. Northern Norway might have been saved, and if the future course of the war had been foreseen the Allies might have stayed. At the moment, however, the disasters in the Low Countries and France required every man that Britain and France could muster. Norway seemed less vital, and was abandoned.

On June 7 the king and his entourage sailed for London, and on June 9 announced that organized opposition had ceased, but that the fight would be continued from abroad. Though small and unprepared, Norway had held out longer than any of the continental states against blitzkrieg, 63 days (Poland had lasted 29 days, France 39, Belgium 19, Holland 4).

3. THE NORWEGIAN NATION UNDERGROUND

The Germans tried anew to set aside the Norwegian government after it had left the country. They bulldozed the Storting's presidential board to request the king to abdicate, and would permit no explanation to accompany the request. This was in June 1940 when German power blazed like a meteor through Europe. The king broadcast home from London that he knew the Storting members had been coerced and that he and the ministry would continue to represent the legal government and would in due course return to Norway.

The London government proceeded throughout the war to govern Norwegian seamen and fleet, to radio news and directions and inspiration to the population at home, and to plan for the day of return to Norway. Its gold reserve was saved and the Bank of Norway did business in London. The free fleet of over 4,000,000 tons was worth more than the gold both in money and in service. Its tankers carried 40 per cent of the oil cargoes of the allies to theaters of action around the planet. Half of that fleet and 3000 sailors were lost, but it had been more useful than an army of hundreds of thousands. Not a single ship free on April 9 turned back to the German quays. All of the old companies pooled their activities in an organization called Nortraship, with headquarters in New York. Their fees and taxes paid the expenses of the entire government, and left a surplus for use in the liberation. Insurance provided much of the means for rebuilding.

Some airforce personnel escaped to England and after a few months went on to Canada. There General Hjalmar Riiser Larsen and Colonel Ole Reistad established Camp Little Norway, and to it flocked scores of eager boys from Norway. They escaped in small boats to the shores of Scotland or through the woods to Sweden, then across Russia or out by plane to England. They returned to pilot bombers over Germany. By the spring of 1944 a Norwegian unit of the RAF had established the highest record for effectiveness and safety.

The British government coöperated wholeheartedly with this active government-in-exile and helped it to build a new navy to operate with the British navy. Britain allowed Norwegian courts to function and gave them the use of British jails. The Bank of Norway was tax-free. The Norwegian king and ministers were honored guests. The Norwegian government continued without a legal break.

This whole situation naturally exasperated and frightened the nazis, and even the Norwegians realized that some form of government must be set up at home. The aim of the Norwegians was to make that government merely an administrative structure which could conduct the necessary details of social organization, but not give moral or practical advantages to the invaders. The proper formulas were difficult to find.

In the early days of the conquest, even while the king was still in the country, the Supreme Court had taken responsibility for appointing an Administrative Council (April 15). Quisling's "prime-ministership" had been abolished that day by the Germans. It had backfired against the nazis because of the popular reaction against Quisling. On April 24 Josef Terboven became Reichskommissar, and Norway was governed as a conquered province. Nevertheless the Norwegian people were honored Nordics, and the Germans wanted desperately to align them with nazism. For that all must be legal, so in September the nazis tried to get legal powers voted by the Storting. This was refused, so on September 25 Terboven proclaimed that political parties were dissolved and that the royal family was "no longer of significance." A State Council of thirteen was established. The next important change came February 1, 1942, when in the Act of State Quisling was again brought forward and made minister-president to form a national government. But this move too failed to win friends.

While the Germans were seeking to build a base from Norwegian law the Norwegians were slowly discovering, as did the Danes later, the political potential in voluntary social organizations. On August 24, 1940 the leaders of the political parties, and of the large organizations of employers, laborers, and producers, agreed to sink all party and occupational differences and to work together for the interests of Norway. In October the small church organizations joined with the state church in the Christian Council for Joint Deliberation, nucleus of an increasingly effective protest group, representing all together almost 100 per cent of the people. In November the sportsmen refused to be organized under nazi leadership and during that winter only four out of 3000 athletic teams participated in contests.

About 90 per cent of the schoolteachers refused to be nazi-organized. Only two out of ninety professors at the university were nazi. Some farm leaders joined the nazi organization, but neither farmers nor fishers would be nazi-organized. The will of the people was clear and these organizations which united for protest soon learned to take positive action.

The nazi regime wanted the support of existing legal institutions, but refused to permit the Supreme Court to examine and pass upon its acts. Hence in December 1940 the chief justice and fifteen members of the court, with the approval of other judges, resigned. Soon the chief justice became the acknowledged leader of the "illegal" resistance movement.

The church at last came out, in February 1941, with a pastoral letter which in ringing tones denounced the lawlessness and brutality of the Hird, the Norwegian counterpart of the nazi brownshirts, and attacked the nazi invasion of Christian rights. A year later, after Quisling had become minister-president, the nazi government became more repressive. When people were stopped from entering Trondheim cathedral for service the bishops of Norway resigned, and on Easter Sunday practically all the clergy did so. But they kept on with their work, if not arrested, and were supported by the people. In February 1942, 12,000 of 14,000 teachers refused to obey orders to nazify the children; 1300 were arrested, and more than half of those were sent under brutal conditions to work with Russian prisoners in labor camps at Kirkenes.

Violence had been tried before without success. In September 1941 a strike of workers gave the nazis the opportunity to arrest and execute two popular labor leaders, though both had opposed the strike.

Through 1942 the noose was pulled tighter and tighter. In September Quisling attempted to establish his long-cherished corporative state, but the answer of the people was mass resignation from the nazified trade unions and the Germans forced

Quisling to give up the scheme. The next step was a roundup of the Jews; of the 1500 in Norway about 800 were captured and sent to camps in Germany. Thirteen returned.

In November 1943 the Germans took action against the recalcitrant students of the university. After threatening all of them some 650 were transported to Germany to have "right ideas" forced into their heads. An international roar of protest went up from many lands, including Finland and Sweden, and the king of Sweden sent Hitler a strong personal note.

The Germans were driven to desperation by the unanimity of opposition. Even Quisling's handful of ambitious mis-minded young men gradually diminished. Month after month more became "rowers," men who rowed away from the sinking ship. Probably never more than 2 per cent of the population had associated themselves actively with the quislings.

The regular press was taken over by the authorities and published the German handouts. One of the attempts to win friends and influence people was to publish each day the picture of a quisling with a statement, "Why I am a member of *Nasjonal Samling*." People ceased to read these lies and half-truths, as they ceased to go to the nazi movies. Underground newspapers appeared, ultimately about 230 with a combined circulation of 250,000–300,000, spreading the news by courier and by chain-letter methods. Radios were confiscated in September 1941, but boys and technicians constructed new sets, sending as well as receiving. Contact with England was never lost.

The whole population helped in resistance. Every office and factory had at least one active worker. Word of decisions and activities could be passed on quickly through trade organizations, church societies, schools. Food was collected for the needy, passports forged, bridges blown up. When the nazis wanted forced labor from the classes of boys born in 1921, 1922, and 1923 the population objected and coöperated in evasion. Birth certificates were lost or changed, offices with records were burned, and the nazis got only 300 of the 80,000 eligible. When a piece of sabotage was to take place in a way that might endanger the community the saboteurs would call the police or the fire department and tell them, for example: "There will be two explosions at the roundhouse at 10:30 and 10:35; wait for the second blast and then don't hurry." The Germans were infuriated with the police, but they were helpless.

Through it all the Norwegians, "the world's most serious people," kept a soul-saving sense of humor. They loved to pass on little jokes like the one about the twelve-year-old boy and the Viking ships. It was September 1940 when German planes were failing in their attempt to bomb England into submission. Across from Oslo some German soldiers were looking at the Viking ships in the Bygdø Museum. As they exclaimed "*Wunderbar, wunderschön*," the boy came up and said, "You like our old ships, do you?" The Germans outdid themselves in admiration. The boy cocked his head on one side and remarked, "Yes, those are the boats our ancestors used when they went over and conquered England every year." Another attitude was represented by the popular question asked by schoolchildren, "Is it true or is it German?"

Often the Germans caught a saboteur or a suspect, and they filled Norwegian concentration camps like the notorious Grini, and sent hundreds to Germany. When they caught up with Lauritz Sand, leader of the Norwegian counterespionage, they tortured him for weeks, and broke twenty bones. But Mr. Sand gave no information. The Norwegians are a stubborn people.

High in the fjelds at Rjukan was the "heavy water" plant and the Germans needed the heavy water for their work in atomic fission. A band of young Norwegians was carefully trained and equipped in England. They succeeded in blowing up the plant and then hid out in the fjelds to the end of the war. Again and again saboteurs destroyed trains or tracks, and they kept the British fully informed about German building and movement in Norway.

The Home Front had no courts, no army, no stately buildings. It had power because of the national will. Its leaders rose through natural selection, no formal election. Not only chief justice Paal Berg, but the postwar prime minister, Einar Gerhardsen, was an active leader, as was many another official. Confinement in a concentration camp became an honor, almost a prerequisite for public approval, and an important item in a man's record in *Who's Who*.

The most tragic chapter was written in the snows of the north. Soviet forces came in from Petsamo and took Kirkenes on October 25, 1944, and a Norwegian force soon joined them. Together they drove the Germans back slowly. But as the Germans left they carried out a thorough scorched-earth policy, slaughtering livestock, destroying bridges, burning buildings, and leaving the people to freeze to death in the Arctic winter. That bitter memory will not be effaced for many generations.

Threats of a similar devastation of all Norway were not carried through. On the eve of the nazi collapse in Germany a secret army of 40,000 men had been built by the Norwegians and at the end the German forces surrendered to this authority. May 5, 1945 was a great day and greater still was June 7. Exactly five years from the day king and government departed from Tromsö Haakon VII and the government of Norway steamed up Oslo Fjord. Norway was once more free.

The people had earned the tribute penned by the poet Arnulf Överland:

> *We owned no ready sword*
> *We lived by faith in peace . . .*
>
> *Farmer and working lad, they fought,*
> *A few men here and there*
> *Against machines and iron tanks*
> *And legions of the air.*
> *They fight until they fall,*
> *Knowing a broken will*
> *Means life without meaning*
> *And the end of all.*

4. DENMARK BOWS TO FATE

In 1864 Denmark had been defeated and disillusioned when none came to her aid, and she lost Slesvig-Holstein after a brave fight. After World War I she regained North Slesvig without lifting a finger. After a half century of debate the country was disarmed and the fortifications of Copenhagen were dismantled in the 1920's. With the military might of Germany at her elbow what could be the use of fighting? Defeatist and carefree the Danish government had considered its position and taken its decision long before April 9, 1940.

In 1937 the social democratic premier, Thorvald Stauning, had told a Swedish audience at Lund that Denmark would not be the watchdog of Scandinavia. On January 1, 1939 foreign minister Peter Munch made a 100 per cent pronouncement for neutrality. When suggestions of a common Scandinavian defense policy were made, Stauning rebuffed them. He was the heir of a pacifist party tradition, and of Denmark's sad experience. When President Roosevelt took the initiative which led to the German request for a nonaggression pact, Denmark dared not offend her great neighbor and signed a ten-year agreement with Hitler on May 31, 1939. It was no check on Germany, no safeguard for Denmark. That pact lasted for ten months.

Danes detested nazism and feared German power, yet they could put no faith in their own strength or their geography or their neighbors. They lived virtually without an army and without a foreign policy, hoping that luck would be with them.

For weeks before the Germans swept in, the Danish minister in Berlin had been sending warnings home, and on April 4 the naval attaché had come home to report imminent danger. By April 8, with endless columns of nazi troops approaching the border, the government considered mobilization. The German minister in Copenhagen countered this by convincing the Danish foreign minister that Germany was friendly and Hitler honorable and that mobilization would be a disastrous affront. By four o'clock the next morning the same emissary was presenting the German ultimatum.

The Germans struck at night, as they did in Norway. An armored division and 80,000 men crossed the Jutland frontier; parachutists dropped in the islands and boatloads of troops entered the ports; soldiers crawled from the holds of "coalboats" which had been lying for days in the harbor of Copenhagen; bombers flew over the city. Denmark had on that day less than 14,000 men under arms. The border troops fought desperately but were quickly overwhelmed; the royal guard would not give up. Lilliput made a gesture, and could do no more. Resistance was suicide, there were neither men nor means to make it effective. The ultimatum not only told the government that Germany was coming to protect Denmark against an English invasion, but threatened to desolate Copenhagen like Warsaw. At 6:30 A.M. the king ordered resistance to cease.

Denmark was occupied and at the mercy of the invaders. The Germans promised not to use Denmark as a base of operations against England, but soon did so. They promised not to interfere with Danish internal affairs, but they stood by that only as long as the Danes submitted to German wishes. In practice the uninvited guests did exercise unique forbearance. They wanted to be "systematically loved" and to show the world how kind they could be to a people who yielded. They would make of Denmark a "model protectorate." They were willing to let the Danes eat well if Germany could have the surplus, for they recognized that both products and surplus would be greatest under pleasant conditions. The nazis tried to be wise in Denmark.

Many in the government of Denmark wanted to be "wise" in return. Stauning was deeply impressed by German success. He urged the people to adapt themselves. In the national emergency a government of all four major parties was established. Peter Munch, the foreign minister, had signed the pact of 1939 but he was not sufficiently flexible, so he was one of the ministers dropped in the reorganization. In his place came Erik Scavenius, foreign minister in World War I, a practical man, and a past master at adjusting to the needs of the moment. Scavenius was neither pro- nor anti-; he was a "realist," accepted facts as they were and ably administered the day-to-day details of German-Danish relationships.

Actual nazis in Denmark were few, but racialists, adventurers, opportunists, and weak time-servers were to be found. No single nazi party unified all these groups. Fritz Clausen, who had fought with the Germans in World War I, tried to raise himself to the position of a little *Fuehrer;* Jens Møller, a veterinary and newly elected member of the Rigsdag, led the German minority in North Slesvig. Altogether about a dozen personal cliques vied for their place in the sun, but all together they could not, even under occupation in 1943, amass 3 per cent of the popular vote.

King Christian X had ordered resistance to cease, but he was no compromiser. He was above party, a noble figure in physique and in heart. He personified the pride and the shame of Denmark, and was beloved by his people as the incarnation of their feelings and as their voiceless leader. Innumerable stories attested to the people the king's patriotic determination. When the Germans demanded that the Danish flag be taken down from a building the king refused. The Germans said, "We will then remove it ourselves." The king: "If you do I shall send a soldier to put it up again." The German: "If you send a soldier we will shoot him." Christian X replied calmly, "I will be the soldier." The flag continued to fly. When the Germans demanded the introduction of the Nürnberg laws against the Jews and the wearing of the yellow armband the king publicly announced that he would wear the "J" too if the Germans carried out their plan. And the king continued his daily horseback ride in the streets of Copenhagen until injured by a fall in 1942.

Among the conservatives brought in to make the government more representative of the people was J. Christmas Møller, dynamic and farsighted. Governmental accommodations to circumstances went too far for him; he withdrew in the fall of 1940, and toured the country speaking directly and inspiringly against the nazi menace. He foresaw the inevitable collapse of nazi overlordship, he had faith in the staying qualities and the eventual victory of the British, and he thought Denmark must help in helping herself. The Germans did not silence him until January 1941, when he had to go underground. He and Frode Jacobsen organized "The Ring" of young people to spread information and prepare for the time when action would be feasible. In the spring of 1942 Møller escaped to England, and there became the central figure in the Free Denmark movement abroad.

In Washington Denmark was fortunate in having one of her ablest diplomats, Henrik de Kauffmann. He it was who on April 9, 1941 signed with Secretary Hull the agreement which placed Greenland under the wartime protection of the United States. He was immediately dismissed under German pressure, but he calmly continued to represent Danish interests, and had to wait only until May 1945 to see this agreement and his whole policy ratified by the Danish Rigsdag. Others of the Danish foreign representatives gradually followed Kauffmann's example. It was the old and permanent Denmark which was represented in the free countries of the world.

The Danes were not as amazed at the German attack as were the Norwegians, hence not as bitter in their disillusionment. For them the disillusionment had come in 1864 and the wound in the heart was partially calloused. The first months of occupation were not too difficult. Danish contempt and hatred of the Germans was shown by the cold-shoulder policy: Danes simply did not see the Germans on the streets, ignored them. The Germans acted correctly and tried to smile. They would force these stubborn Nordic brethren to be friends. Some of them were reported to have gone insane through exasperation with the Danish slow-down, and the thousands of petty irritations practiced by these annoying people who did not appreciate the blessings of German protection. Some of the Germans, boys who had been given happy vacations in previous days of Danish hospitality and adopted into Danish families, felt disillusioned when they found that their nazi leaders had lied to them and that they had invaded the country of people whom they loved. Others played happily the role of "protector."

German requisitions on Denmark amounted to little in 1940 and prices were good. Some 340,000 pigs were sent to Germany, 15 per cent of the whole stock. As the war continued, the German need of supplies from Denmark increased. Food was taken in increasing quantities, though the Danes still had plenty, and probably ate better throughout the war than any other people in Europe. But fertilizers could not be obtained, nor sufficient fodder, hence the land was despoiled and livestock was slaughtered too fast. Industries, especially shipyards, were put to work on German orders.

As much as possible the Danes kept control of production. When the Germans wanted to bring in workers to construct an airfield on Jutland the government decided that it would rather do the work with Danish labor. The influx of German workers was prevented, but the alternative involved payment for the work by Denmark. The Danish state advanced millions of kroner for the purchases of agricultural supplies and for construction work. The Germans promised to send coal and other materials in exchange, but at the end of the war German deliveries were far behind and the cost was left to Denmark.

The Danish people had felt anti-nazi and anti-German for years, but they had thought it necessary to yield. Gradually they changed their minds and their policy. They were chagrined as they saw their Norwegian cousins fighting, and their British customers and friends enduring the devastation of bombs. Abroad a Danish Council was set up in London in September 1940 to coördinate the work of 3000 Danish sailors serving the Allies; 40 per cent of the merchant fleet escaped German control. Christmas Møller roused hope at home. An underground press managed to give to the people forbidden news from beyond the curtain of censorship. As fast as one paper was suppressed three others jumped into print, or mimeograph. Party differences had been subordinated to the national interest and a Committee of Nine organized to represent the diverse elements in an extralegal body.

In January 1941 the Germans asked the king to appoint a government of other parties omitting the social democrats. This he immediately refused to do, for the exclusion of the largest party would violate the constitution. Then came in June Hitler's attack on Russia and the demand for a supporting Danish "free corps." Recruitment attracted only a fraction of the "scum" of youth into the Schalburg Corps. This special guard incorporated criminal elements and became a curse on the domestic front. When the communist party was proscribed and the Danish government was required to sign the anti-comintern pact (November 1941) it was too much for the Danish minister in London. In December 1941 he left government service to work with the Free Danes.

The entrance of the United States into the war, despite the early disasters in the Pacific, gave new hope to the Danish opposition. The death of Stauning on May 3, 1942 did not change the official government attitude. When Wilhelm Buhl, minister of finance, became premier he expressed appreciation of German behavior and urged coöperation. Yet dissatisfaction increased and sabotage gained momentum. On the king's birthday, September 26, Hitler had sent greetings which Christian acknowledged by a curt telegram of simple thanks. The Fuehrer was furious.

The Russians continued to "reject the inevitable," the British counterattacked at El Alamein, the Americans and the British landed in North Africa. At the end of October 1942 Scavenius was called to Berlin and told to set up a government friendly to the Germans. For this he could not gain coöperation of the parties and ended by picking a government of his own, with himself as both premier and foreign minister. He had rank, but behind him the Committee of Nine was to exercise control.

Authority was in the hands of Werner Best, Hitler's diplomatic representative, and General von Hanneken, military commander. Yet neither the conciliation policy of Best nor the brutality policy of von Hanneken convinced the Danes. Sabotage increased and a number of organizations arose to promote it. Contacts were strengthened with Sweden and England. An election was due for the Folketing in the spring of 1943, and the Germans reluctantly consented to its being held. That opportunity was exploited by the Danes to show themselves and the world where they stood. All the old parties (except the forbidden communists) combined to give the voters a clear choice, for or against democracy. Ninety per cent voted, the highest proportion ever, and 95 per cent of these voted for democracy. An out-and-out resistance party, *Dansk Samling*, won three seats. Definitely nazi tickets won only 2 per cent of the votes. The Danes lifted their heads with new faith in each other.

During the summer of 1943 the nervous nazis tried to guard against the rising tempo of sabotage, and the more they did so the more obstinate became the Danes. Explosions came nightly. Strikes broke out everywhere. At Odense shipyard workers struck against the German guards on a ship under construction. The owners sided with the workers and paid their wages during the strike. Opinion was so solid that a jittery German officer fired into the crowd in the city and was in turn trampled to death. Reprisals merely incensed the population the more. Late in August, both hope and patience gone, the Germans discarded the idea of the "model protectorate." King, government, and Rigsdag had refused to declare a state of emergency. The Germans took over with a proclamation of martial law, Sunday morning, August 29, 1943.

Hundreds of underground workers and suspects were arrested, many of them prominent business and professional men and women. The tiny garrisons put up again a brief and futile fight. The navy went down with éclat. Orders were issued to escape with the ships to Sweden if possible, otherwise to scuttle. A few escaped, a few fell into Germans hands, most were scuttled. As the Germans dashed to the navy yard at Copenhagen one drawbridge was up; the Danish chauffeur found an exceptionally slow and circuitous way around, and by the time they arrived there were no ships left.

Scavenius could not get together a new government and the king refused to appoint a ministry that lacked the approval of the Rigsdag. From August 29 Denmark was governed by the German military, and Danish officials merely maintained the administration. The death penalty was ordered for spies, saboteurs, and any suspicious person. Danish soldiers were interned, and martial law continued to October 6.

What had gone wrong? Why had the model protectorate refused to coöperate with the German protector? It must be the Jews! said the Germans. In Denmark there were but 6–7000 Jews and there had never been a "problem." But now the Germans were applying the heel and in the night of October 1–2 the entire Jewish population was to be rounded-up. Word leaked out in advance, and by bicycle and car, by boat and raft and swimming, some 6000 of the intended victims were spirited to Swedish boats and over to the Swedish shore. The nazis bagged only 600, most of whom died in Buchenwald.

The Danish sense of decency and justice was outraged. The king protested in vain, and the people intensified their efforts to destroy German production and transportation. The nazis in turn increased violence and allowed the Schalburg Corps to run wild. When a nazi Danish informer was eliminated, a loyal Danish hostage was executed. After an act of sabotage the Schalburgers would blow up some popular public building. Kaj Munk, minister and poet of international note, was assassinated, and many others.

By June of 1944 the Germans were attempting to control sabotage with a curfew from 8 P.M. to 5 A.M. Perhaps it could have worked in the winter, but hardly in the warm light nights of a northern June. And especially right after the long-awaited invasion of Normandy! One afternoon thousands of workers at Burmeister and Wain shipyards just went home, writing an official explanation that they were not on strike, but that if they could not work in their gardens in the evenings they would do so by day. The gardens were much more important to them than was production for the nazi military machine. Soon the flight to the colony gardens was general and the idea spread to twenty-two other towns. The Germans shut off Copenhagen's supply of gas and electricity and cut off food supplies. But after five days and nights of fighting behind barricades the people were still not intimidated or subdued.

When the "strike" began the Freedom Council took over. This Freedom Council grew out of the success of democratic coöperation in the elections of 1943, and was already a strong centralizing power in the August days. Basically it rested upon one-man representation from each of the four big resistance organizations: The Ring, the youth organization already mentioned; *Frit Danmark* (Free Denmark), a newspaper organization widespread through towns and parties in the whole country; Denmark's Communist Party; and the Christian political and activist *Dansk Samling* (Danish Union).

The leader of the Special Forces and a few other individuals were from time to time members, changing as one or another was caught or forced to flee. But the group as a whole was never caught. It was a close-knit secret committee, usually of six men, coöperating wholeheartedly despite divergent political attitudes. Only one thing was fundamental: freedom. The Freedom Council became recognized as the guiding, coördinating authority in the resistance movement. After the government was shelved on August 29, 1943, the Council grew into a government of the Danish people. It rested on neither law nor force, but it was obeyed because it personified the common will.

Hence it was that the Freedom Council took up the spontaneous movement of June 1944 and laid down the demands to the Germans: curfew must be abolished, the Schalburg Corps suppressed, public services restored, and no reprisals. After five days of chaos the nazis had to yield to the unanswerable unanimity of the nation. From this time on the position of the nazis weakened steadily in France, in Russia, at home in Germany, and in Denmark. Sabotage increased and the number of underground newspapers rose like an inflationary curve. The Danish police were set aside by the nazis in September and 1900 of them were transported to concentration camps. The Danes kept order by self-restraint. When a German officer remarked, "What discipline," a Dane replied, "Not discipline, but culture." Then the German police were established.

Sabotage was planned and executed with consummate skill, to delay production and to stop transport, yet to do little permanent damage. Key pieces of machinery broke or disappeared to halt the work of a whole factory; a section of railroad was removed, or a single car of soldiers dynamited. One detachment passing from Norway to the western front was delayed a week in transit through Jutland. Forty or more single acts of railway sabotage might occur in one night. The Danes counted up 2156 acts of sabotage against railways, and 2548 major acts against factories. No conceivable force could keep track of it. Regular connections were maintained with England and with Sweden, and parachutists landed nightly with orders and equipment. Denmark was a peaceful battlefield, with people smiling by day and fighting by night. And the Danes had thought of themselves as pacifists!

When the Germans collapsed in May 1945, and British troops entered Denmark, the Danes knew that they too had played a part in the Liberation.

5. ICELAND OCCUPIED

When Denmark fell under the shadow of the nazi bombers on April 9, 1940 her distant possessions were left to themselves. The Faroe Islands were taken under British protection and provisioning.

Since 1918 Iceland had been autonomous, united with Denmark through the king and the foreign ministry. On April 10,

1940 the Althing met and gave over the royal power to the government of Iceland. Sveinn Björnsson was made regent, and Iceland was prepared to go alone. But the country had no army, no navy, and lay in an exposed and strategically important position. As the Germans extended control over western Norway the British worried increasingly that they might establish another flanking position against Britain in Iceland. For once the British acted first. On May 10, 1940 a British naval force landed troops and took over the protection of the country, promising to respect Icelandic independence and to see it restored at the conclusion of hostilities.

Iceland was as much in the American sphere as in the European, and when Russia was plunged into war in June 1941 the north Atlantic island took on new significance as a station on the supply route from North America to Murmansk and Archangel. Hence, on July 8, 1941, by previous arrangement with the British and the government of Iceland, American forces landed to take over defense responsibilities.

No more than Denmark did Iceland wish to be occupied, but the people realized that they faced only two alternatives. They did not want or invite either the British or the Americans, yet they felt that if they had to be occupied by Germans or by Anglo-Saxons they had been granted the lesser of the two evils. Forty-five thousand foreign soldiers in a country of 125,000 people created inevitable social problems and some unfortunate incidents occurred. They were, however, individual incidents and there was neither general opposition nor sabotage, but rather friendly coöperation and a number of marriages. The occupation was as friendly as an occupation could be.

The Keflavik airfield was made into a base for transatlantic planes and the harbor of Reykjavik became a lively center of trade. Iceland's fish were paid for by the Americans and sent to Britain on lend-lease, and supplies which had come from Denmark and England now came from the United States. Prices rose and Iceland prospered. Submarine activity offshore, the sinking of a few Icelandic ships, an occasional nazi plane—but

Iceland essentially felt the war indirectly rather than directly, and through an artificial prosperity rather than through destruction.

6. SWEDEN STEERING BETWEEN THE ROCKS

"Each of our countries in full agreement with the others should follow the tried policy of impartial neutrality to which all the Northern States have declared their allegiance . . . the peoples of the North are imbued with a common desire to live in peace with all others. They are also inspired by a common determination to live as free nations." These are the words of King Gustav V, on October 19, 1939.

Sweden, last of the northern neutrals, had the will, the skill, and the luck to stay neutral. How could it be done, and what did it mean?

The Swedes were practical not theoretical in their neutrality, dogmatic occasionally in speech but never in action. As King Gustav said, they wanted peace, but also freedom. In the Winter War of 1939–40 they did not pretend to be neutral, but did all they could for their neighbor short of fighting. It was a bold policy and it abandoned solidarity with Denmark and Norway who declared neutrality. When that war was over Finland asked Sweden and Norway for a defensive alliance and both expressed willingness. Then came a Russian warning and the German invasions in the North. The agreement did not materialize. Later discussions of a Swedish-Finnish union were likewise blocked by Russian objections.

The ninth of April 1940 posed bitter problems for Sweden. She was neighbor and kin to Denmark and Norway as well as to Finland. But she had emptied her armories for Finland, and there was little left. The situation was changed by Denmark's immediate acceptance of the German occupation, and more importantly by the fact that the kind of aid given Finland, if extended now to Norway, would certainly lead to immediate war. The German minister assured the Swedish government on the fateful morning that Sweden would not be attacked *If* . . .

The government decided that in this desperate situation Sweden must maintain a real neutrality. That required decisions on many points left vague in the Hague regulations on neutrality and undecided in Swedish practice. The Swedish method was to be legally strict in all interpretations and then, outside the law, to take whatever ameliorative measures she dared in Norway's favor. Transportation of war material, for example, could be either granted or refused, and it was totally prohibited. Transit of troops and equipment was prohibited by the Hague convention and was not even brought in question for some time. When the Germans tried to smuggle munitions through Sweden the customs authorities detained the cars, then returned them to Germany. Sweden had already established a policy of refusing export licenses for arms and munitions to warring powers.

Strict neutrality demanded that Germany and Norway be treated exactly alike, at least publicly. When Sweden refused to permit transportation of war materials for Norway's benefit the Norwegians protested. The Norwegians were also often bitter about the treatment of Norwegian refugees who escaped to Sweden hoping to arm themselves and return to fight. In both cases Sweden was attempting to apply the rules equally, rules which for Norway's sake it was important to maintain. There can be no question that the Swedish government was friendly in heart to the Norwegian cause, and that the Swedish people were overwhelmingly sympathetic. Nevertheless tension was at fever pitch, and the Norwegians, understandably enough, could tolerate no obstacles. Incidents resulted which will leave deep scars for years.

Governments and peoples of course differed in both attitudes and knowledge of facts. The Norwegian people wanted the Swedes to jump to their side. The Norwegian government knew that it was far better for Norway that Sweden remain neutral. In a postwar Norwegian publication is an interesting memoir from Foreign Minister Halvdan Koht to the British government arguing the importance of Swedish neutrality.

Koht complained that Sweden did not observe toward Norway the same kind of neutrality that she had toward Finland [which Sweden did not call neutrality], but he insisted that in no case should Sweden be driven into war. If Britain insisted, for example, on Sweden's stoppage of ore traffic to Germany it might drive Sweden in on Germany's side. That would be tragic. If on the other hand Sweden should enter the war on the side of the allies they would all have Russia to fear. Norway had had a warning that the U.S.S.R. would not tolerate the influence of a great power, especially Great Britain, in north Norway; for the same reasons they would react against British influence in Sweden and British sea power in the Baltic. The result of Sweden's "aid" might well be a Russian attack on both Sweden and Norway.*

In another case, after Norwegian protests to Sweden the Norwegians discovered that they had a weak legal basis to stand on, and that if their protest had been accepted it would later have reacted against them in a changed situation.† Farsighted governmental thinking and experience was a thing completely apart from popular feeling, and obviously not something to publicize. Unfortunately the result was increased popular misunderstanding.

The Swedish people on their side wanted to maintain peace, but they also wanted to help the Norwegians as they had helped the Finns. The pro-Germanism which had existed during World War I had been weakened by the excesses and the anti-democratic propaganda of nazism. It was almost snuffed out by the attacks on Denmark and Norway. Press and public writhed inwardly at the compromises and the appeasement of the government. The whole position was demeaning for a proud people. At the same time almost no one was ready for war.

Wide differences of opinion and a profound confusion were

---

* Memoir to British and French governments, May 19, 1940, *Norges Forhold til Sverige under Krigen 1940–1945*, I, 21–23. *Ibid.*, 235–236.
† Counselor Bull to Koht, May 5, 1940, *Norges Forhold*, I, 20.

reflected in a blend of patriotic bravado and a sense of futility. "It is a little land" (*Det är ett litet land*), was a common confession of weakness and disappointment. Many felt that they had let their neighbors down. Yet as a young Norwegian put it, "Sweden's only crime is that she was not invaded." Per Albin Hansson, respected prime minister, expressed the opinion of the majority, but not all, of the Swedish people in a speech of April 12:

> Our emotions are shaken by what has happened to our Scandinavian brother peoples . . . I am convinced that the Swedish people are ready to endure heavy sacrifices for their peace and self-determination . . . to preserve that which is dearest to all of them, freedom and independence.

A significant lack in the speech was that there was no reference to any sense of obligation to other peoples.

The "special regard for Sweden" entertained supposedly by the big nazi Hermann Göring was used by the Swedes whenever possible. Göring's first wife had been Swedish and he had spent some pleasant visits there. To him, therefore, a private Swede hopefully proposed in mid-April the withdrawal of both German and Norwegian troops from the Narvik area and occupation there on a trusteeship basis by Swedish troops. Germany was interested. The idea was passed on to Norway's foreign minister Koht, who was at first cool, later became favorable. The plan was approved by London on June 1. Koht and Günther signed an agreement on it at Luleå, Sweden, on June 3, and this was presented to Germany. It was too late. On June 7 General Ruge was ordered to cease hostilities in Norway and both the allies and the Norwegian government left the country. A potentially unique chapter of war history was not written.

On the withdrawal of the Norwegian government to London the Swedes were confronted with a situation without exact parallel. Rules had to be worked out, and under the most urgent pressure. The Germans immediately claimed that since Norwegian opposition had now ceased the Swedes could have no objection to German transit through Sweden to Norway for the German forces of occupation. The Norwegians, however, were continuing to fight, and their allies, the British, were vitally concerned about German strengthening of Norwegian coastal bases. The Swedes had to think hard and to squirm.

Sweden had permitted one German train, of Red Cross personnel and material, to pass through Sweden to Narvik in late April. If there were soldiers aboard it was due to German deceit. Otherwise no traffic of a dubious nature was approved until the change of situation in June. Even then the government was at first determined to deny the German request, and delayed day after day.

The situation rapidly grew worse for the allies. It was the month of Dunkirk, and until Winston Churchill infused new vitality into the British government it looked as if there might not always be an England. The Swedes were told officially in London that Britain might have to make the peace on whatever terms she could get, that her policy would be guided by common sense, not bravado.

The Germans kept pressing for every possible concession, backing requests with threats. Von Ribbentrop demanded rail passage through Sweden for German soldiers on leave and the right to transport materials; refusal he said would be regarded by the Fuehrer as an unfriendly act. Germany was riding high, and Sweden wanted to live. The government accepted the first step in appeasement. On June 19 the German government was informed that Sweden agreed. In the next weeks the details were negotiated, and transit began over Swedish roads of general goods (not war materials) and "leave soldiers" without arms.

To the protesting governments of Britain and Norway Sweden replied that she would rigidly inspect the trains, and that all was within the limits of neutrality. The British asked as compensation that Sweden resign to them her contract for American planes, but Sweden refused. To the Norwegians Sweden said specifically that "all neutrality policy had its limits in the possibilities open to the neutral state." Opportunism, nothing doctrinaire.

In the summer and autumn of 1940 some 480 cars of goods passed to and from Norway over the Swedish route. One car of German personnel and 20 cars of material crossed Sweden to Finland in September and 142,000 men went through to Germany and 136,000 back to Norway (to January 13, 1941). In addition there was some "horseshoe" traffic over Swedish lines from Norway and back again to Norway because of the lack of a through railway from Trondheim to Narvik.

When the Germans attacked Russia in June 1941, there came new demands on Sweden, and the Germans were allowed to send one entire division across Sweden to Finland. This concession aroused heated controversy within the government, and may have been approved on direct personal appeal by King Gustav. It was counted as aid to the Finns, and was frankly admitted to be a departure from neutrality, but a "one-time" departure, not to be repeated.

What the Swedes did for the Norwegians during the early months did not seem much to their hard-pressed neighbors, but it was significant. They forbade export to Norway of arms, ammunitions, and gasoline, but permitted (between April 9 and June 10, 1940) export of 24,000 steel helmets, 850 compasses, 4500 maps; 46,000 pounds of clothing, 770,000 pounds of foodstuffs, and large quantities of hospital material. In the years of occupation and hardship which followed, Sweden sent hundreds of prefabricated houses for the shelter of the homeless and vast quantities of food to maintain the "Oslo breakfast" for the school children of Norwegian cities. They kept cottages near border escape routes from Norway equipped with food and fuel. They took in hundreds of youths who fled from fear or who used Sweden as a way-station to get to England or Camp Little Norway in Canada, there to gird themselves for effective fighting. Large numbers of Norwegian youth continued their education in Upsala or Stockholm, and several hundred more were trained in Sweden as "police" to take over in northern Norway when opportunity permitted.

For the Danes also, particularly for the Jews whom they helped to escape from Denmark just prior to the round-up of October 1943, the Swedes opened homes and opportunity to work. Altogether more than 15,000 Danes were sheltered in Sweden when the war ended. Some 35,000 refugees from the Baltic States were given shelter; 70,000 Finnish children were given shelter and schooling through Swedish foster-homes.

It was the Swedish Count Folke Bernadotte who in the spring of 1945 arranged for the release from German prison camps of the Danish police and many of the Norwegian political prisoners (19,000 people in all). Shiploads of food were taken as gifts from the Swedish people to Greece, and the Swedish Red Cross was helpful in distressed areas throughout Europe. It was a Swedish captain and crew who turned back in all but suicidal conditions to rescue the men of the sunken *Jarvis Bay* in the north Atlantic. Talk of obligation to others was at a minimum, but there were daily acts of helpfulness and sacrifice. Occasionally even a stiff-necked official might close one eye while a fugitive slipped in or out. The people's conscience and sense of northern brotherhood spoke in a vigorous opposition press and in the little acts of every day.

Sweden's job of taking care of herself was complicated. She lay surrounded by German and Russian power, first allied in aggression, later slaying each other. She normally sold to Germany her iron ore, and received from Germany steel plate for ship construction and for building, and much of her coal. Her chief peacetime customer was Britain, already cut off. She imported foodstuffs and other necessary goods from countries beyond the North Sea. Her industry and her life depended on commerce.

Both warring groups recognized this situation, a repetition of World War I. Britain tolerated the continuance of iron ore export to Germany and the manufacture for the nazis of ball bearings and other vital goods. Arms and ammunition the Swedes did not sell. Safe-conduct agreements with Germany allowed five ships per month to enter and leave Gothenburg for the west, but even this traffic was subject to the whims of the nazis, who repeatedly stopped it for weeks or months at a time. Eleven ships and one hundred lives were lost in this *allowed* commerce.

Despite such strangling pressure Sweden maintained the trade agreement made with England in December 1939, and did not allow the export of strategic materials southward to increase. In 1939 her ore export to the German area amounted to 11,300,000 tons, in 1940 to 9,300,000 tons, in 1941, to 9,400,000 tons, and in 1942 to a well-controlled 8,200,000 tons, and it continued to drop. By 1942 total exports were down to 47 per cent of normal, imports to 45 per cent. Food was rationed, *akvavit* had to be made from wood instead of from potatoes, and cars were driven by wood gas instead of gasoline.

Sweden was willing to adjust to circumstances, but she had no intention to submit to whatever might happen. Government and people made it clear as the northern air that they would battle any invader. Neutrality tradition was strong, but it had always been an armed neutrality, and there remained a pride in the exploits of Charles XII. Sweden was much stronger in a military way than any other of the northern lands. She restocked the supplies sent to Finland, increased production from the great Bofors munitions plant, and called her men to the colors. Her iron ore and her heavy industry strengthened her position, though she lacked coal.

Sweden's defense budget was $50,000,000 in 1938–39, $400,-000,000 in 1939–40, and $600,000,000 in each of the next two years. She built an efficient flexible system of mobilization, providing for a steady neutrality guard and the quick assembly of 600,000 men, and 110,000 "Lottas" (Wacs) in case of danger. On several occasions that force was fully mustered, and it may have been that trigger-readiness which made a bold man in Berlin fear that the conquest of Sweden would be too costly for what it would repay. The Swedes were reputed to have the best anti-aircraft guns in the world and they used them; during 1940 they shot down thirty German planes which had flown over Swedish territory. In the summer of 1942 repeated U-boat attacks in the Baltic were found to be Russian, but no country would admit responsibility. The Swedes did their best at self-defense. At the end of 1942 Sweden had 23 destroyers with 6 more building; 27 submarines with one building; one mine-carrying cruiser almost ready; 8 old coast defense vessels, and 20-odd torpedo boats.

A pamphlet of *Directions for Citizens of the Kingdom in Event of War* was issued, the essence of which was: "Resistance shall be made in all situations. Any information that resistance should be abandoned is false." This was distributed in June 1943; by that time Sweden felt surer of herself and of others, and her neutrality had changed tone.

In the months immediately after April 9, 1940 Sweden had yielded to many distasteful German demands. Despite frightening pressure she many times refused. On the surface she was rigidly correct and impartial. Yet Sweden modified her neutrality toward both sides. It was a weather-vane policy. The difference was, as the record shows, that Germany won her concessions by force or threat of force; concessions to Britain and the United States were made for reasons of trade or because of real sympathy with their cause. Concessions to Germany, because of their nature, were usually immediately known while concessions to the allies were, because of their nature and the Swedish position, usually secret until the end of the war. It made for Sweden a bad press in the western countries, a reputation worse than she deserved.

Sweden's merchant fleet agreement with England of December 1939 was made solely for Sweden's own economic benefit, but it gave to Britain the use of 600,000 tons of Swedish shipping (for commodity use only) until it was sunk. Two-thirds was gone by 1943. Courier planes flew regularly above the clouds from Stockholm to England, and they carried businessmen of the west, and Norwegian escapees, and "others."

From the Swedish west coast swift 100-foot motor ships carried to Britain, in greatest secrecy, much-needed ball bearings. SKF smuggled to Britain and Russia $20,000,000 worth of bearings and machinery, about half as much as was sold openly to Germany, with whom Sweden had to trade in order to get coal. But by the spring of 1944 both Britain and the United States were pressing Sweden for the cancelation of her agreements to sell ball bearings to Germany. The Swedish product was only 3 per cent of Germany's needs, but that 3 per cent was of high quality and important. The Swedes had already cut the German quota and did not care to cut further on a contract which the allies had known about when made. They kept on selling until October 15, 1944, when they ceased completely. To the United States as early as 1940 were smuggled the designs for the Bofors anti-aircraft gun, which was modified somewhat and manufactured by thousands in the United States.

The Swedish press did not have to go underground, and the old law on the freedom of the press was its protection. Occasional issues were confiscated after publication because the government feared particular articles might provoke retaliatory measures from the nazis. The Germans were often exasperated by the vitriol of the Swedish press, and returned it with interest, calling the Swedes "swine in dinner-jackets." But for the most part such papers as Torgny Segerstedt's crusading *Handels-och Sjöfartstidning* kept up a steady attack on the Germans, and kept reminding the Swedish government that a United Nations victory was vital for the continuance of Swedish democracy. There were, on the other hand, several papers owned outright by Germany, as was true also in Denmark, and a news service under nazi control. Stockholm was a buzzing information center where newspapermen and spies from east and south and west grabbed for morsels of fact or opinion for their papers or their governments.

The elections of September 1944 gave significant indication of Swedish feeling, and undoubtedly stiffened the back of the government. The outcome of the war was by then fairly clear. The socialists elected half of the second chamber, 115 out of 230, but lost 100,000 votes and 19 seats. The communists raised their vote from 100,000 to 300,000 and their Riksdag seats from 3 to 15. The conservatives polled almost 500,000 votes and held 39 seats. The coalition government continued and Per Albin Hansson was still prime minister; neutrality was obviously approved. Yet the strong communist trend indicated, at that moment, an increasing urge for action, for in the fall of 1944 Russia represented the most vigorous anti-nazism.

As the conflict advanced to its final stages Swedish neutrality all but ceased to be neutrality. In August 1943 the goods traffic between Germany and Norway was limited more strictly, and was stopped in April 1944 after Sweden found large numbers of military maps of Sweden in some German shipments. German couriers were given circumscribed routes. After September 1944, only hospital cars were allowed to move through Sweden from north Finland to Germany. The Swedes were angered by German attacks on Swedish fishing boats, and by some shooting within Swedish territorial waters. All Swedish waters were next closed to German warships, and the ore traffic was brought to a halt by the stoppage of insurance and credit.

Even the normal credit operations for wartime trade had been drawn so as to provide Sweden with imports from Germany large enough to balance her exports over each six-month period. Sweden was not going to be caught with a defeated debtor unable to pay. In the autumn of 1944 she sacrificed both trade and import possibilities when she ceased all credit, and prohibited foreign trading to her Baltic ports. She also announced that she would not harbor war criminals. It was all clear indication that she had little to fear from Germany, and that the war would soon be over. It was also a boost to the allies in speeding that end.

How neutral was Sweden? If by neutrality one means impartiality, there was none. Sweden did first what she had to do in order to placate Germany; later she did all she dared to help the allies. Neutrality was the policy of the possible, frankly opportunistic, even "cold-bloodedly selfish," as one Swedish official stated. It was Sweden's way of struggling for survival, just as war was the way of other countries of struggling for survival. In judging the justice of the policy one must remember that it was impossible for Sweden to get foreign aid, coal, or foodstuffs, except from Germany or with German consent. Peacetime trade was as much with Britain as with Germany, but this was war, and peacetime trade was curtailed by geographic circumstance. To paraphrase a Swedish statesman with geographical insight, "Sweden lay where she lay."

There was a strong German influence in Sweden as there had been for centuries. Swedish scholars and businessmen and soldiers admired the achievements of the German nation, and Swedish conservatives had a certain sympathy for German "order." But feeling had changed since World War I. It was social democrats, not conservatives, who now held political power in Sweden, and liberal thought was stronger. Very few Swedes favored the nazi ideology, and the nazi party in Sweden could not elect a single member of the Riksdag. What many foreigners interpreted as pro-Germanism was more two other things: 1. the supercaution of a small nation before the overmight of a ruthless power; 2. anti-Russianism, which was age-old in Sweden, and which saw in Germany the only real protection against the threat from the east.

With regard to Sweden's relations with Great Britain there are two fundamental factors, both of which are frequently forgotten or distorted. First is the admiration and love of Britain felt in Sweden, more in commercial Gothenburg and Malmö than in governmental Stockholm, but deeply everywhere. There is no reason for calmly taking it for granted that Sweden should naturally love Britain. Political sympathy with Britain was a fact of as great significance as the respect felt for German science. The second factor is that, love or no love, Sweden had also to fear Britain. Both Britain and France in the winter of 1940 wanted definitely to involve Sweden in the war and to use her territory as a base against Germany. Churchill describes some of the schemes in his memoirs. It is easy to say that in the long run Sweden had everything to fear from Germany and nothing to fear from Britain. She did fear that Britain might involve her in war, and rightly or wrongly she was determined to strike at whomever struck her first.

Who was responsible for the Swedish neutrality policy? Probably two men bore the brunt of leadership: King Gustav and Prime Minister Per Albin Hansson. Gustav V had been at the helm in World War I, and had then been rather strongly pro-German. He had, however, used his influence to keep Sweden out of war, and to unite the Scandinavian countries in a common neutrality policy. He was conservative in political sympathy, yet democratic in manner, "no friend of theatrical royalty." He was shrewd, experienced, and widely acquainted. Like the kings of Denmark and Norway (altogether that was a remarkable trio in strength of character, as well as in height and age!) he was beloved and respected by the people, and his firm stand for neutrality was influential.

"Per Albin," the prime minister, was a man of the people, one with them and yet their leader, liked and respected by the king. He stood wholly for the interests of the Swedish people, thoroughly neutral, isolationist.

These top figures could of course have been overruled. They dominated policy because they represented the will of the overwhelming majority of the Swedish people on major issues. The foreign minister, Christian Günther, had been brought in after the outbreak of the Winter War in Finland, displacing Rickard Sandler who favored a more vigorous policy. Günther played throughout the war the role assigned him: to administer and defend the already determined policy. Of the others, not responsible for policy, many who out of their own security complained of weakness and compromise nevertheless preferred these things to war.

Neutrality as a principle of foreign policy had in Sweden the deep roots and the strength of the Monroe Doctrine in the United States. Swedish neutrality, as a policy, favored neither

Germany nor Britain, it aimed solely at the best interests of Sweden. Concern was more for the immediate present than for the future, uncertain at best. Appeasement there was in external action, much of it, but not in internal opinion. The Swedes had no intention to follow in the wake of any great power, and no intention to compromise their own well-founded democracy.

7. FINLAND INVOLVED AGAIN

The Finns had no historic basis for thinking that the treaty of March 1940 would establish eternal peace between them and the Russians. In the Winter War they had fought alone and lost. Next time they must have allies.

Friends were good to have in the British Isles and across the Atlantic, but they could not help much in a crisis. Scandinavian unity was good, but recent experience showed it to be a thing of the spirit rather than of the battlefield. In March 1940 Norway and Sweden agreed to an alliance with Finland, but were frightened off by a scowl from Russia.

Only one state had the power and the location and the potential interest to be of real help to Finland against Russia, and that was Germany. Contrary to wartime propaganda there was little love for Germany in Finland: German soldiers in Finland in the revolution of 1918 had created as much animosity as appreciation. German indifference during the Winter War angered the Finns deeply. Nazism was an ideology utterly foreign to Finnish thinking and conditions. Ties with Britain and the United States were closer economically, politically, philosophically. Ties with emigrants in the United States were especially strong. But Germany was close and powerful, and the realistic Finns knew that sooner or later Germany would battle Russia. And Russia was Finland's inveterate enemy. What more natural than a "marriage of convenience"?

Many Finns were therefore glad when, in September 1940, Germany requested leave to send troops through Finland to Norway. They quickly agreed, without prescribing limitations or thinking through the potential dangers. Didn't they already allow transit to Russian troops, and had not the Swedes made a similar agreement with Germany?

The Germans had no illusions that the Finns loved them, and Hitler complained to Molotov that the pro-Russian attitude of Germany during the Winter War had further alienated Finland. The Germans nonetheless coolly planned their northern "Operation Barbarossa" with expectation of Finnish collaboration. The Russians evidently sensed this if they did not know it, and the question of Finland occupied hours in the Molotov discussions in Berlin in November 1940. Molotov entered a mild demurrer against the passage of German troops through Finland to Norway, while the nazis calmly admitted that Finland was in the Russian sphere.*

By June of 1941 it was easy for the Germans to have a number of ships in Finnish ports, one armed division on its way north, and another division on its way south. Both could be aimed eastward. When the Germans attacked Russia on June 22 it was inevitable that the Russians should think of Finland as a German base. The evidence from both Finnish and German documents, however, indicates that the Finns were unaware of German plans, and that they had made no political agreement.

On the other hand, the Finns were perfectly aware of the probabilities of war and welcomed them. On June 15 a northern sector of Finland was assigned to German command. The Finns could hardly have been surprised when the Russians bombed Helsinki. On June 25 they recognized a state of war, and the Swedes gave permission for passage from Norway of one German division to aid on the Finnish front. Finns were not allied with Germany, but, as Hitler announced, they were fighting "side by side."

The first days of the war, even the first months, went well for the Finns. By July 10 Marshal Mannerheim, hero of the

* See Raymond J. Sontag and J. S. Beddie, ed., *Nazi-Soviet Relations 1939-1941*, especially pp. 234-247.

war of independence and of the Winter War, could sign a jubilant and aggressive "order of the day" calling for the liberation of Karelia. By September 14 the old frontier of Finland on the Karelian isthmus had been rewon and 200,000 refugees (almost half) from the year before were moving home again, resettling the land. By the end of 1941 practically all the territory lost in 1940 had been reconquered and in places the armies were deep in Russian territory, and had cut the main railway south from Murmansk.

Germany had succeeded in drawing Finland into war and in getting Russia to strike the first blow. The nazis won an important northern flanking position. They could not, however, persuade the Finns to join fully in their war. In August 1941 the Germans asked Finland to aid in an attack on Leningrad but the Finns refused. Some 1400 Finnish volunteers had gone south to train with the SS, and the government asked that they be sent back. The Germans, however, held them to their term of enlistment and they fought as the only group of Finns in the Ukraine. In every way possible Finland emphasized that she was not a partner of the nazis, insisted that she was fighting a separate war against an old enemy.

The "separate war" idea was reasonable enough from the Finnish angle of vision. It was somewhat similar to the American position in the War of 1812 when the United States fought against Britain, but did not consider herself an ally of Napoleon. In Finland's case she could not see why her position was any different in 1941 from what it was in 1939–40. But the situation was changed by two facts: Germany was now fighting with Finland, and Finland's Russian enemy was now the ally of Britain, and soon would be an ally of the United States. With this latter fact Finland had nothing to do, but with the German coöperation she did. Both facts made for most complicated relationships. Finland remained the same, while Germany, Britain, and the United States all changed their attitudes toward Russia!

Russia could not accept the separate war idea, and she pressed

England to declare war on Finland. The Germans from the other side pressed Finland to break relations with England. This the foreign minister, Rolf Witting, awkwardly and foolishly did, and then an official and most friendly party was given to the departing British diplomats. In the fall of 1941 Churchill tried to find a way to assuage the Russian urgency and to freeze the situation on the Finnish border. Russia, Britain, and the United States were deeply concerned lest the Finns and Germans advance eastward and break the last slender rail connection carrying supplies south from Murmansk.

First Britain asked that Finnish troops withdraw behind the 1939 border, then on November 28 sent an ultimatum demanding that Finland cease all military operations. Churchill in a private letter to Marshal Mannerheim suggested that a public statement would not be necessary, but merely a private pledge that the Finns would go no farther. Mannerheim replied "that Finland would finish up only the operations then under way." This was on December 2. The Marshal thought it was acceptance of Churchill's proposition, but it was poorly worded, and did not specify what was meant by "the operations then under way."

The government reply of December 4 was more vague, simply restating the war aims of Finland as the liberation of the territory conquered in 1940 and "the neutralizing of those areas from which the enemy prepared to destroy Finland." On December 6 Finland officially reincorporated the lost areas, but no more. On the same day Mannerheim announced that the strategic objectives had been attained, and ordered "that the offensive operation be ended and defensive measures initiated."

It was understandable enough that Finland could not publicly announce that under no circumstances would her forces advance another step, but the answers were too uncertain to satisfy Britain. A declaration of war was issued from London on December 6 to take effect at noon on December 7. That same day Pearl Harbor blew the United States wholly into the war.

The United States had maintained her friendly relations with Finland despite the growing antagonism with Germany. It was the United States minister in Helsinki who handled the correspondence between British and Finns and who sought for adjustment. But the United States was interested in that delicate thread from Murmansk, the Russian supply line, and in diminishing the German influence in Finland. Beginning as early as August of 1941 Secretary Hull warned Finland of the possible consequences of collaboration with the nazis. Increasing pressure was applied in the fall and during 1942 until, beginning August 1, Finnish consulates in the United States were closed. At the end of the year the Finnish Information Service in the United States was throttled and the legation staff was restricted in travel. Still the Finns took no new aggressive steps, but still there was no definite assurance that they would not. The Americans were annoyed and worried, and the Russians wanted action.

In March of 1942 the vigorous socialist Vaino Tanner was made minister of finance, and became a spokesman for the government. In February 1943 President Risto Ryti was reëlected, and in March a change in cabinet brought in Professor Edwin Linkomies as prime minister and Henrik Ramsay as foreign minister, but Tanner stayed and there was no essential change in policy.

In 1943 the long-continuing war became increasingly burdensome for Finland, and the prospects for the future did not improve. Internal differences of opinion came to the surface. In July a Finnish-American Society was established, with Eljas Erkko, former foreign minister and managing editor of *Helsingin Sanomat*, as president. In August, thirty-three leading men signed an appeal for peace, and another group drew up a counter appeal. The Swedish Finns were split on the issue, and so were the party groups. In February 1944 K. A. Fagerholm, prominent social democrat, called for a "realistic" reappraisal of Finland's position. After a new appeal from Secretary Hull, the leading social democratic newspaper said that the American warning should be heeded and a peace approach made to the Soviet Union.

Throughout the spring of 1943 there had been talk of peace negotiations and the United States had offered to mediate. Nothing resulted, partly because the Finns, out of a sense of loyalty, informed the Germans of their desire to get out of the war. The nazis immediately blocked shipments of food to Finland and cut in half the promised oil and gasoline; they demanded a political pact to bind the Finns more closely. Parliament refused to sanction such a pact and it was definitely rejected. Eventually Ribbentrop accepted assurances and dropped the retaliations. The same thing was repeated in the autumn of 1943. It showed the spirit of the Finns, but it showed also the German stranglehold on the Finnish economy. Not even her Scandinavian friends could provision Finland.

As trade with her Scandinavian neighbors declined and as trade beyond the Baltic area was choked off, Finland could get only from Germany the necessary quantities of potatoes, grain, textiles, fertilizers, oils, machinery, and munitions of war. In the prewar years her imports from Germany were about 20 per cent of the total; in the years 1941–1944 this import jumped to 75 per cent. Her normal exports to Germany were about 15 per cent and these jumped to 65 per cent.

In the fall of 1943 a question was raised by the Americans through the Finnish chargé in Lisbon: What might be expected of Finland if a United States force landed in northern Norway? The Finnish government replied that they would not fight the Americans, that they would begin negotiations to get the Germans to withdraw, that the United States should prevent the Russians from entering Finland, and that Finland would need certain supplies of food. This would have been an excellent "out" for Finland; it would have avoided the Finnish obsession of being left alone at the mercy of the Russians. But no more was heard of it.

From February to April 1944 actual peace discussions got under way. To Juho Paasikivi, Finnish diplomatic troubleshooter, Mme. Kollontay, Russian minister in Stockholm, gave an outline of Russian terms:

1. Finland must sever relations with Germany and intern the German forces in Finland; Russia would be willing to help.
2. The 1940 treaty must be reinstated and Finnish troops withdrawn to the 1940 border.
3. Russian prisoners must be returned immediately.
4. Questions for discussion: demobilization, reparations, Petsamo.

The Finnish government thought the terms too harsh, but asked for approval to seek peace on the best possible terms. Parliament approved 105–80, with the minority more definitely of the opinion that some of these terms were inacceptable. Even the minority wanted the government to report any scheme for peace on a basis of "independence, freedom and safety."

The British, President Roosevelt, and King Gustav all publicly advised acceptance of the Russian terms. But the Finns, after Paasikivi had obtained "clarification" in Moscow in April, considered them impossible. Most of all they worried about the obligation to intern the Germans, and Russia would not begin negotiations until the Finns accepted that stipulation. The reparations figure was set at $600,000,000, which a Finnish economist reckoned at 45 per cent of the country's total productive capacity for a five-year period. "The Finns would have to learn to live without eating." The government presented its negative conclusion to a secret session of parliament on April 12 and won a unanimous vote of confidence.

In June 1944 the skies grew dark over Finland. Western armies were advancing through France, and Russia was launching a direct offensive in the north. On the sixteenth of June the Finnish minister to Washington, Hjalmar Procopé, was given his passports; on the twentieth Viipuri, key border fortress in the southeast, fell; on the twenty-second a new peace approach to Moscow was made through Stockholm; and the same day von Ribbentrop flew in from Berlin. The German foreign minister dissuaded the Finns from making peace with Russia and promised strong military assistance and food supplies. All that

Germany wanted in return was a commitment from Finland to stand with Germany to the end.

The Finns then pulled out of the hat a commitment which did not commit. Instead of having parliament vote an agreement with Germany, which would have lasting legal effect, President Ryti gave the required pledges in a personal letter to Hitler. He personally and alone took responsibility for not making a separate peace with Russia. The social democrats opposed this plan in the cabinet meeting, but stayed in the government even when it was done. On June 30 the United States finally broke relations with Finland.

In July 1944 the drive of the western armies across France made imminent the doom of Germany. Germany not only could not send Finland the needed support, but withdrew her air force and some of her infantry regiments. No one would permit the Finns to have their private war. They yielded at last, not so much to their own defeat as to a world situation.

President Ryti resigned on August 1 so that his personal pledge to the Germans could be canceled. Four days later Marshal Mannerheim was made president, and the Germans were warned of the desperate situation and the political change. Another message was sent to the Russian minister in Stockholm. The preliminary conditions of the Russians were more stringent than before, but on September 2 the parliament voted 108–45 to accept them. The Finns had to cease firing on September 4; the Russians not until September 5; and the Finns must demand that the Germans evacuate Finland by September 15 (1944).

The Finnish delegation went to Moscow and was presented with a treaty which left a hardy people room to exist and no more. It was ratified by a unanimously dejected parliament on September 23. The eastern boundaries of 1940 were restored, which once more sheared off 10 per cent of the arable land and once more threw nearly 450,000 people back into a smaller and a war-worn country. The Petsamo area in the far north was ceded to Russia, excluding Finland from access to the Arctic and taking from her the rich nickel mines of the north. Hangö was renounced by the Russians in return for a fifty-year lease on the Porkkala peninsula, which gave the Russians a strangling strategic position around the corner from Helsinki, and permitted them to control a section of railroad from Helsinki to Turku (Åbo). Finland was obligated to try in court and to punish the "war responsibles," and to disband all "fascist-minded" organizations. The reparations figure was set at half the figure mentioned in the spring, but $300,000,000 in American dollar values of 1938 was a stupendous sum for Finland. Could the country survive?

The Germans disappointed the Finns by refusing to depart peaceably, and amazed them by the atrocities and devastation they left in their wake as they were slowly pushed out. On to April 1945 there was bloody fighting and the towns and farm-steads of the northern third of Finland were laid waste. The lone chimneys of burned homes still marked the north country in 1949.

The Finns had tried to treat their German partners fairly. Both had a common cause against the U.S.S.R. and it was natural for Finland to sign the anti-Comintern pact. Some Finns admired all things German, but neither the country nor the government was "pro-German" or "pro-nazi," any more than Germany was "pro-Finnish," or any more than the United States was "pro-Russian" while engaged as an ally of the U.S.S.R. in war. This distorted aspect has been overemphasized because Finland was on the other side, and because she was small and her policies little known. Her anti-Russianism was her own, more ancient and more consistent than Germany's anti-Russianism; her anti-communism had been tempered in her own internal fires; her democracy was a thing unknown in Germany and maintained throughout the war. No alliance or pledge was made by Finland to Germany until Ryti's letter of June 1944. Finland's "pro-Germanism" was composed of loyalty to the one state that helped her, and of the military and economic dependence which grew with the war itself. By the time the

Finns had driven the Germans out of the country there was only hatred and disillusion left.

Finland had not been careful enough in her neutrality, and had allowed Germany to compromise her. Once involved in war she was dependent on Germany not only for guns but for potatoes and grain; she could not get out of the war largely because no one else could feed her. She clung to the notion that a single nation could wage a separate war while the world chose sides; she was just as mistaken as were those nations who thought they could have separate peace. She fought skillfully and with a bravery which made the shields ring in Valhalla. Politically she played her cards so badly that the Russians feared her, the German "brothers-in-arms" distrusted her, and her sincere friends in Britain and America could not know what to count on. It was both a miracle and a tribute to her stubborn strength that she survived as a nation.

8. SCANDINAVIA AND THE COSTS OF WAR

The costs of war can never be stated precisely. Only some of the lesser but tangible items can be measured. The sensitivity of the Scandinavian countries to European and world conditions was evidenced as early as October 1939; Finland's income was reduced 20 per cent, food rationing was begun in Norway, gasoline rationing in Denmark, and export of eggs from Sweden prohibited. Sweden's minister of finance, Ernst Wigforss, warned the workers of what happens when their products cannot be sold; the old standard of living could not be maintained. The cost of living index, which had held fairly even from 1937 to 1939, began to rise rapidly. (See p. 283.)

The financial situation in the occupied countries is illustrated by Norway. There the note circulation on April 9, 1940 was under 600,000,000 kr. But the Germans opened a Wehrmacht credit in the bank in Oslo, and by 1945 the note circulation was over 3,000,000,000 kr. In 1940 there were 113,000,000 kr. deposits on current account; on May 7, 1945 the amount was

COST OF LIVING INDEX

	Den.	Nor.	Sw.	Fin.	Ice.
1937	100	100	100	100	
1939	104	105	105	105	102
1942	156	152	145	174	212
1945	162	160	150	292	277

5,900,000,000 kr. It made little difference that the exile government in London had paid its way, this inflation remained as a ball and chain on the country. Denmark faced a similar problem, for she had sent Germany her foodstuffs, and Germany never caught up in payments either in coal or in money; at the close of the war the debt stood at 7,640,000,000 kr. (about $1,500,000,000).

Shipping losses were stupendous. Of Norway's 4,850,000 tons a fleet of 4,000,000 tons was abroad on April 9, though some of it was caught in the ports of Denmark, or Germany, and later in Vichy France. Of that 4,000,000 tons, much of it in modern tankers, just half survived the war. Insurance made good the losses, but could not rebuild the ships, except a few. Hence earning capacity was lost for years to come. Over 3000 sailors had perished. The whaling fleet, small and specialized, was particularly hard hit, losing nine out of thirteen of its "floating factories."

Denmark had a merchant fleet of 1,176,000 tons in 1939, but only 921,000 tons in 1945. Finland had 645,000 tons in 1939 and was down to 330,000 tons in 1946. This loss was due to the sinking of 113,000 tons, reparations payments to Russia of 82,500 tons, and confiscations by Germany, Britain, and the United States of about 120,000 tons. Sweden had 1,582,000 tons in 1939; even in her neutrality she lost about 250,000 tons, but since she was able to build anew she ended the war with about 1,600,000 tons. Iceland had only 31,000 tons in 1939, but she felt keenly the loss of some of her fishing boats and one of her two large passenger vessels.

Loss of life was especially large in Finland and Norway. The Finnish toll in two wars was 78,000, 2 per cent of the population. Finnish losses, furthermore, included 17,800 square miles of territory, reparations of $300,000,000 in goods (in terms of 1938 dollars), and the destruction of some 1600 houses in the Russian wars, and of 25,000 in the deliberate devastation by the Germans as they retreated in the north. There was additional destruction in the area ceded to Russia. The damages inflicted by the Germans were reckoned at $120,000,000.

In Norway the destruction led to staggering reparations claims against Germany. Damage to industry and commerce was estimated at $100,000,000, that to ocean shipping at $395,-000,000, railway and other transport at $215,000,000, man-years lost to the national economy or used in the war against Germany at $761,000,000, additional costs of German occupation at $2,738,000,000, and other items which all added up to $5,-217,000,000.

Such figures are impressive, but Mars presented a bill which was larger still, incomprehensible in worldly statistics, including items like disillusionment and mistrust between neighbors. War had changed Scandinavia.

8. The Search for Security

The impact of war on Scandinavia was not only devastation and debt. It was not only psychological disillusionment. It was revolution in political position. Scandinavia had been drawn into the vortex of international conflict, and had little hope of escape. The situation had been created by forces beyond her control; her problem was one of adjustment.

1. THE AFTERMATH OF WAR

The residue of war was an avalanche of "threats from within": social and economic disorganization, overextension of budgets, inflation, and the ever-present shadow of communism.

During the war a wise Norwegian woman worried about what youth would do after the war—youth trained in sabotage, boys who had been encouraged to give full rein to their destructive inclinations. Instead, in Norway, Denmark, and Finland, it appeared that the sobering discipline of the underground and of national disaster actually created a more mature and purposeful youth. After celebrating liberation through the summer of 1945 the Norwegians settled down to work. But restlessness pervaded the atmosphere, as illustrated by the youth riots in Stockholm in 1948. These seemingly aimless outbreaks could be explained only by the combination of youth and spring, social uncertainty and postwar *malaise*.

Economic disorganization resulted from the abnormal channels into which industry and commerce had been thrown by the war. The disorganization was to a large extent hidden or absorbed by the demand for workers in new industries and in reconstruction work. But thousands of men had to rebuild their homes instead of plow their fields, and production had to be directed into essentials and diverted from the unnecessary: in Oslo, for instance, houses could not be painted nor rugs replaced; all possible labor and materials for such things were sent to northern Norway to put that desolated region on its feet once more. Work there was in plenty, and work provided a healthy social outlet and discipline. Tensions there were, of course, and the Swedish metal workers in 1945 staged the largest strike since 1909; they settled at last for an infinitesimal gain. Particularly in the three countries which experienced war directly the first postwar years showed both a willingness to work and a willingness to endure restrictions. Production was the important thing for the moment, and adjustments of wages and of profits could await a later test of strength. The love of country and the obvious need evoked a no-strike pledge from Norwegian workers and labor stoppages were notably rare throughout Scandinavia.

Refugees created varied problems. In Sweden 35,000 Balts were absorbed into the busy economy, though not so easily into the society. They remain officially classed as Russian citizens, greatly to their annoyance, and they live in fear that Sweden may yield to Russian pressure to send them to their fate in the U.S.S.R. Incidents occur to keep fear alive: two boys were reportedly kidnapped by Russians and taken back, and occasionally a boy or a young woman is threatened and hounded by Russian agents. The Swedish government has stood firm, however, and has returned only the group who reached Swedish shores in uniform. The Balts appreciate the hospitality of Sweden, and the opportunity to retain their language and their own schools, but they feel no real safety. They try for visas to the United States, to the Argentine, or to South Africa, and some sail the Atlantic in small boats without the formalities of passports and visas.

In Finland the refugees from Estonia and Ingermanland have

been in greater danger; if born in Russian territory the Finns are bound by treaty to send them back, and the Russians keep finding and demanding such unfortunates. The greater problem in Finland has been the resettlement of the 450,000 Finns from the Karelian area ceded to Russia in 1940 and again in 1944. Forest lands have been cleared for some, but many have had to be squeezed into established communities, with hardship to themselves and to the owners of lands already too small.

Denmark, in the spring of 1945, was flooded with 210,000 refugees, fleeing from Eastern Germany before the dreaded Cossacks. The Danes took the hardheaded and farsighted attitude that these people would never make good Danish citizens, and that it was safest not to let them mix at all with the population or to get established in jobs. They could not even do road work (most of them were women, children, and old men anyway). They were kept in prison compounds, fed well, and returned to Germany as fast as Danish diplomacy could persuade the powers to receive them in one zone or another; the Russians would not take them. Not until February 1949 were the last of them transported from Denmark. The cost of keeping them had been high, but the Danes were satisfied with their policy.

More disturbing to Denmark, because she could do little about them, were the 300,000 German refugees who had crowded into South Slesvig, an area which was partly Danish, and which many Danes hoped could be re-annexed, as North Slesvig had been in 1920. They did not want to annex all those extra Germans; they feared either a "yes" or a "no" in a plebiscite, for they did not want Denmark to be rejected, yet they did not want a hungry population to vote merely for Danish butter. Premier Knud Kristensen was the chief spokesman for Danish expansion, and he lost out in the fall of 1947. The issue remained, a twentieth-century remnant of that centuries-old Slesvig-Holstein complexity which Palmerston said only three people had ever understood: one of them was dead; one had gone crazy; he was the third, and he had forgotten it.

The luxuries of partisan political strife had been laid aside during the war, and coalition governments had acted in the spirit of national unity, whether in regular legal form as with Sweden, Finland, and Iceland, underground as with Denmark, or in exile as with Norway. Freedom brought the return to party programs, reinforced by deepened convictions. In the special case of Finland a coalition government continued until the summer of 1948, and in her case alone was there any real bitterness in the resumption of one-party responsibility. In each case the social democrats were the strongest single group (technically not quite so in Finland), and they took over the administration. This parallelism in the five countries facilitated inter-Scandinavian coöperation, especially in the field of social legislation.

It was exactly in social legislation that these countries headed into contradictions and troubles. The governments assumed new responsibilities for guiding the economy, but it was a puzzling and uncertain time for all economies. The governing parties had promised everyone a long and happy life of security, and they swelled the budgets for social affairs. They legislated two- and three-week paid vacations for workers, yet they had to insist on extraordinary production and to persuade people to wait for some of the promised beneficence. Where the leash was not held tightly, inflation, as in Finland and Iceland particularly, robbed the people of the advances which looked good on paper. Finland had not enough goods, and by 1948 prices soared to eight times the prewar levels. Only the automatic increase of wages prevented chaos.

In Denmark and Norway, and even in Finland, people were understanding and optimistic. In Sweden, where war had not disrupted life as much, people were surprised and disgruntled to find that peace brought little relief. Sweden was ready for business in a big way, but found it difficult to do business. Her war-built dollar reserve was exhausted in two years, too much of it going for purchase of plastics and nylons and other consumer goods, instead of basic production goods such as machinery. Swedish products could be sold for credit, but not enough for dollars; and credits were extended to the danger point. In 1946 torrential rains drowned important crops; 1947 followed with killing drought. The drought affected the vital water supply and curtailed power. Government planning for abundance degenerated into planning and controls for existence. People complained of "red-tape Sweden" (*Krångel Sverige*), and Stockholm in 1948 was placarded with signs "Save for worse times ahead" (*Spara för sämre tider*).

Such was the northern milieu in which communists tried to spread suspicion and dissension. They had behind them in 1945 all the prestige of the magnificent Russian resistance to the Germans, and in Norway the Russian prisoners doing labor for the nazis left a good impression. In Denmark the communists enjoyed prestige for their effective work in the underground. In all these countries they won election support, 1944–1946, of from 8 to 15 per cent of the voters. In Finland they combined with left-wing socialists and won still greater support and a strong ministerial position. In Iceland they had two members of the cabinet.

Then the communists began to overplay their hands, both internally and internationally. In Denmark, for example, where the food rations were twice the European average, they induced a group of workers to demonstrate against a shortage of potatoes. In Iceland they rioted and the communist members of the government withdrew in protest against the continuance of United States use of Keflavik airport. By the end of 1947 their votes and their influence were declining significantly. The decline became a toboggan slide with the Soviet coup in Czechoslovakia and the Russian demands for a mutual assistance pact with Finland.

The entire North was aroused. In the spring of 1948 a massive anti-communist student meeting protested in Oslo. Thousands of party members resigned. The social democratic parties of Denmark, Norway, and Sweden staged a joint campaign against communists in April, trying to wash themselves clean of the taint of fellow-traveling. Men with border-line records were extruded from party councils. Even in Finland, after she signed the agreement with Russia, the communist minister of interior, Y. Leino, was tried for old crimes and forced from office, despite the fact that he was married to Hertta Kuusinen, probably the most powerful communist in the country. The Finnish elections of July 1948 cut the communist-popular democrat strength by 25 per cent, and when they wanted still to hold important places in the coalition government the other parties revolted and allowed the social democrats alone to form a cabinet, though they had only 54 members out of 200 in the diet, and would have to live on the sufferance of others.

Communism was recognized as anti-democracy, anti-Scandinavia. In the Swedish elections of September 1948 the communist members of the Riksdag were reduced from fifteen to eight. The Norwegian election of October 1949 returned to the Storting not one of the previous 11 communist members. Two weeks later the Icelanders showed that they too had changed their minds, though in less spectacular degree; the new Althing would have one fewer communist, two fewer social democrats, and three more agrarian progressives. Threats from within were still present, but minds were clearing and backs were stiffening.

Threats from without loomed also. In fact, as the inner threats were increasingly known and brought under control, the external threats grew in potential danger. The eclipse of Germany was in itself a release; the North could breathe again when Hitler's power was destroyed. The tragedy was that as Germany disappeared the Russian giant looked more huge than ever. Western Europe was weakened both absolutely and relatively. The result was that the whole area had to lean increasingly on the young giant across the Atlantic.

Russian pressure exerted itself first in trade relationships. The Soviet state was a potentially rich market, and supposedly more stable than individualistic America, which would be plagued by the business cycle. Important, too, Russia, directly or indirectly, could supply oil and coal and other necessary materials which could no longer be obtained through Germany. All the northern states, like the United States, wanted to develop trade with the U.S.S.R., and each country made trade agreements with her.

Most extensive and most controversial of all these agreements was that made by Sweden, providing for a credit to Russia of one billion kronor ($278,000,000). Swedish business did not object to the agreement as such, but was aghast at the amount. The United States made an official protest, basing her objection on the ground that this large credit would prevent Sweden from continuing her natural trade with other countries. The real fear was that Sweden would become enmeshed in bilateral trade on a governmental basis, and therefore involved politically with Russia. Facts belied the fears. In the first place the total trade contemplated over a six-year period was but 15 per cent of Sweden's export, and no more than filled the gap left by the loss of German trade. Second, the agreement merely guaranteed credit, and left the contracting for goods to individual transactions between the U.S.S.R. and Swedish industries. The Swedish government did bring pressure on some industries to sell to Russia, but the total contracts made amounted to only one-third of the available credit (280,000,000 kr. or $80,000,000 by the end of 1948; increased slightly in 1949).

The heavy hand laid on Finland would have crushed a less resilient nation. The $300,000,000 reparations (in 1938 dollar values) were not only severe in themselves, but they were required in goods that Finland was not accustomed to produce: ships, electrical equipment, machinery, and only one-third in forest products. But the Finns immediately set to work to build the necessary plants and to meet the demands. They would work and pay, and in eight years they would be free. Occasionally they fell slightly behind schedule in some items, but the totals they fulfilled every year. The Russians maintained constant oversight and compulsion, but after the first four years, in the face of American aid to western Europe and their own leniency to Rumania and other satellites, they canceled half of the second half of the reparations due from Finland.

Politically the Russians pressed hard on the Finns. After the armistice in 1944 General A. Zhdanov hinted at the need of a military pact between Russia and Finland. In conversations of the Russians with Mannerheim and Paasikivi the topic recurred. It was dropped for a time, until once when Premier Mauno Pekkala in Moscow tried to say something kindly to Stalin. Molotov asked Pekkala afterwards, "did I understand you to say that Finland is now ready to enter a pact such as Zhdanov suggested in 1945?" Pekkala replied negatively and said that he had no powers to act. In January 1948 when General Savonenkov was appointed the Russian minister to Helsinki the Finns knew the time had come.

Stalin made further evasion impossible by sending a personal letter of invitation to alliance to President Paasikivi. The Finns dragged out the negotiations for weeks. They took full advantage of the simultaneous uproar over the Czechoslovak affair, and they won a wording for their pact which was as mild and safe as any such agreement could be. In its final form it did little but state in a legal document the condition of affairs which geography and power made inevitable. All the states along Russia's border to the south had acquiesced. How could Finland refuse to say that she had no aggressive designs on her big neighbor? And the Finns were sure enough of themselves to be willing to discuss. They knew that neither tricks nor confusion could succeed in Finland. But they did have to be careful about the phrasing of terms.

Finland promised to defend her territory against "Germany or another state allied with her," to enter into discussions with Russia in case of war or threat of war, and to accept Russian aid. Finland insisted upon accepting no responsibility for action outside her own territory. Promises of noninterference in internal affairs were mutual; the term was ten years; the date was April 6, 1948.

It was in July, after this treaty had been ratified, that the elections clipped the wings of communist power in the Parliament. Repeated attempts at crippling strikes, communist-inspired, failed to shake the government. The Finns continued to live dangerously, undaunted. In the summer of 1949 the communists started a series of strikes in key industries like lumber and metals, evidently intending to cripple the entire economy and overthrow the government. But noncommunist workers refused to quit work, violence did not succeed, troops were thrown in quickly, the illegal strikes were condemned by the federation of labor, and the offending unions were expelled. Able leadership and the solidarity of the majority preserved the government and the national independence.

Soviet compulsion on the other northern countries was comparatively gentle. Fulminators in the press and over the radio from time to time attacked them for planning to give bases to the United States, or for maltreating Estonian refugees, but most charges were not taken seriously. At Easter time, 1948, rumors of a possible military move against Denmark and Norway brought quick defensive moves in those lands, and nothing happened. The Russian desire for "coöperation" with Norway in the defense of Spitsbergen, mentioned in 1944, was suggested again in 1947. The Norwegians carefully pointed to the United Nations and to their own defensive strength; they thought they could deflect any probable threat; the Russians noted their attitude and once more laid the matter on the shelf. Constant pressure but no violence remained the method, at least temporarily.

Another outside pressure very different, but very real, was the inadequacy of dollar valuta. It was a disease, a lack of dollar corpuscles in the economic blood-stream. The trouble was only partly the excess spending of 1945 and 1946; it was largely the destruction and wastage of capital goods, the reorientation of trade which accompanied war, and the reorientation of political power. Germany had been second only to Britain as market and source of supply for the northern countries. After 1945 Germany no longer functioned in either capacity. The goods needed in the North could be had only from the United States; but the United States needed only small quantities of the goods produced in the North. So Scandinavia could not get the dollars with which to buy her needs. The old-fashioned multilateral trade was of little use, because other possible purchasers lacked dollars too. And, dollars were needed for what little could be had from occupied Germany.

Without dollars Finland could not build the factories to pay her reparations, Denmark could not buy the fertilizer to make her fields yield crops, Sweden could not buy the machinery to make her industry function. The trouble was not laziness, as some Americans thought, nor socialistic programs: it was an international disease of war-devastated economies and artificial barriers to the interchange of goods. The same disease was affecting England, France, the Netherlands, and other countries.

To aid Europe as a whole to reconstruct its economy, to stimulate a new flow of trade, to make the western democracies function in order to save them from communist revolution, the United States first granted loans and then inaugurated the Marshall Plan, or ERP. To war-devastated countries like Denmark and Norway generous aid was given as grants, with loans in addition; to more fortunate countries like Sweden the aid was in the form of loan only. Sweden also was obligated to extend credit aid to other countries. (See table, p. 193.)

The important thing was that the aid, whether grants or loans, enabled these countries to buy production goods, food, and tobacco, and to speed up the process of recovery. The first ECA loan went to Iceland in July 1948, a $2,300,000 credit for a ship to "increase the production and processing of fish oils and their related products and their exportation." Denmark estimated that each dollar of the support given her was multiplied four times in Danish production; Norway on the basis of this aid and her own efforts raised her industrial production index in 1948 to 140 as compared with 100 in 1939. By the end of 1948 progress was evident throughout the North. Sweden during the course of 1949 achieved the trade balance set as a

EXPORT–IMPORT BANK CREDITS TO FINLAND,
1939–1949

December 13, 1939	
March 1, 1940	$ 35,000,000.00
December 12, 1945	4,971,000.00
January 16, 1946	35,000,000.00
January 21 and 22, 1947	35,000,000.00
February 19, 1947	2,580,000.00
February 14, 1948	1,950,000.00
May 12, 1948	675,000.00
November 3, 1948	10,000,000.00
Miscellaneous small grants	50,204.68
Total	$125,226,204.68

INTERNATIONAL BANK FOR RECONSTRUCTION
AND DEVELOPMENT, CREDIT TO FINLAND

August 1, 1949 .... $ 12,500,000.00

goal for 1952. Finland alone, because of Russian objections, was not within the ERP, but a series of special loans to Finland by the United States helped toward the accomplishment of the same object. This positive evidence of the will and the ability of democratic nations to coöperate in mutual aid was a body blow to the disruptive tactics of the communists.

To the American citizen and taxpayer this five billion dollar per year program was intended to aid people in distress, to give business assistance to important working partners, and to help build a political bulwark against Russian aggression. The Scandinavians could appreciate the last two motivations, but found it difficult to believe in Uncle Sam's altruism. They saw other aspects of American policy which seemed like stupid contrariness. For example, the United States was giving aid to Denmark to rebuild her export industry and agriculture, but the American forces in near-by Germany bought their meat from the United States, saying it had higher caloric value. The United States was helping Norway to reconstruct her merchant fleet, but curtailed the earnings of that fleet by requiring that at least

50 per cent of ERP goods be shipped in American bottoms. The Swedes objected that the United States was "dumping" wood pulp on the European and South American markets at forty dollars per ton less than the Swedish price. Despite these disturbing problems the Scandinavians were coöperating wholeheartedly in the total program which they knew was of inestimable value.

Trade difficulties and the dearth of dollars slowed progress and forced unnatural controls. Imports had to be curtailed drastically and exports artificially stimulated. Danes could not replace their broken cups and saucers, they could not buy new silver made in their own workshops without bringing in for trade an equal amount of old silver. But foreigners with dollars could buy handsome porcelain and silver. In most of these countries permits had to be obtained to export anything (even a toy wooden pig), and only the man with dollars could expect to get many permits. He was often so frustrated by red tape and high prices that he did not buy. Foreign exchange was under strict control: Sweden in 1947 allowed the government to demand from Swedish citizens, in return for Swedish kronor, their holdings abroad in "hard currency" countries. By such stringent measures, and usually with popular approval nevertheless, the Scandinavians have made progress in reëstablishing their society.

In September 1949 reform from without was added to regulation from within; the devaluation of the pound sterling had its immediate counterpart in Denmark, Norway, Sweden, and Iceland. The Scandinavians considered that the move had been forced by the United States, and they felt some resentment. They had no choice but to go along because their own dollar shortages were severe and because they must on account of their trade with Britain keep their currencies aligned with the pound. They hoped that trade might be resuscitated by the move, but they had already pared their imports to the bone. They feared that they could not increase exports to the dollar lands sufficiently to counterbalance the increased price of the goods they needed. They accepted devaluation, however, as another of the stringent measures necessary in the struggle for readjustment.

By the end of 1948 Norway's desolated Finnmark was two-thirds restored and her fleet was almost back to prewar capacity. Narvik was being rebuilt in concrete on a larger scale, and new piers installed for the ore traffic. Denmark was reclaiming her heath and Finland her forests. Iceland was improving her means of processing fish. Sweden was electrifying more railroads, building new power plants. All the countries were planning thoughtfully and striving energetically, expanding educational facilities and extending social legislation as fast as finances permitted.

To war's aftermath of threats and reconstruction problems must be added reorientation in Scandinavian foreign relations. War had changed both Scandinavia and the world, and wartime alignments tended to continue. Norway was a functioning member of the United Nations from the first, operating through her government in London. Her representatives played a part in the framing of the charter of the new world organization and Norwegian Trygve Lie became its first Secretary General. In none of the northern countries was there any question this time about participation as there had been with the League of Nations. All had learned that an international organization was the only hope for them and for the world. The only issue was how to make coöperation effective. Youth was interested in world government, but statesmen concentrated on doing what they could with the machinery at hand.

Denmark during the war had no legal government abroad and could not take part in the wartime United Nations and the San Francisco Conference. But upon liberation in May 1945 she joined immediately. Iceland and Sweden had not been in the ranks of the warring states but were in the first group of new states admitted to the United Nations, in the autumn of 1946. Finland's status remained puzzling. She should belong to the world organization and every one professed to want her, but she was caught in the rivalry of East and West. When the United Nations refused to admit certain of the Russian satellite states the U.S.S.R. retaliated by delaying the inclusion of Finland.

In the council chambers of the United Nations, in its secretariat and in its affiliated organizations, the Scandinavians served with intelligence and success. Here was a forum and a working institution in which the Scandinavian will to peace and the Scandinavian genius for coöperative action could express themselves. When the Council of Europe was set in motion in 1949 the Scandinavians joined that, too, ready to use it to the limit of its possibilities.

In relations with specific states Scandinavia had to readapt her policies. At the moment Germany was neither a military threat nor an economic asset. Britain was so completely enveloped in her own problems, her own austerity, that she could not give her customary assistance to the North. Britain and Germany together normally bought half of Scandinavia's exports and supplied half of her imports. Now, for the great new needs of reconstruction, Scandinavia had to look elsewhere. There was but one direction to look, despite the fact that before the war the United States accounted for less than 10 per cent of either exports or imports of the Scandinavian countries.

In the new world the wideness of the Atlantic Ocean was of little importance. Ships and airplanes and telephones bridged it. Scandinavia found it possible to expand her earlier contacts with the United States and counted increasingly on America as an economic ally.

Although economic and cultural relations had firm foundations the Scandinavians found themselves confused in the realm of American politics and diplomacy. They could see little rhyme or reason in American political parties. The Finns and others could not understand how Americans could so wholly oppose Russia at one moment, then wholeheartedly ally with her, then reverse the field again. The vagaries of Congress on the Marshall Plan, approving it, reducing it, reëstablishing it, dismayed everyone. After much propaganda about interest in democracy the logical Northerners could not see how responsible leaders could dream of including Franco Spain in the Atlantic Pact. And they puzzled about other contradictions between what Americans professed and what they performed, especially in the matter of race.

Nevertheless the Scandinavians recognized that in the essentials their interests and those of the United States were identified. They tried to understand America and attempted to have America understand them.

2. INTER-SCANDINAVIAN COÖPERATION

Scandinavian union has never succeeded, but the Scandinavian idea has persisted. Coöperation on the basis of individual autonomy has grown as the old triple and dual states have broken apart. This coöperation was momentarily disrupted by World War II, but the sense of interdependence was deepened.

During the war underground groups in Denmark, filled with a realization of their own futility, agitated for a binding federal union with Sweden and Norway. Support came from high quarters, and the leaders were sanguine. But the Swedes wanted Finland included, while the Danes objected to extending their risks to a Russian border state. The Danes wanted to include Iceland, and the Swedes were loath to push the boundaries into the Atlantic. The Norwegians were the most reserved, inclined to feel that their heroic resistance and their coöperation with Britain and the United States placed them in a different league.

In the wartime discussions and in the continued talks after the war the Swedes were in a delicate position. They favored some kind of union, but they must be practical. They were the most numerous, the most wealthy, and the strongest militarily; they feared that active advocacy might arouse jealousy and destroy any possibility of success. And they were not sure. Some thought that a Scandinavian league in 1939–40 might have prevented the attacks on their neighbors; others thought that a league would have meant only the immediate involvement of Sweden along with the others.

The idea of union could not overcome nationalistic separatism. Memories of the Kalmar Union and of the emotional but impractical Pan-Scandinavianism of the nineteenth century made people pause. Men recalled the mass meetings of students of the North, such as that at Christiansborg in 1845 when 247 speeches on brotherhood bound young men soulfully together. It was only "talk-brotherhood," as was proved by the wars of 1849 and 1864. The twentieth century was skeptical.

In coöperation short of legal commitments the Scandinavians went far. (Examples have been cited in several connections herein.) Academic interchange was frequent—exchange of professors and students, scholarships, international folk high schools, mutual examination of textbooks in history in order to eliminate contradictions and causes of bitterness. Since 1919 the Norden societies have done effective work in publishing Scandinavian books and journals, holding lectures, and promoting visits between the various countries. State support has aided some of their activities. Bands of school children vacationed in their neighbor-lands. Cities of similar size in the different countries were named "brother-cities," and aided one another in the postwar period (Copenhagen was "brother" to Helsinki and Stockholm; Gothenburg was "brother" to Bergen, etc.).

Increasingly conventions of professional groups like lawyers, doctors, historians, were held on Scandinavian rather than national bases. Social reforms were planned in common (cf. p. 116), and ministers of state met to discuss innumerable common problems. Labor unions built a feeling of solidarity. Orchestras and athletic teams traveled back and forth as freely as between the states of the United States. Sports are a major concern of the Scandinavians, and in 1948 Sweden took great pride in ranking second to the United States in the Olympics; if taken together the Scandinavian countries outranked the United States (an extraordinary feat for 17,000,000 people).

The advantages of economic coöperation were recognized

Hardinge, British statesman, to Sir Arthur Nicolson, ambassador at St. Petersburg, spoke frankly in terms of broad truth:

As for the Baltic and North Sea agreements they will hold good for us so long as they are not violated by others. If in time of war the Straits [Skagerak, Kattegat and Öresund] remain open that is all we want. If Germany tries to close them we shall regard ourselves as absolutely free to do what we like and even to ignore the integrity of Norway should we require a naval base on the Norwegian coast. For these reasons the agreements are hardly worth the paper they will be written on as we know that Germany has made preparations to invade Denmark in case of war with us.*

The attitude here stated was the standpoint of Russia, Germany, Great Britain, and France. It led to the attack on Finland in 1939 and it almost led to French and British action in Sweden and Norway in the winter of 1940. It led to British violation of Norway's waters on April 8, 1940, and to the German invasion of Denmark and Norway on April 9. It brought British and later American occupation of Iceland, and throughout the war it threatened the integrity of Sweden. The law of nations was still the law of force.

The Scandinavians are more aware of this "realism" of diplomacy and warfare than are Americans. At the same time they are proud and freedom-loving, and hate to admit that their longboats must sail in the wake of anybody's super-carrier.

To try to preserve Scandinavian independence, in January 1949 Sweden "tacked" on her sailing route: she offered to extend her neutral defense area to include Norway and Denmark. Like many a diplomatic move it looked like one which might have averted trouble in the past war, but was inadequate to help in the next one; "too little and too late." But Norway and Denmark were eager to preserve Nordic solidarity, and statesmen wrestled for weeks seeking a formula for common action. The foreign ministers and the prime ministers met—in Karlstad, Copenhagen, Oslo. Experts were called upon. Party

* February 5, 1908, *British Documents on the Origins of the War, 1898–1914*, VIII, 165–166.

leaders joined the discussions, and the dream of a "Scandinavian parliament" was almost a reality.

But the new project foundered on the rocks of differing interests. Norway felt she must have aid from the West. Sweden stood adamant on unfettered neutrality. Denmark could not find a compromise solution. The United States was agreeable enough to the idea of a united Scandinavia, but averse to a Scandinavia pledged to absolute neutrality. This would but "widen the soft spot." The United States feared, as did many within the Scandinavian countries, that such a solution would merely prepare the North for a sudden pounce by a ruthless aggressor. The Scandinavian Pact failed to materialize and Norway and Denmark regretfully joined the Atlantic Pact while Sweden withheld, at least for the moment. The Atlantic Pact regards the defense of each of its members as a concern of all. For that group neutrality is abandoned in favor of solidarity.

The neutrality of Sweden is rooted in tradition and in recent experience; the country has kept out of war for 135 years and naturally thinks it may be possible to avoid it in the future. She clings to neutrality as to a religious dogma. Her point of view was attacked by a writer in the London *Economist*, who complained that Sweden counts on western help but will do nothing to prepare for it. He continued:

Swedish policy will remain ambiguous, inconsistent and, above all, opportunist, a policy of armed neutrality, of economic and cultural collaboration, of limited obligations, of membership of UNO —and insurance against its failure. Thus the strongest state in Scandinavia is the weakest.[*]

If one lets Sweden speak for herself he gets a different emphasis. The position can be paraphrased as follows, in words based on newspaper comment, government statements, and conversations with hundreds of Swedes from "John Q. Carlson" to high officials:

"We are with the West, and Britain and the United States

[*] 15 May 1948, pp. 801–802.

ought to understand that. We will attack no one, and if we are attacked we will fight as long as we can. We went so far as to offer to include Denmark and Norway in our sphere of defense, and to regard an attack on either of them as an attack on ourselves. This was the same kind of proposal the United States made to various states in the North Atlantic Pact. We thus magnanimously agreed to abandon our more than century-old neutrality, keystone of our foreign policy. We who possess the only real military and naval strength in the North were ready to pledge common action. But the offer was spurned, chiefly because of American pressure. Now we are forced to retire into neutral isolation, for otherwise we irritate our great eastern neighbor, and possibly force her to take more positive action in Finland—which would be disastrous for our good Finnish friends, and bring Russian guns to the Åland Islands, the Gulf of Bothnia, and to our northern border in easy reach of the iron mines of Kiruna and Gällivare.

"Even if we should be so bold as to align with the West, what good could it do either the West or ourselves? The United States could not get aid to us in time to count, and, from what we gather, the strategy of the West is to retire to the Atlantic shores of Europe in case of Russian attack, or at least to the Rhine and the North Sea. In any case we would be left to our fate.

"And neutrality is not impossible. Yes, the odds are against it, but it has worked since 1814, through World War I and World War II, and it just might work again. We can be no worse off for trying it.

"Do you speak of a moral responsibility to band together with others of like belief? How can an American raise such a question on Sweden's conduct? Was not the United States more neutral and isolationist than Sweden until she suddenly became a dominant world power? Nations must look out for themselves. The great states do, and so must the small."

Such an argument has logic, plausibility. It represents deep conviction. Within Sweden, however, some voices are raised against it, notably that of Herbert Tingsten in *Dagens Nyheter*. But his is a voice crying in the wilderness, winning converts certainly but slowly. If Sweden should eventually abandon her independent stand it will be through the pressure of events, because of changed conditions. The failure of the Scandinavian Pact and the tying in of Norway and Denmark with the Atlantic powers do in themselves change the situation, but so far there is no weakening in the Swedish government position. One official spokesman said simply, "We thought we could afford to take that position." Prime Minister Erlander has said that "each people must make its decisions on the basis of its own experiences," and that the possibilities for continued neutrality are increased by United States assurances that bases will not be demanded in Norway. Professor Bertil Ohlin, leader of the People's Party, disclaimed "primitive isolationism" and referred to the "sharpening of opposition between East and West which increases Sweden's risks and demands strengthening of the country's defenses."

This emphasis on defense is a significant aspect of Swedish policy—these Vikings have become peace-loving, but they are not yet pacifist. They claim the strongest army in continental Europe; they could put 700,000 men in the field and equip 12 divisions with up-to-date weapons. The Swedes are the only people in Europe manufacturing their own jet planes. They have a good navy and trained sailors. They threaten the direst consequences to anyone who attacks them; they are digging munitions factories and power stations underground, and steadily expanding their defenses. They reckon on holding off an invader for at least two or three weeks. Their defense will be desperate even if alone.

But Sweden did not want to be alone. The government announced that the January 1949 offer to include Denmark and Norway in her neutrality sphere continued open. Why did her neighbors and cousins reject that offer and line up with the Atlantic states? The answer is to be found in Norway.

Norway is interested in Scandinavian union, but less so than

Sweden, much less so than Denmark. Norway is youngest of the northern trio, her modern independence dating only from 1905; she is the least populous and the least prosperous. The pride and sensitivity of her nationalism are only the keener. At the same time Norway has a peculiarly broad world outlook, vision and contacts expanded by a migrating people and a merchant fleet that sails and serves the seven seas. Her interests and friendships extend to England and the United States as well as eastward to Sweden and southward to Denmark. She fronts to the west in a coastline of over 1000 miles, and the family ties of the North do not bind her fast. *Arbeiderbladet*, the social democratic daily of Oslo, put the national attitude in a nutshell:

Individually, the countries of Europe are powerless. Jointly and in coöperation with America they can protect their freedom. And only when they stand united do they have any prospect of achieving an amicable and lasting relaxation of east-west tension.

Most important of all is that Norway has been convinced by crushing experience that neutrality is an obsolete concept, a hope without reality. And if neutrality is useless, if one must depend on allies in war, then supply of war materials is vital. That is why the question of American aid in armament was crucial for the Scandinavian pact. If the United States would supply arms to a neutral unaffiliated North then these states had everything to gain and nothing to lose by forming their own separate group. When the United States said she could not guarantee to ship arms and other war potential to states not committed to help in the common cause, then Norway said she would go with the West. In that sense the United States did torpedo the projected Scandinavian Pact.

Theoretically it might be possible to have both a Scandinavian Pact and a Norway allied with the West. Practically this was not possible because Sweden insisted on a neutral North; only for the sake of keeping Scandinavia together and entirely free from outside ties was Sweden willing to extend her risks. Sweden has greater military strength both immediately and in productive capacity than Denmark and Norway put together. She could not, however, adequately supply her neighbors without help from outside.

Sweden therefore demanded absolute neutrality for all Scandinavia. Norway was just as stubborn in insisting upon strong ties with the West. The marvel is that they negotiated as long as they did, and Denmark may be the answer to that.

Denmark is strategically the Achilles heel of the North. Without mountains or wide protecting seas the land is open to quick and easy invasion by air or land or water. The narrow channels of the Belt and the Sound connect the North Sea with the Baltic and would be a must for Russia to control. The great city of Copenhagen and the fertile agricultural lands are both vulnerable and attractive. Denmark can furnish butter and beef for millions. The Danes know that they could not alone defend themselves against a powerful aggressor for even two days; they share the recent bitter experience of Norway. "The choice," says conservative leader Ole Bjorn Kraft, "is between isolated helplessness and planned coöperation with other democracies."

Denmark would like a pact which would give her the near strong arm of Sweden, and which would be backed at the same time by Norway, Britain, and the United States. In the negotiations on the pacts Denmark stood in the middle, trying hard to effect a compromise. But when the showdown came, when Norway and Sweden could not agree, the Danes reluctantly but definitely took their place with the Atlantic powers.

The defense of outlying possessions plays a subordinate but contributory part for Denmark and Norway; Sweden has no outside responsibilities. For Denmark the Faroe Islands must be considered, but primarily Greenland. Right now it is not likely that the United States would withdraw from bases there held since the agreement of 1941; the island is a vital stepping-stone on the northern great circle air route to Europe, or from Europe. It is also an important weather observation center. For

Norway a tender spot is Spitsbergen, far up toward the North Pole. There sit some 2300 Russian coal miners. Furthermore it bears remembering that in the far north Russia borders Norway by land. It is a short border, but it reminds the Russians that Norway is their only immediate neighbor on the west who has not signed a "nonaggression" pact.

Iceland and Finland, the western and eastern flanks of the Scandinavian bloc, enter less into discussion because their positions are clearer. Iceland, placed in the middle of the North Atlantic and of greater strategic importance than Greenland, has no choice but to join the western group.

The Russian bear hugs Finland tightly, through control of reparations and the mutual assistance pact of 1948. The communist party, too, is not in Finland a mere annoying fragment, but a vigorous minority party which has already had a taste of power in a coalition government. It thirsts for more, and the social democratic government, with but a quarter of the seats in the Diet, exists on sufferance of the bourgeois parties. The Finns are in no position to speak out frankly, and they realistically accept what is inevitable. They know that if Sweden were to join the Atlantic group the Russians might call it a threat and force their "protective troops" into Finland, and therefore to the borders of Sweden. Yet the Finns are daring and many of them would be glad to risk the showdown that Sweden's adherence to the Atlantic Pact might bring. Some hold a more sanguine hope: that a unanimous Scandinavian participation with the Atlantic states would so strengthen the West that the effect would be to push the East-West boundary definitely to Finland's *eastern* border.

The entire North has been forced to reconsider its historic policy, to reassess its position in the world of power politics. Differing circumstances and differing hopes have led the five nations in different directions. In none of them are people unanimously happy over the decisions taken, but only in Sweden is there so much as a bare possibility of early change. Sweden, strongest of all, and central geographically, is psychologically and strategically in a key position. Within Sweden the opposition thinks the government decision is based on a series of fatal fallacies. Some outsiders agree, and some even in America think that all Scandinavia should have followed the Swedish lead.

What are the basic considerations or problems which these peoples have had to evaluate and decide?

Problem number one is: can any state, big or little, stand alone, can it even look after its own welfare? Belgium threatened no one in 1914, and was neutralized by international agreement. Belgium, like Holland and Denmark and Norway and many a larger state in World War II, was peacefully going about its business when it was suddenly overwhelmed. By the piecemeal, "artichoke" tactics a large state can conquer any number of small states. It has been done. It can be done again.

Problem number two is: in the next war can there be any neutrality? In World War I neutrality worked for Scandinavia. In World War II it worked for none but Sweden, because of the desperation and the strength of the conflicting powers, and because of a few quislings. The fifth column for World War III has long been forming, and is insidious and powerful. In country after country it has declared that it will support the U.S.S.R. rather than its own nation. In a next war there will be no quarter.

Problem number three is concerned with geography: can war leave one area—in this case the Scandinavian—untouched while destruction swings in another direction? With present techniques of under-sea and air warfare any such hope becomes folly. In a possible war between East and West, wherein each is really trying to get at the other, Russia would need the submarine bases of the deep, rock-walled Norwegian fjords, and she would need the iron and steel of Sweden. Britain and the United States would have to prevent Russia from getting them. Russia would need the food and productive capacity of Denmark and Sweden. What of air war, the great destructive direct thrust of the near future? The shortest route by air from Moscow to Akron (or the other way!) passes directly over southern Sweden. Neither desert bases in Africa nor the oil of the Middle East can change that fact.

This whole problem is summed up in the difference of opinion between the Norwegians and the Swedes. Norway's foreign minister, Halvard Lange, conceives of Scandinavian defense as a part of the problem of the defense of all the western democracies; the Swedish ministers think that Scandinavian defense can be treated as a separate and independent problem.

Problem number four poses a question for both Scandinavia and the United States: could the West count on the good will and the aid of Scandinavia without any previous agreement? History gives all too clear an answer to that. For all the anti-nazi sentiment in the world how many states jumped to the aid of their neighbors in 1939–1941 until each was himself attacked? In this the policy of Sweden was not different from that of many another; Sweden was simply more fortunate. What reason is there to expect that Sweden or any other state would act in a different way the next time? Weakness and appeasement have shown themselves in the postwar period, and increased pressure is likely to bring them out still more. How can the West feel sure of any state which is unwilling to declare itself?

As for sympathies of course there is no question at all. Every people in Scandinavia is overwhelmingly pro-West. No one needs to ask a Swede, "Whom are you neutral against?" Finland is a good friend of the United States and of Britain. But friendship does not guarantee either the will or the possibility to help at a critical moment.

Problem number five simply reverses the question of number four: can Scandinavia count on the good will and aid of the United States with or without specific commitments? Again there is no shadow of doubt about the basic good will, nor of the practical interest of the United States in the maintenance of the northern democracies. But could the United States, without careful preparation and coördinated plans, give to Scandinavia assistance any more effective than Britain gave Poland in 1939? There is confidence in the North that the United States will come later if not sooner to the rescue. The popular mind indulges in an almost fantastic overestimation of America's ultimate power, and governments enjoy their lesser illusions. Both the smallness of the small and the greatness of the great become exaggerated, and the need for teamwork, for coöperation in responsibility and action, is minimized. The United States has the will, but she lacks the geographic position, the manpower, even the economic resources, to keep order in the world through her own power. General Marshall, while Secretary of State, said that the card he needed for the game with the Russians was a sufficient number of divisions of soldiers. Yet perhaps most important of all is that no country alone can possess that moral authority which can come only through the common action of all peace-loving peoples.

Problem number six is the question: can a nation choose its side at the last moment? It is unthinkable right now that any country in the North would *choose* Russia. But nervous antagonists cannot wait for the other to "get the draw" on one; friend or foe is forced to act with equal speed and equal ruthlessness. In 1940 the British mining of Norwegian waters almost led to war between Norway and Britain; the simultaneous and much better prepared German operation prevented that other tragedy. Norway and Sweden both threatened to fight earlier in 1940 if France and Britain sent troops across their territory to Finland. Finland did get caught fighting on the side of nazism, as the United States back in 1812 got caught fighting on the side of Napoleon. In war there may well be two enemies, and a people may find itself maneuvered into fighting the lesser enemy instead of the greater.

Are not some of these problems being considered in an atmosphere of wishful thinking in an illusion that the world is the same as it was a generation or a century past? But the elimination of Germany has created (at least temporarily) a power vacuum immediately to the south of Scandinavia, in the very heart of Europe. The aggrandizement of power around two new centers has transformed political relationships. The old balancing and juggling—neutrality—is now much more difficult if not impossible.

The real revolution of the twentieth century is the idea and the reality of an enlarged and unified society. This transcends changes in technology and in class relationships. The proudly independent nation states of the nineteenth century have in actuality lost their sovereignty. The United Nations is still weak, but has hopeful potentialities. Meanwhile groupings of states have assumed power. Faith in neutrality is disappearing, even in Scandinavia. The Swedish offer to extend her neutrality sphere to include Denmark and Norway is a partial recognition of the changed status. Many Swedes realize that they are whistling in the dark when they talk about an independent stand. Throughout the West there has come an increasing realization of cultural affinities, an appreciation of common values worth preserving.

How defend those values? That is the practical question. Who is responsible for defending them? That is the moral question. Both must be faced and answered. For the United States the answers have been thrust upon us by outside forces. For the peoples of the smaller states of the "in-between" area the pressures are different and the decision more difficult. But decision cannot be avoided.

One great consoling fact in the tense postwar world is that relations between the United States and Scandinavia stand on a firm foundation of friendship and fundamental common interest.

Appendix I. Some Vital Facts about Scandinavia

ON SPELLING AND PRONUNCIATION

Mention of three extra letters makes it possible to spell Danish, Norwegian, and Swedish without artificial anglicization. (The complications of Finnish and Icelandic are disregarded.)

å   is pronounced like o in cold. Basically Swedish, used in Norwegian, and, since the spelling reform of 1948, in Danish.

ä   is like the ai in fair.

ö   (Swedish) ⎱ are like the ö or oe of German; there is no real
ø   (Danish) ⎰ English equivalent.

AREA AND POPULATION

Country	Area in Square Miles	Year	Population Number
Norway	124,556	1946	3,126,000
		1948	3,198,000
Sweden	173,394	1947	6,842,046
		1948	6,924,888
Denmark	16,569	1947	4,165,600
		1948	4,190,000
Finland	130,159	1946	3,849,097
		1948	3,965,000
Iceland	39,768	1948	138,502

Source: Area: *Encyclopaedia Britannica Atlas*. Population: Norway, Denmark, and Finland, the official statistical yearbooks; Sweden, Memorandum from Ministry of Foreign Affairs; Iceland, *Encyclopaedia Britannica Book of the Year, 1950*.

POPULATION OF LARGE CITIES

Country	City	Population	Population with Suburbs
Norway (1946)	Oslo	289,000	420,000
	Bergen	108,933	
	Trondheim	56,444	
	Stavanger	49,218	
	Drammen	26,589	
	Kristiansand	24,110	
	Haugesund	18,119	
	Ålesund	18,012	
	Moss	17,008	
Sweden (1948)	Stockholm	726,418	910,000
	Göthenburg	344,017	377,423
	Malmö	186,217	201,970
	Norrköping	83,302	
	Hälsingborg	70,776	
	Orebro	64,543	
	Uppsala	60,370	
	Borås	55,938	
	Västerås	55,912	
	Linköping	51,834	
	Eskilstuna	51,742	
	Gävle	45,316	
	Jönköping	42,423	
Denmark (1945)	Copenhagen	731,707	1,078,892
	Aarhus	107,393	137,722
	Odense	92,436	104,391
	Aalborg	60,880	81,084
	Esbjerg	43,241	
Finland (1946)	Helsinki	358,195	
	Turku	93,735	
	Tampere	93,665	
	Lahti	41,344	
	Pori	39,064	
	Oulu	35,292	
	Vaasa	33,105	
	Kuopio	29,553	
Iceland (1948)	Reykjavik	53,384	
	Akureyri	6,144	

Sources: Norway, Sweden, Denmark, Finland, the official statistical yearbooks; Iceland, *Encyclopaedia Britannica Book of the Year, 1950*.

GOVERNMENT

NORWAY

Ruler: King Haakon VII, from November 27, 1905.

Cabinet: Labor, appointed November 1, 1945; continued after election of October 1949.

Members of the Cabinet:

Prime Minister	Einar Gerhardsen
Minister of	
Foreign Affairs	Halvard M. Lange
Agriculture	Kristian Fjeld
Church and Education	Lars Moen
Defense	Jens Christian Hauge
Social Affairs	Aaslaug Aasland
Justice	O. C. Gundersen
Communications	Nils Langhelle
Commerce	Erik Brofoss
Finance	Olav Meisdalshagen
Industry, Handicraft, Shipping	Lars Evensen
Supply and Reconstruction	Nils Hönsvald
Fisheries	Reidar Carlsen
Labor	Johan Olsen

Representation in the Storting (Parliament)

Parties	Elected October 8, 1945 for a four-year term	Elected October 9, 1949
Labor	76	85
Conservative	25	23
Liberal	20	21
Communist	11	0
Agrarian	10	12
Christian People's	8	9
Total	150	150

Sources: W. Mallory, *Political Handbook of the World, 1949; Royal Norwegian Information Service.*

SWEDEN

Ruler: King Gustav V, from December 8, 1907.

Cabinet: Social Democratic, appointed July 31, 1945. As reconstructed to October 1948.

Members of the Cabinet:

Prime Minister	Tage Erlander
Minister of	
Foreign Affairs	Östen Undén
Justice	Herman Zetterberg
Defense	Allan G. F. Vougt
Social Affairs	Gustav Möller
Communications	Torsten Nilsson
Finance	Ernst J. Wigforss (David Hall from June 1949 to October 1949; Per Edvin Sköld from October 1949 to —)
Education	Josef Weijne
Agriculture	C. E. Sträng
Commerce	John A. Ericsson
Civilian Supply	Karin Kock-Lindberg
Interior	Eije Mossberg
Ministers without Portfolio	Nils Quensel
	Gunnar Danielsson
	Per Edvin Sköld
	Sven Andersson

Representation in the Riksdag (Parliament)

Parties

First Chamber

Social Democratic	84
Conservative	23
Farmers'	22
Liberal	17
Communist	3
Independent Conservative	1
Total	150

Second Chamber
(Election of September 1948 for 4 years)

Social Democratic 112
Conservative 57
Farmers' 30
Liberal 23
Communist 8
    Total 230

Source: W. Mallory, *Political Handbook of the World, 1949.*

DENMARK

Ruler: King Frederik IX, from April 20, 1947.

Cabinet: Social Democratic.

Members of the Cabinet:

Prime Minister	Hans Hedtoft, appointed November 11, 1947

Minister of
Foreign Affairs	Gustav Rasmussen
Finance	H. C. Hansen
Economical Coördination	Vilhelm Buhl
Agriculture	Kr. Bording
Interior	Jens Smörum
Housing and Health	Johs. Kjaerboel
Transport and Public Works	Carl Petersen
Justice	Niels Busch-Jensen
Education	Hartvig Frisch
Fisheries	Christian Christiansen
Social Welfare	Johan Stroem
Defence	Rasmus Hansen
Ecclesiastical Affairs	Frede Nielsen
Labor	Marius Soerensen
Commerce	Jens Otto Krag
Minister without Portfolio	Fanny Jensen

Representation in the Rigsdag (Parliament)

    Parties

Landsting (Upper Chamber)
Election of April 1, 1947

Social Democratic	33
Liberal	21
Conservative	13
Radical Liberal	7
Communist	1
Faroe Representative	1
Total	76

Folketing (Lower Chamber)
Election of October 28, 1947

Social Democratic	57
Liberal	46
Conservative	17
Communist	9
Radical Liberal	10
Danish Unity Party	0
Party of Justice	6
Copenhagen Liberals	3
Faroe Representative	1
Total	149

Source: W. Mallory, *Political Handbook of the World, 1949.*

President: Juho K. Paasikivi, elected by Parliament on March 9, 1946; assumed office on March 11, 1946; reëlected Feb. 15, 1950.

Cabinet: Social Democratic, appointed July 29, 1948.

Members of the Cabinet:

Prime Minister	Karl August Fagerholm
Minister of	
Foreign Affairs	Carl Enckell
Agriculture	Matti Lepisto
Trade and Industry	Uuno Takki
Finance	Onni Hiltunen
Interior	Aarre Simonen

Education	Reino Oittinen
Social Affairs	Waldemar Liljeström
Justice	Tauno Suontausta
Supply	Onni Toivonen
Communications and Public Works	Onni Peltonen
Defense	Emil Skog

Minister in

Foreign Affairs	Uuno Takki
Communications and Public Works and Supply	Erkki Härmä (Emil Huunonen from July 30, 1949 to –)
Agriculture and Interior	Jussi Roatkainen
Social Affairs	Tyyne Leivo-Larsson
Cabinet Chancery, Finance and Minister without Portfolio	Aleksius Aaltonen
	Unto Varjonen (appointed July 1949)

Representation in Eduskunta (Parliament)
Election of July 1948 for 3-year term

Parties

Agrarian	56
Social Democrats	54
Democratic Union (Communists and Socialist Union)	38
Coalition Party (Finnish Conservatives)	33
Swedish People's	14
Progressive (Finnish Liberals)	5
Total	200

Source: W. Mallory, *Political Handbook of the World, 1949.*

ICELAND

President: Sveinn Björnsson, assumed office August 1, 1945 for four-year term; reëlected, 1949.

Cabinet: Coalition. Conservatives—2, Social Democrats—2, Progressives—2. Appointed February 4, 1947.

Members of the Cabinet:

Prime Minister	Stefán J. Stefánsson
Minister for	
Social Affairs	Stefán J. Stefánsson
Foreign Affairs and Justice	Bjarni Benediktsson
Commerce and Communications	Emil Jónsson
Minister of	
Finance and Fisheries	Jóhann Th. Jósefsson
Agriculture and Industries	Bjarni Ásgeirsson
Education and Air Communications	Eysteinn Jónsson

A new Cabinet took office on December 6, 1949:

Cabinet: Independence Party.

Members of the Cabinet:

Prime Minister	Olafur Thors
Minister of Social Affairs	Olafur Thors
Minister of Justice and of Foreign Affairs	Bjarni Benediktsson
Minister of Finance and of Commerce	Bjorn Olafsson
Minister of Fisheries, of Industry, and of Aviation	Johann Th. Josefsson
Minister of Agriculture and of Communications	Jon Palmason

Representation in Althing (Parliament)

Upper Chamber

Election of June 1946

Party	
Conservative	7
Progressive	4
Communist	3
Social Democrat	3
Total	17

Lower Chamber

Conservative	12
Progressive	10
Communist	7
Social Democrat	6
Total	35

Althing as a Whole

Election of October 1949

Conservative (Independence Party)	19
Progressive (Agrarian)	17
Communist	9
Social Democratic	7
Total	52

Source: W. Mallory, *Political Handbook of the World, 1949;* Associated Press.

MONETARY TABLE

VALUE OF SCANDINAVIAN COINAGE IN UNITED STATES CENTS

	1946–1949	After Devaluation September 19, 1949
Danish Krone	20.9	14.5
Norwegian Krone	20.1	13.9
Swedish Krona	27.85	19.3
Icelandic Krona	15.37	10.7
Finnish Markka	.0735	.0625 (after July 5, 1949)
		.0431 (after Sept. 19, 1949)

In plural form these units of coinage and currency are:
Kroner for Denmark and Norway
Kronor for Sweden
Kronur for Iceland

NATIONAL INCOME

Country		In 1938 Dollars		
		1938	*1947*	*1948*
Denmark	total	1,200,000,000	1,130,000,000	1,290,000,000
	per capita	316	276	307
Norway	total	740,000,000	770,000,000	810,000,000
	per capita	255	248	253
Sweden	total	2,310,000,000	2,810,000,000	2,850,000,000
	per capita	367	413	413
Finland	total	660,000,000	590,000,000	690,000,000
	per capita	178	151	173
United Kingdom	total	18,020,000,000	17,990,000,000	20,040,000,000
	per capita	378	363	401
United States	total	29,030,000,000	46,490,000,000	47,740,000,000
	per capita	521	665	683

Source: U.N., Dept. of Economic Affairs, *Economic Survey of Europe in 1948* (Geneva, 1949), p. 235. This table, giving statistics in terms of 1938 dollar values, should be compared with the absolute figures in the text, pp. 148–150.

COST OF LIVING INDEX

Country	1937 = 100		Last 3 months of 1948
	1946	1947	
Denmark	160	167	170
Norway	163	163	163
Sweden	144	152	160
Finland	449	706	811
Iceland (Reykjavik)	286	326	322

Source: U.N., Dept. of Economic Affairs, *Major Economic Changes in 1948* (Lake Success, Jan. 1949).

LIVESTOCK

Country	Year	Horses	Cattle	Swine	Poultry	Sheep	Goats
Norway	1938	193,383	1,398,714	429,000	3,525,529	1,778,395	307,599
	1947	224,545	1,225,024	258,635	3,767,458	1,698,026	154,956
Sweden	1938	617,000	3,036,000	1,371,000	11,304,157	406,000	50,000
	1947	550,952	2,796,637	1,188,892	8,361,364	420,774	21,330
Denmark	1938	564,000	3,183,000	2,845,000	27,600,000	147,000*	8,600
	1947	594,000	3,013,552	1,830,022	18,886,000	n.a.	n.a.
Finland	1937	380,000	1,925,100	504,200	2,814,960	1,072,300	10,372
	1946	404,000	1,672,000	254,000	1,167,000	1,099,000	n.a.
Iceland	1938	49,000	37,000	600	90,000	592,000	1,700
	1946	54,000	38,000	n.a.	n.a.	509,000	750

* 1937.

Sources: 1938, *Encyclopaedia Britannica Atlas.* Postwar, Official Statistical Yearbooks except for Iceland; Iceland, *Statesman's Yearbook, 1948.*

NUMBER AND TONNAGE OF MERCHANT MARINE
(after *Lloyd's Register*)
(Above 100 gross tons)

Country	1939		1947		1948	
	No.	Gross Tonnage	No.	Gross Tonnage	No.	Gross Tonnage
Norway	1,990	4,835,000	1,685	3,762,000	1,865	4,262,000
Sweden	1,238	1,582,000	1,198	1,830,000	1,250	1,974,000
Denmark	709	1,175,000	607	1,024,000	667	1,123,000
Finland	432	626,000	241	288,000	297	457,000
Iceland	70	31,000	108	42,000	130	60,000

Sources: Official Statistical Yearbooks; Memorandum from Norwegian Ministry of Foreign Affairs.

SHIPBUILDING
(after *Lloyd's Register*)

Country	1938		1947		1948	
	No.	Gross Tonnage	No.	Gross Tonnage	No.	Gross Tonnage
Norway	42	54,654	45	36,854	49	47,000
Sweden	40	166,464	52	222,598	56	246,000
Denmark	35	158,430	15	60,695	20	99,000
Finland	9	16,597	28	9,779	17	2,397

Sources: *Lloyd's Register;* Official Statistical Yearbooks; Memoranda from Norwegian Ministry of Foreign Affairs, and Finnish Ministry of Foreign Affairs.

INDUSTRY

Country	Year	No. of Establishments	No. of Workers	Value of Production (in $)
Norway	1938	4,503	144,118	496,371,507
	1946	5,532	166,733	854,807,600
Sweden	1938	19,092	644,360	1,955,690,661
	1945	22,074	639,432	3,224,581,794
	1947	—	—	5,069,166,666
Denmark	1938	6,303	180,569	671,473,255
	1947	7,221	213,808	1,283,083,400
	1948	—	—	1,383,000,000
Finland	1937	4,246	207,506	459,689,617
	1946	5,691	236,723	824,191,176
	1948		260,000	1,645,000,000

Sources: 1938, *Encyclopaedia Britannica Atlas*. Postwar, Official Statistical Yearbooks; *European Recovery Program, Denmark: Country Study;* Memorandum from Norwegian Ministry of Foreign Affairs.

MINERAL PRODUCTION

NORWAY

Mineral	1938 Tons	1948 Tons
Silver ores	14,907	8,111 (1947)
Copper ores and concentrates	35,105	23,005
Pyrites even cupreous	1,027,776	808,964
Nickel ores	34,220	1,673 (1947)
Iron ores and Titaniferous iron stone.............	1,474,478	316,790
Zinc ores and lead ores	15,089	11,454
Rutile concentrates	124	100
Molybdenite	775	143

Source: *Norges Bank Bulletin*, March 1949.

SWEDEN

Mineral	1938 Short tons	1946 Short tons
Iron ore	15,352,860	7,553,700
Silver and lead ore	14,920	30,360
Copper ore	16,745	61,160
Zinc ore	72,568	68,990
Manganese ore	6,701	13,860
Arsenic ore	287,193	114,070
Sulphur pyrites	205,458	308,220
Gold	2,172,170 oz.	75,213 oz.
Silver	7,059,377 oz.	591,914 oz.
Coal		536,994 tons

Sources: 1938, *Encyclopaedia Britannica Atlas, 1945*; 1946, *Statistisk Årsbok för Sverige, 1948*.

FINLAND

Mineral	1938 Short tons	1946 Short tons
Copper ore	387,400	734,332
Copper	13,483	22,174
Gold	3,858 oz.	9,314 oz.
Pyrite ore	113,514	195,263
Pyrites (sulphur content) ..	48,811	
Silver	57,900 oz.	137,623 oz.

Sources: 1938, *Encyclopaedia Britannica Atlas; 1946, Minerals Year-book,* 1946.

AGRICULTURAL PRODUCTION

NORWAY

Crops	1938 Acres	1938 Tons	1947 Acres	1947 Tons
Wheat	86,329	79,145	72,047	50,925
Rye	13,321	12,125	3,319	2,206
Barley	147,736	137,016	96,643	89,220
Oats	210,451	216,822	187,106	144,995
Mixed grains	11,075	11,795	9,462	8,158
Potatoes	132,259	1,033,516	140,498	1,012,513
Root crops (fodder)	44,522	807,765	43,520	578,280
Hay	1,667,801	3,306,569	1,323,119	2,743,161

SWEDEN

Crops	1938 Acres	Tons	1948 Acres	Tons
Wheat	759,103	905,539	779,973	774,186
Rye	497,599	446,101	394,965	354,874
Barley	272,204	293,763	216,969	212,617
Oats	1,646,566	1,522,056	1,209,920	873,612
Mixed grains	629,158	731,597	695,833	630,908
Legumes	61,772	46,958	61,686	44,998
Potatoes	338,178	2,064,057	365,399	2,509,398
Root crops (fodder)	162,827	2,830,817	150,254	2,293,058
Sugar beets	125,377	2,021,508	117,499	1,993,179
Hay	3,394,467	5,884,959	3,258,073	5,052,589

DENMARK

Crops	1938 Acres	Tons	1947 Acres	Tons
Wheat	330,923	517,750	59,776	59,965
Rye	363,100	316,911	259,480	197,642
Barley	998,786	1,525,253	1,151,679	1,464,846
Oats	940,961	1,282,636	846,757	961,095
Mixed grains	757,463	890,769	792,405	773,594
Potatoes	199,094	1,604,508	261,128	2,012,469
Root crops (fodder)	1,017,635	26,475,041	974,123	18,288,480
Sugar beets	97,064	1,554,023	108,442	1,603,957
Hay	568,433	1,350,758	1,120,071	447,864
Chicory	——	——	1,549	11,243
Straw	——	——	——	3,998,593

FINLAND

Crops	1938		1946	
	Acres	Tons	Acres	Tons
Wheat	322,530	282,079	389,531	196,376
Rye	582,735	405,757	362,009	158,759
Barley	300,846	219,358	345,332	166,141
Oats	1,143,363	900,579	792,862	367,896
Mixed grains	23,505	——	13,672	6,183
Legumes	27,568	——	25,595	11,316
Potatoes	226,252	1,455,036	191,060	982,279
Sugar beets	12,795	144,401	8,918	53,158

ICELAND

Crops	1939 Tons	1946 Tons
Hay	269,024	221,100
Potatoes	13,160	8,200
Turnips	2,856	650

Sources: 1938 figures are from *Encyclopaedia Britannica World Atlas*; others as follows: Norway—*Statistiske Översikter*, 1948, pp. 69, 72; Sweden—*Statistisk Årsbok för Sverige*, 1949, pp. 90–91, 92–93; Denmark—*Statistisk Aarbog*, 1948, pp. 44, 47; Finland—*Annuaire Statistique de Finland*, 1946–47, p. 88; Iceland—*Statesman's Yearbook*, 1948.

DEFENSE

	Army		Navy			Air Force		Approx. Annual Postwar Budget
	Under Arms	Mobilizable	Personnel	Mobilizable	Vessels	Personnel	Planes	
Denmark		100,000	1,500	4,000	2 coastal torpedo craft, submarines, etc.			
Norway	13,000 annual recruits	40,000 to 60,000 plus Home Guard of 100,000	4,500	15,000	60 (none larger than destroyer)	4,500 to 13,500	150 to 200	c. $64,000,000
Sweden	40,000	700,000	—	—	5 coastal battle-ships (of which 2 obsolete) 3 modern cruisers 13 modern destroyers 18 motor torpedo boats 25 submarines 2 mine layers 44 mine sweepers — small patrol boats		1,000	c. $154,000,000
Finland ...... (in accordance with limitations of treaty of peace with Allies, July 1947)	34,400	—	4,500	—	(10,000 tons)	3,000	60	c. $13,000,000

WORLD TRADE: VALUE OF IMPORTS AND EXPORTS
(In millions of dollars, current F.O.B. prices)

		Total Exports	Total Imports
Denmark	1938	335	307
	1947	480	548
	1948	550	668
Sweden	1938	463	472
	1947	895	1299
	1948	1073	1191
Norway	1938	193	262
	1947	380	695
	1948	427	671
Finland	1938	181	163
	1947	323	313
	1948	406	447
Iceland	1938	17	10
	1947	45	67
	1948	63	62

Source: U.N., Department of Economic Affairs. *Economic Survey of Europe in 1948* (Genoa, 1949), Table XVI.

Appendix II. Suggested Reading

The prolific Scandinavians make a brief bibliography difficult; these peoples write books and buy them and read them on a scale beyond that of the United States or any other nation. Their colorful and hospitable countries are inviting subjects for foreign travelers, students, journalists, and these write more books. The Scandinavian records are thorough and of long standing, so the historical picture can be fairly accurate. The problems are of choice and emphasis.

Each of these countries has published recently, through government or private channels, a book of descriptive summaries of various aspects of its society: *Denmark 1947* (Copenhagen: Ministry for Foreign Affairs and Danish Statistical Department, 1947); G. B. Lampe, ed., *Norway* (Oslo: National Travel Association of Norway, [1948]); *Sweden, Ancient and Modern* (Stockholm: Swedish Traffic Association, 1938); *The Sweden Year-Book 1938* (Uppsala, 1938); *Sweden, A Wartime Survey* (New York: American-Swedish News Exchange, [1943?]); Urho Toivola, ed., *The Finland Yearbook 1947* (Helsinki: Mercatorin Kirjapaino . . . , 1947); Thorsteinn Thorsteinsson, ed., *Iceland 1936* (3rd ed., Reykjavik: Landsbanki Íslands, 1936). In addition are the statistical yearbooks, the directories, and the *Who's Who* publications; the facts are well in order.

Pictorial-descriptive surveys are numerous and excellent, and among them might be mentioned Knud Gedde, ed., *This Is Denmark* (Copenhagen: Gjellerup, 1949); Lennart Sundström, ed., *The Face of Sweden* (Stockholm: Lindquists Förlag, 1948); *Finland in Pictures* (Helsinki: Werner Söderström, 1947); Karl Fischer, ed., *Norway Today* (Oslo: Tanum, [1938?]).

There is no satisfactory complete history of the Scandinavian countries together, either in English or in the Scandinavian languages. An able Swedish historian is at work on such a volume, and an American has done an excellent pioneering work in a seg-

ment of the field: Bryn J. Hovde, *The Scandinavian Countries,
1720–1865* (2 vols., Boston: Chapman and Grimes, 1943; reissued
by Cornell University Press, 1948). The emphasis here is on social
and economic forces. A book of lectures by individual specialists
similar in scope to this volume, is Henning Friis, ed., *Scandinavia
between East and West* (Ithaca: Cornell University Press, 1950).

Of the separate national histories an old but useful treatment of
Norway is Knut Gjerset, *History of the Norwegian People* (2
vols., New York: Macmillan, 1932). An up-to-date volume, first in
a series on the Scandinavian countries, is Karen Larsen's sympathetic
History of Norway (Princeton, for the American-Scandinavian
Foundation, 1948). Wilhelm Keilhau, Norwegian economist-his-
torian, issued during the war a handy little volume, *Norway in
World History* (London: MacDonald, 1944).

On Denmark there are two histories in English: J. H. S. Birch,
Denmark in History (London: John Murray, 1938), and John
Danstrup, *A History of Denmark* (Copenhagen: Wivel, 1948),
both political in emphasis.

The histories of Sweden are likewise predominantly political:
Ragnar Svanström and Carl Frederik Palmstierna, *A Short History
of Sweden* (London: Oxford, 1934); and Andrew A. Stromberg,
A History of Sweden (New York: Macmillan, 1931).

For Finland a useful survey is J. Hampden Jackson, *Finland*
(London: Allen and Unwin, 1938) and also, though somewhat
more specialized, John H. Wuorinen, *Nationalism in Modern Finland* (New York: Columbia, 1931).

Knut Gjerset, *History of Iceland* (New York: Macmillan, 1924),
is the most thorough treatment in English, but Professor Skuli
Johnson has edited a recent 170-page booklet, *Iceland's Thousand
Years* (Winnipeg: Icelandic Canadian Club, etc., 1945).

A variety of periodicals in English enables one to keep up to
date. Most important is the *American-Scandinavian Review*, a
quarterly published by the American-Scandinavian Foundation in
New York. It is literary in tone, but contains articles on current
affairs and quarterly news summaries. *The Norseman*, published
in London, contains excellent articles with more of a political-
economic emphasis, and is particularly concerned with Norway.
The Danish Foreign Office Journal is a new and well-edited quarterly, with factual articles. Denmark, Norway, and Sweden each
maintain a first-rate news reporting service for the United States.
For commercial news and articles the *Swedish American Monthly*
(published by the Swedish Chamber of Commerce of the U. S. A.,
New York) and *Norwegian American Commerce* (published

monthly by the Norwegian American Chamber of Commerce, New York) are both useful. For still more exact information direct from Finland there is a *Bank of Finland Monthly Bulletin* and a quarterly, *Unitas*, published by the Nordiska Föreningsbanken, both in Helsinki.

1. THE HERITAGE

The fascinating record of Scandinavian history, told in detail in series upon series of volumes in the Scandinavian languages, is summed up in a few good English-language books. The early story is well told in Haakon Shetelig and Hjalmar Falk, *Scandinavian Archaeology* (translated by E. V. Gordon, Oxford: Clarendon Press, 1937). A detailed account of the Vikings abroad is given by Thomas D. Kendrick, *A History of the Vikings* (New York: Scribner's, 1930), and a briefer interpretation of the life at home by Axel Olrik, *Viking Civilization* (New York: American-Scandinavian Foundation, 1930). Insight into the contributions of the Vikings is provided by Charles Homer Haskins, *The Normans in European History* (Boston: Houghton Mifflin, 1915). Halvdan Koht's *The Old Norse Sagas* (New York: American-Scandinavian Foundation, 1931) introduces one to a group of literary-historical masterpieces, and Henry Goddard Leach's *A Pageant of Old Scandinavia* (Princeton, for the American-Scandinavian Foundation, 1946) gives a wealth of excerpts from the old literature. Another valuable anthology is Elli Tompuri, *Voices from Finland* (Helsinki: Sanoma Oy, 1947). The sagas themselves may be had in many modern editions and translations; among the most interesting and valuable are: The Saga of Egil Skallagrimson, The Saga of Burnt Njal, and The Poetic Edda and the Prose Edda.

Much of the magnificent literature of modern Scandinavia is easily obtainable in English translations. Hans Christian Andersen's fairy tales are as popular with children as are Henrik Ibsen's dramas with adults. Holberg and Strindberg are dramatists who deserve wider American appreciation. Selma Lagerlöf (*Gösta Berling*) and Knut Hamsun (*Growth of the Soil*) are well known. The Norwegian American Ole Rölvaag (*Giants in the Earth*, New York: Harper, 1927) deserves to be still better known. Halldór Laxness' *Independent People* (New York: Knopf, 1946) is a good example of the modern Icelandic novel. Most significant of the recent writers are Sigrid Undset (*Kristin Lavransdatter*) and Johannes V. Jensen (*The Long Journey*). As an introduction to the modern group H. G. Topsöe-Jensen, *Scandinavian Literature from Brandes to Our Day* (New York: Norton for the American-Scandinavian Foundation, 1929), will serve. The American-Scandinavian Foundation through the *Review* and its annual publications nourishes an American appreciation of Scandinavian literature, publishing anthologies of short stories as well as longer works.

Laurence M. Larsen has edited a collection of the old laws in *The Earliest Norwegian Laws* (New York: Columbia, 1935).

A phase of the cultural heritage, neglected necessarily but unfortunately in this volume, is surveyed in Carl Laurin, Emil Hannover, and Jens Thiis, *Scandinavian Art* (New York: American-Scandinavian Foundation, 1922). A recent book, Iona Plath, *The Decorative Arts of Sweden* (New York: Scribner's, 1948), deserves mention especially for its illustrations.

A few volumes in recent history will serve as doorways into a larger library: Werner von Heidenstam, *The Swedes and Their Chieftains* (New York: American-Scandinavian Foundation, 1925), one in a number of works of historical fiction; Nils Ahnlund, *Gustav Adolf the Great* (Princeton, for the American-Scandinavian Foundation, 1940); Halvdan Koht and Sigmund Skard, *The Voice of Norway* (New York: Columbia, 1944); Nils Herlitz, *Sweden, A Modern Democracy on Ancient Foundations* (Minneapolis: University of Minnesota, 1939); Oscar J. Falnes, *National Romanticism in Norway* (New York: Columbia, 1933); Theodore Jorgensen, *Norway's Relation to Scandinavian Unionism 1815–1871* (Northfield: St. Olaf College, 1935); Halvdan Koht, *The Life of Ibsen* (2 vols., New York: Norton for American-Scandinavian Foundation, 1931); Stefan Einarsson, *History of Icelandic Prose Writers 1800–1940* (Ithaca: Cornell University Press, 1948); Franklin D. Scott, *Bernadotte and the Fall of Napoleon* (Cambridge: Harvard University Press, 1935); Lawrence D. Steefel, *The Schleswig-Holstein Question* (Cambridge: Harvard University Press, 1932).

2. SCANDINAVIAN-AMERICAN CROSSCURRENTS

A brilliant piece of saga interpretation and collation by Einar Haugen, *Voyages to Vinland* (New York: Knopf, 1942), describes the earliest contacts of North and West. The great protagonist for the fourteenth-century voyages and the Kensington Rune Stone is Hjalmar Holand, and his best book is *America: 1355–1364* (New York: Duell, Sloan and Pearce, 1946).

On the seventeenth-century migration the standard authority is Amandus Johnson, *The Swedish Settlements on the Delaware 1638–*

1664 (2 vols., Philadelphia: University of Pennsylvania, 1911, and an abridged edition in 1944). There were Finns as well as Swedes, as shown by John H. Wuorinen, *The Finns on the Delaware 1638–1938* (New York: Columbia, 1938).

The general works on immigration give much space to the Scandinavian element, and there is a rich and increasing special literature. Best work in the field to date has been done by the Norwegian Americans ably guided by Theodore C. Blegen, who is largely responsible for the value of the *Norwegian-American Studies and Records,* of which some fifteen volumes have been published since the mid-1920's by the Norwegian-American Historical Association, Northfield, Minnesota. This organization has also issued special volumes such as Ole Munch Raeder's *America in the Forties* (1929), Ole Rynning's *True Account of America* (1926), and Carleton C. Qualey's *Norwegian Settlement in the United States* (1938); most important of all are Dean Blegen's own *Norwegian Migration to America 1825–1860* (1931) and its second volume, *The American Transition* (1940).

A Swedish American group, growing out of the centennial celebration of 1948, is preparing to publish the letters of Gustaf Unonius on the nineteenth-century Swedish migration, and other studies are likely to follow. Valuable work already done on the Swedes includes George M. Stephenson, *The Religious Aspects of Swedish Immigration* (Minneapolis: University of Minnesota, 1932); Adolph B. Benson and Naboth Hedin, eds., *Swedes in America* (New Haven: Yale, 1938); Helge Nelson, *The Swedes and Swedish Settlements in North America* (2 vols., Lund: Gleerup, 1943); Nels Hokanson, *Swedish Immigrants in Lincoln's Time* (New York: Harper, 1942); Jonas O. Backlund, *Swedish Baptists in America* (Chicago: Conference Press, 1933); Florence E. Janson, *The Background of Swedish Immigration 1840–1930* (Chicago: University of Chicago, 1931). A selection of stories from an essay contest of 1948 is published as *The Will to Succeed, Stories of Swedish Pioneers* (New York: Bonniers, 1948).

On the subject of cultural interchange the best general overview is Halvdan Koht's *The American Spirit in Europe* (Philadelphia: University of Pennsylvania, 1949). Only a few preliminary studies have been made in a field ripe for investigation by careful research: Harald Elovson, *Amerika i Svensk Litteratur 1750–1820* (America in Swedish Literature . . . , Lund, 1930); Adolph B. Benson, "Cultural Relations between Sweden and America to 1830," *Germanic Review,* XIII (1938), 83–101; Brynjolf J. Hovde, "Notes on the Effects of Emigration Upon Scandinavia," *Journal of Modern His-*

tory, VI (1930), 253–279; Kenneth Bjorck, *Saga in Steel and Concrete: Norwegian Engineers in America* (Northfield, Minnesota: Norwegian-American Historical Association, 1947); E. H. Thörnberg, *Sverige i Amerika, Amerika i Sverige* (Sweden in America, America in Sweden, Stockholm: Bonniers, 1938); Franklin D. Scott, "American Influences in Norway and Sweden," *Journal of Modern History,* XVIII (1946), 37–47.

A number of personal interpretations add somewhat to the literature on the interaction between Scandinavia and the United States, for example, Jacob A. Riis, *The Making of an American* (New York: Macmillan, 1908); Frederika Bremer, *America of the Fifties* (New York: American-Scandinavian Foundation, 1924), and a recent visitor's comment, Herbert Tingsten, *Problem i U. S. A.* [*sic*] (Problems in the U. S. A., Stockholm: Bonniers, 1948).

Diplomatic relations have likewise suffered from too little cultivation, but there are a few studies: Soren J. M. P. Fogdall, *Danish-American Diplomacy 1776–1920* (Iowa City: University of Iowa Studies in the Social Sciences, VIII, No. 2, 1922); Knute Emil Carlson, *Relations of the United States with Sweden* (Allentown, Pennsylvania: H. R. Haas, 1921); Brynjolf J. Hovde, *Diplomatic Relations of the United States with Sweden and Norway 1814–1905* (Iowa City: University of Iowa Studies, VII, No. 4, 1921).

3. FUNCTIONING SOCIAL DEMOCRACY

On government a good description is available in Ben A. Arneson, *The Democratic Monarchies of Scandinavia* (New York: Van Nostrand, 1939, revised edition, 1949), and further elaboration in articles such as Richard C. Spenser, "Party Government and the Swedish Riksdag," *American Political Science Review,* XXXIX (1945), 437–458. Changes in parties and personnel can be followed in Walter H. Mallory, *Political Handbook of the World* (New York: Harpers for Council on Foreign Relations, annual) or in the *Britannica Book of the Year* (Chicago: Encyclopaedia Britannica, annual).

Just before World War I a useful volume on the economy of the five states was published as a joint enterprise: *The Northern Countries in World Economy* (Copenhagen: Munksgaard, 1937, rev. 1939). There are as yet few special studies to bring facts up to date, but one exception is William C. Chamberlain, *The Economic Development of Iceland Through World War II* (New York: Columbia, 1947). Significant studies on particular subjects include

Arthur Montgomery, *How Sweden Overcame the Depression* (Stockholm: Bonniers, 1938); Brinley Thomas, *Monetary Policy and Crises; A Study of Swedish Experience* (London: G. Routledge, 1936), and Christopher L. Paus, *Report on Economic and Commercial Conditions in Norway* (London: H. M. Stationery Office, 1934, 1936, 1938), a practical guide for merchants.

On social and economic policy the most popular account is Marquis Childs's *Sweden, The Middle Way* (New Haven: Yale, 1936, rev. 1947 and issued in Penguin Books, 1948). A very useful survey covering many phases of social policy was published as "Social Problems and Policies in Sweden," the May 1938 number of *The Annals of the American Academy of Political and Social Science* (vol. 197). For Denmark a good introduction is Peter Manniche, *Denmark, A Social Laboratory* (Copenhagen: G. E. C. Gad, 1939), and a more detailed and recent treatment may be found in *Social Denmark* (Copenhagen: *Socialt Tidsskrift*, 1947). For Norway see John Eric Nordskog, *Social Reform in Norway* (Los Angeles: University of Southern California Press, 1935) or O. B. Grimley, *The New Norway* (Oslo: Griff, 1937). "Recent Social Developments in Finland" are surveyed in the *International Labour Review* (January–February 1948, pages 1–14) by Niilo A. Mannio, long an official in the social ministry.

Special studies which lead one farther are Helen F. Hohman, *Old Age in Sweden* (Washington: Social Security Board, 1939); James J. Robbins, *The Government of Labor Relations in Sweden* (Chapel Hill for American-Scandinavian Foundation, 1942); Walter Galenson, *Labor in Norway* (Cambridge: Harvard University Press, 1949); Alva Myrdal, *Nation and Family* (New York: Harper, 1941); John Graham, Jr., *Housing in Scandinavia* (Chapel Hill: University of North Carolina Press, 1940); Leonard Silk, *Sweden Plans for Better Housing* (Durham: Duke, 1948).

Economic and social history is well treated in *Det Norske Folks Liv og Historie* (The Norwegian People's Life and History; 11 vols., Oslo: Aschehoug, 1930–1938). A popular one-volume account of "Swedish Work and Life" by the well-known economic historian Eli F. Heckscher, is also untranslated—*Svenskt Arbete och Liv* (Stockholm: Bonniers, 1941).

Several of the above-mentioned volumes deal with the coöperative movement, but in addition should be cited Frederic C. Howe, *Denmark, The Coöperative Way* (New York: Coward-McCann, 1936); Henning Ravnholt, *The Danish Coöperative Movement* (Copenhagen: Det Danske Selskab, 1947); Anders Hedberg, *Consumers Coöperation in Sweden* (Stockholm: Nordisk Rotogravyr,

1948); and the *Report of the Inquiry on Coöperative Enterprise in Europe, 1937* (Washington: Government Printing Office, 1937).

The folk high schools receive attention in Peter Manniche's *Denmark*, and also in Andreas Boje and others, *Education in Denmark* (London: Oxford, 1932). See also Noëlle Davies, *Education for Life* (London: Williams and Norgate, 1931), on the influence of Grundtvig; and Sören Kierkegaard, *Philosophical Fragments* (New York: American-Scandinavian Foundation, 1936). On education in Sweden see Christina Staël von Holstein Bogoslovsky, *Educational Crisis in Sweden in Light of American Experience* (New York: Columbia, 1932).

4. ECONOMIC PLANNING

An up-to-date general book on planning is Seymour E. Harris, *Economic Planning* (New York: Knopf, 1949), but of the Scandinavian countries he deals only with Norway. *Sweden's Economy, a Long Term Program* (Stockholm: Swedish Institute, 1948) summarizes the Swedish plan presented to the OEEC. Svenska Handelsbankens *Index* (Stockholm, serial) both in articles and supplementary pamphlets gives useful information and criticism; one of special value is the pamphlet of June 1946 by Börje Kragh, "Sweden's Monetary and Fiscal Policy Before and After the Second World War." Another valuable article is L. R. Klein, "Planned Economy in Norway," *American Economic Review*, XXXVIII (December 1948), 795–814. Best of all are the pamphlets "Country Studies" for *Denmark, Sweden, Norway*, and *Iceland*, published by the Economic Coöperation Administration (Washington, 1949). On earlier phases of planning see Brinley Thomas, *Monetary Policy and Crises; A Study of Swedish Experience* (London: Routledge, 1936), and Arthur Montgomery, *How Sweden Overcame the Depression* (Stockholm: Bonniers, 1938).

5. NEUTRALITY AND DIPLOMACY TO 1939

No comprehensive work has been done on the history of Scandinavian neutrality, but there is a host of special studies. One of the most useful for the early period is Carl J. Kulsrud, *Maritime Neutrality to 1780* (Boston: Little, Brown, 1936), and on neutrality in general the four-volume work by Philip C. Jessup and Francis Déak, *Neutrality, Its History, Economics and Law* (New York: Columbia, 1935). An Uppsala dissertation by Nils Söderquist, *Le Blocus Maritime* (The Maritime Blockade, Stockholm: 1908) has about 90 pages of documents, and is useful for the period since 1300. Hans Lennart Lundh has done a first-rate essay on Swedish policy in 1865–66 in "Svensk Neutralitetspolitik Åren 1865–1866," published in *Studier Tillägnade Curt Weibull* (Studies dedicated to Curt Weibull, Gothenburg, 1946).

In the great series edited by Professor Henry T. Shotwell for the Carnegie Endowment for International Peace, on the social and economic effects of World War I, the Scandinavian volumes have been abridged, translated, and brought together in one volume: Eli F. Heckscher, Wilhelm Keilhau, Einar Cohn, T. Thorsteinsson, *Sweden, Norway, Denmark and Iceland in the World War* (New Haven: Yale, 1930).

For the period of the Long Armistice and the League of Nations a good general treatment is Shepard S. Jones, *The Scandinavian States and the League of Nations* (Princeton: Princeton University, 1939). Norman J. Padelford has examined "The New Scandinavian Neutrality Rules" of 1938 in *The American Journal of International Law* (XXXII, October 1938, 789–793), and the rules themselves are given in the same issue, pp. 141–163. The Norwegian Edvard Hambro, now Registrar of the International Court at The Hague, deals with the same subject in "Les Sanctions et l'Attitude Actuelle des États du Nord après l'Assemblée de la Societé des Nations de 1938," *Le Nord*, I (1938), 340–350. On the development of opinion in Sweden between the wars Herbert Tingsten has made a significant contribution in *Svensk Utrikesdebatt mellan Världskrigen* (Swedish debate on foreign policy between world wars, Stockholm: Institute of Foreign Affairs, 1944), translated and published by the Oxford University Press in 1948. Eric C. Bellquist has ably reviewed *Some Recent Aspects of the Foreign Policy of Sweden* (Berkeley; University of California Press, 1929).

6. WORLD WAR II

On the recent war the literature grows steadily, both in the Scandinavian countries and in the United States.

A general treatment written by an Englishman during the war contains much political history background, and is useful, though unfair at some points: Rowland Kenny, *The Northern Tangle* (London: J. M. Dent, 1946). A sympathetic American Quaker has interpreted Swedish history as a struggle for peace: David Hinshaw, *Sweden, Champion of Peace* (New York: Putnam, 1949).

On the diplomacy of the war in the North probably the most

valuable work yet put into English is *Finland and World War II*, a nationalistic Finnish approach, but honestly done by a group of Finns who knew the story and who had access to the documents; it is edited by John H. Wuorinen (New York: Ronald, 1948). Valuable confirmatory evidence is provided through the German documents edited by Raymond J. Sontag and J. S. Beddie, *Nazi-Soviet Relations 1939-1941* (New York: Didier, 1948).

The early phase of the Danish occupation is told in Sten Gudme, *Denmark, Hitler's Model Protectorate* (London: Gollancz, 1942), and in Paul Palmér, *Denmark in Nazi Chains* (London: Lindsay Drummond, 1942). Perhaps the best survey in English to date covering the whole war is the one edited by Borge Outze, *Denmark During the German Occupation* (Copenhagen: Scandinavian Publishing Co., 1946).

The spectacular struggle of the Norwegians is told by many participants, and in many ways. President of the Storting Carl J. Hambro has described the beginnings in *I Saw It Happen in Norway* (New York: Appleton-Century, 1940), and Theodor Broch, mayor of Narvik, has told the story of the prolonged fighting in the north in *The Mountains Wait* (St. Paul: Webb, 1942). The general internal opposition is described by a foremost historian, Jacob S. Worm-Müller in *Norway Revolts Against the Nazis* (London: Lindsay Drummond, 1941). The church attitude is told by Bjarne Höye and Trygve M. Ager, *The Fight of the Norwegian Church Against Nazism* (New York: Macmillan, 1943). Amanda Johnson has put together much of the total story in *Norway, Her Invasion and Occupation* (Decorah: Decorah-Posten, 1949). And one of the documents of permanent value is the human, gripping diary from the concentration camps by Odd Nansen, *From Day to Day* (New York: Putnam, 1949).

The neutrality of Sweden aroused a quantity of discussion pro and con—unlike the neutrality of Switzerland or Eire which was accepted rather calmly. Much personal bitterness mars the book by Joachim Joesten, *Stalwart Sweden* (New York: Doubleday, Doran, 1943). Joesten also had an article "Phases in Swedish Neutrality" in *Foreign Affairs*, XXIII (January, 1945), 324-329, followed in the next number with a valuable article by Bruce Hopper, "Sweden: A Case Study in Neutrality," *ibid.*, XXIII (April 1945), 435-449. The wartime services of Sweden to the Allies are praised by Ralph Wallace in "The True Story of Swedish Neutrality," *Reader's Digest* (September 1946), pp. 89-96. Rowland Kenny's *Northern Tangle* is useful on this subject.

Additional facts continue to come to light, especially through the diplomatic documents of Norway and Sweden, whose experts have consulted with each other prior to publication. Sweden has issued four "white books," *Handlingar Rörande Sveriges Politik under Andra Världskriget* (Documents on Sweden's Policy during the Second World War, Stockholm: Norstedt, 1947–48), and a popularized one-volume *Sveriges Förhållande till Danmark och Norge under Krigsåren* (Sweden's Relations with Denmark and Norway during War Years, Stockholm: Norstedt, 1945). Norway has issued several volumes of investigations of the government at home and abroad, and, on the subject of Swedish neutrality, *Norges Forhold til Sverige Under Krigen 1940–1945* (Norway's Relations with Sweden during the War 1940–1945, 2 vols., Oslo: Gyldendal, 1947–1948).

Hans W. Weigert has an article, "Iceland, Greenland and the United States," in *Foreign Affairs* XXIII (October 1944), 112–122.

7. THE SEARCH FOR SECURITY

The material on this subject is not yet packaged in articles and books. The facts and ideas expressed in this volume on recent trends are based on interviews with officials, on conversations on trains and planes, in factories and offices and around dinner tables, on newspapers and parliamentary debates, on business reports—on living for most of the year 1948 in the North.

There are some written materials, however, to aid the American reader. Sigyn Alenius, a keen young Finnish journalist, has written a pamphlet *Finland between the Armistice and the Peace* (Helsinki: Söderström, 1947). Eric Bellquist has well condensed the facts in "Political and Economic Conditions in the Scandinavian Countries," *Foreign Policy Reports*, May 15, 1948 (New York: Foreign Policy Association). On the diplomatic aspects a good article is that by Erik Seidenfaden, "Scandinavia Charts a Course," *Foreign Affairs* (XXVI), July 1948, 653–664.

Greenland is surveyed and brought up to date in an article by V. Borum, "Greenland" in the *Danish Foreign Office Journal* (1948), No. 1, pp. 14–20, No. 2, pp. 11–19. For a recent survey of Iceland see Helgi P. Briem, *Iceland and the Icelanders* (Princeton, 1945). A report of the Danish mission which visited Greenland in 1948 will probably be available soon.

On the economic problems of the postwar period, and the attempts of the European Recovery Program to meet those problems, the Economic Coöperation Administration issues a pamphlet "Country Studies" on *Denmark, Norway, Sweden,* and *Iceland* (Washington: ECA, 1949).

8. BIBLIOGRAPHIES

The *American-Scandinavian Review* publishes book reviews of the more important books of general interest, and occasionally extensive lists of Danish, Norwegian, Swedish, and Icelandic books for American libraries. The news services often include mention of books and articles. An incomplete but useful catalog *Scandinavia, A List of Books by Scandinavians and about Scandinavians,* was issued in 1949 by The Scandinavia Book Service, P. O. Box 99, Audubon Station, New York 32.

For Sweden Naboth Hedin has compiled a *Guide to Information about Sweden* (American Swedish News Exchange, 630 Fifth Avenue, New York 20, 1947). This pamphlet bibliography includes both articles and books, carefully classified by subject. This is complemented by a pamphlet, *Books about Sweden, 1946–1949* (New York: American Swedish News Exchange, 1949).

INDEX

(The Scandinavian letters å, ä and ö, ø are here alphabetized as if they were simple a or o.)

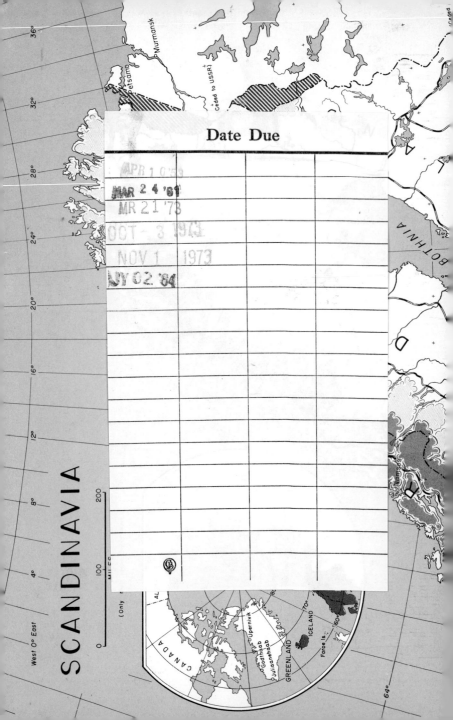